Theodore Roethke

Photograph by Mary Randlett

NEAL BOWERS

Theodore Roethke
The Journey
from I to Otherwise

University of Missouri Press
Columbia & London
1982

for Nancy, who makes things possible

Copyright © 1982 by
The Curators of the University of Missouri
University of Missouri Press, Columbia, Missouri 65211
Library of Congress Catalog Card Number 81–10410
Printed and bound in the United States of America

Library of Congress Cataloging in Publication Data

Bowers, Neal, 1948–

    Theodore Roethke: the journey from I to otherwise

    Bibliography: p. 220
    Includes index.

    1. Roethke, Theodore, 1908–1963. Criticism and
Interpretation. I. Title.
PS3535.039Z59   811'.54   81–10410
ISBN 0–8262–0347–7   AACR2

Acknowledgment is gratefully made to Beatrice Roethke Lushington for her permission to quote from unpublished materials at the University of Washington Library.

Poetic excerpts from the book *The Collected Poems of Theodore Roethke*, Copyright © 1937, 1954, 1957, 1958, 1959, 1960, 1961, 1962, 1963, 1964, 1965, 1966 by Beatrice Roethke as Administratrix of the Estate of Theodore Roethke; Copyright © 1932, 1934, 1935, 1936, 1937, 1938, 1939, 1940, 1941, 1942, 1946, 1947, 1948, 1949, 1950, 1951, 1952, 1953, 1954, 1955, 1956, 1957, 1958, 1961 by Theodore Roethke are reprinted by permission of Doubleday & Company, Inc.

Acknowledgment is made to the following periodicals for allowing these poems to be reprinted: *Commonweal*, "The Conqueror" and "Statement"; *Sewanee Review*, "Second Version"; *The Atlantic Monthly*, "Genius"; *The New York Times*, "After Loss" © 1939 by The New York Times Company, reprinted by permission; and *Poetry*, "Song" © 1963 by The Modern Poetry Association, reprinted by permission of the editor. "Her Dream" is reprinted by permission from *The Hudson Review*, Vol. XIII, No. 1 (Spring 1960). Copyright © 1960 by The Hudson Review, Inc.

Acknowledgments

Over the years, this study progressed from idea to finished product largely because of the generosity and support of a great many people. Though it is perhaps impossible to acknowledge everyone who helped, the following list includes all those who made a substantial contribution to the project.

Mrs. Beatrice Roethke Lushington and Professors Robert Heilman, David Wagoner, and Richard Blessing provided unique insights into my literary subject and helped to focus the study more sharply during its early stages.

Professors John T. Fain, Aubrey Williams, Lewis Tatham, Malcolm Glass, Edward Irwin, and Don Der guided my initial interest in Roethke and offered something even more valuable than expertise—friendship and encouragement.

I owe a special thanks to Iowa State University for funding two summer research projects that led to the completion of this book. I also owe a great deal to my friends and colleagues at Iowa State who have been so supportive of my work: Professors Frank Haggard, Donald Benson, Charles L. P. Silet, Gretchen Bataille, and Richard Hernstadt.

Mrs. Karyl Winn, Curator of Manuscripts at the University of Washington Libraries, helped me make the best use of the Theodore Roethke Manuscripts Collection, and she was ably assisted by Robert Mittelstadt, Christine Taylor, and Richard Berner.

I would be remiss, indeed, if I neglected to acknowledge my wife, Nancy, an astute reader who made this book better than it was.

A Note on the Manuscript Material

Whenever material from the unpublished Theodore Roethke Papers is quoted in this study, it is cited within the text using the University of Washington's numbering system. For example, a quotation followed by (28 #24) would indicate that the quoted material was found in Box 28, Folder number 24 in the Roethke Collection. Whenever relevant, the date of the unpublished material, if known, is mentioned within the text itself.

Grateful acknowledgment is given to Mrs. Beatrice Roethke Lushington and to the University of Washington's Suzzallo Library for permission to quote from the manuscripts.

N.B.
Ames, Iowa
September 1981.

Preface

This book represents the culmination of nearly five years of work, and I would like to think that Roethke—who in one of his notebook entries remarked, "Perhaps the poet's path is closer to the mystic than we think"—would approve of the final product. What I hope to show here is that Roethke's path is not only close to, but one and the same with, the mystic's, and, consequently, that mysticism affords one of the best routes into Roethke's collected work. This approach may assist not only in understanding individual poems, but also in perceiving the coherent nature of the total body of Roethke's poetry.

The basic premise of this study is that Roethke's manic-depressiveness, which troubled him most of his life, produced in him a propensity for mystical insight. The up and down phases of his psychosis, similar to the periods of expansion and contraction of consciousness characteristic of natural or affective mysticism, altered his perception of the world and led him to believe that there is another level of reality, one more real and meaningful than that which is normally perceived. Acting on this belief, Roethke undertook a struggle to find his place in the true scheme of things, a search for identity which closely resembles the mystic's movement toward the Absolute through the stages of awakening, purgation, illumination, dark night of the soul, and union.

In the poetic account of his struggle, Roethke employs the three symbols most often used by mystics to convey some sense of their ineffable spiritual experiences: the outward journey, inward growth, and the consummation of a love relationship. These represent not only different descriptions of Roethke's search for identity but also major divisions within his collected poetry. Roethke moves outside himself, within himself, and into another person, following each path as far as he can and then beginning again, passing through the various mystical stages and ultimately confronting death and union in his final poems.

I should acknowledge at the outset my own initial misgivings about the topic of mysticism, because I suspect that many readers will regard the term itself with a certain amount of apprehension, if not suspicion. Even now, it is difficult to discuss the subject with friends and colleagues without detecting here and there a raised brow of skepticism. The problem, as I have come to see it, is definitional. Very few people know what mysticism is. Therefore, the first obstacle I have had to overcome is the fundamental one of meaning. Although developing a workable definition was no small chore, I trust that in the course of the introductory section I have at least dispelled any erroneous ideas that mysticism has anything at all to do with the occult, magic, voodoo, witchcraft, astrology, or even organized religion. I have endeavored to replace such misconceptions with the awareness that mysticism, stated most simply, is man's most basic religious impulse, his desire to perceive and to unite with the Absolute—with God, if you prefer. Unquestionably, that impulse is bound up with Roethke's quest for identity. In fact, the mystic's desire and Roethke's longing are the same thing.

Once a workable definition has been developed, I have then to apply the concepts of mysticism to a reading of the poetry. This process, of course, constitutes the bulk of the study. The approach is chronological, in terms of the individual books that compose the collected work, and I have generally disregarded the chronology of the poems within any particular volume, choosing instead to follow the sequence of Roethke's arrangement. In terms of emphasis, all of Roethke's poetry receives equal attention, although I have been particularly careful to discuss the poems of *Open House* and to relate them to the rest of Roethke's work. Those early poems are too often regarded in a cursory manner and dismissed as inferior apprentice pieces. However, I find in them the embryo of all the later poetry.

I was especially fortunate in the course of my work to have access to the Roethke notebooks and manuscripts housed in the University of Washington Library in Seattle. In addition to the 277 notebooks in which Roethke jotted down everything from the roster of his tennis team at Penn State to random thoughts on his finances and rough drafts of poems, the collection contains teaching notes, letters, recordings, book lists, clippings, photographs, and even a pair of ankle-top suede shoes, size 12. It is impossible to overstate the importance of this kind of material to the scholar intent on understanding the poet, down to the size of his feet, and there can be no doubt that this study would have less right to lay claim to the reader's attention without the manuscripts on which it so heavily relies.

Of all the material contained in the collection, none attracts the scholar and holds his attention more than the notebooks. Consequently, I have, throughout this study, drawn liberally from these working pages of Roethke's for supportive material. Sometimes the quoted passage is no more than a phrase, sometimes a paragraph or more, but it is always provocative and revealing. The notebooks provide a rare glimpse into the mind of the poet, disclosing a good deal not only about his craft and his working methods but also about the man himself.

Aside from the notebooks, I have relied heavily upon the poetry manuscripts found in the collection. Whenever possible, I have included in my explication of Roethke's collected work examples of these uncollected and frequently unpublished poems and have, when space allowed, quoted them in their entirety. My intention has been to offer the most complete analysis of Roethke's poetry possible and to make available to the reader previously unpublished or unobtainable material.

I am, as all scholars must be, indebted to those who have preceded me, particularly to Karl Malkoff, Richard Allen Blessing, and Rosemary Sullivan. However, though their studies have stood as models of good scholarship, I have generally had to rely on my own resources in the relatively uncharted territory of Roethke's mysticism. Despite the fact that each of these excellent critics acknowledges mysticism as an important element in Roethke's poetry, none pursues it very far beyond the acknowledgment. William Heyen has gone farther down this road then anybody else in his article "The Divine Abyss: Theodore Roethke's Mysticism," but his focus is limited to Roethke's last poems, particularly to "The Abyss," and he attempts no coherent view of all of Roethke's poetry. Another perceptive critic, Jay Parini, comments on Roethke's interest in mysticism and presents an excellent account of his quest for illumination, but his analysis deals primarily with Roethke's posthumous volume, *The Far Field*, and he essays no general examination of the topic. This is the space into which I thrust this study, hopeful that it will contribute to a fuller understanding of Roethke's work and that it will earn a place alongside those worthy studies that have preceded it.

Contents

I. Introduction

1.

Roethke's Mysticism

"There really is something to the idea that a knowledge of the man throws light on his poems."—Roethke Notebooks (34 #34)

Theodore Roethke wrote only one poem in his life, a song of himself, or perhaps more accurately, a song of his search for self, comprised of six volumes published over a period of twenty–three years, the ultimate sequential poem.[1] The implicit comparison to Whitman is an apt one, for, like Whitman, Roethke counted himself among the happy poets, and like *Leaves of Grass*, Roethke's total body of poetry has a unity that overshadows any differences in style and content from poem to poem. Because of this extraordinary unity, the critic soon discovers that he must take Roethke's poetry in its entirety if he is to reach a satisfactory understanding of its individual parts. This is not to say that the poems of any particular volume cannot stand on their own, but simply that each volume of poetry grows out of its predecessor, and individual poems frequently stand in very close relation to one another. Such interdependence creates serious obstacles for the reader who does not take the time to examine the part in the context of the whole; and therefore, it is not surprising to encounter those who consider Roethke obscure or narrow. It is also not surprising that the best studies of Roethke are those that examine the total body of his poetry, perceiving in it some unifying element—Karl Malkoff's "spiritual autobiography" or Richard Allen Blessing's "dynamic vision."[2] This study is aligned with the latter group in attempting to explicate Roethke's poetry in the context of yet another unifying element, the mystic quest.

If there is one point of agreement among the various critics, it is that Roethke's poetry is a journal, the record of a man's attempts to discover his identity and his place in existence. Even the casual reader can agree with Ralph Mills that "the primary thematic concern in Theodore Roethke's poetry is

with the evolution and identity of the self."[3] The poetry reflects "a struggle out of the slime," "a slow spiritual process"
similar to the unfolding of a flower, "an effort to be born, and
later to become something more."[4] Roethke's protagonist is a
man who flees himself to find himself, who wishes his flesh
away and becomes a protean shapeshifter, but who ultimately
returns to his life, to his "rags and rotting clothes."[5] As
Roethke himself put it, "The human problem is to find out
what one really is, whether one exists, whether existence is
possible."[6] The following study is in the mainstream of Roethke
criticism in maintaining that Roethke's poetry represents a
man's search for identity. But more than that, it maintains that
Roethke's search follows the path of mysticism, that his poetry
may be viewed in terms of a mystic quest, a search for identity
and ultimate reality that closely parallels the struggles of the
mystic toward God or the Absolute. In this respect, Roethke's
search for self is not an egocentric journey, and his preoccu-
pations with his own life and his own personal history do not
identify him, as some critics would have it, as a narrowly
confessional poet. The self he drives toward throughout his
poetry is larger than Theodore Roethke, larger than any individual. It is the ultimate unity that subsumes Roethke and
everything else, the ultimate Self.

   Although several critics have touched upon Roethke's mysticism, no one has seemed eager to deal with it in detail, perhaps because no one feels very comfortable with the term *mysticism* and because most critics would agree with Richard Allen
Blessing that Roethke was "not much of a mystic if, indeed, he
was one at all."[7] Nevertheless, certain mystical qualities are so
apparent in the poetry, particularly in the final book, *The Far
Field*, as to be unavoidable. Jay Parini's chapter "The Way of
Illumination," in his book *Theodore Roethke: An American Romantic*, affords an excellent analysis of Roethke's push toward illumination in his last poems. However, Parini's analysis is limited to *The Far Field*, and he does not undertake as thorough
an examination of Roethke's mysticism as the one presented in
the following chapters of this book.

   Roethke's interest in mysticism is undeniable, for his working notebooks abound with references to mystical doctrine.

Such references frequently take the form of apparent outlines or notes transcribed from other sources, as in the following:

> The inward flight
> and frozen night
> ....
> St. John of the Cross
> Suffer
> ....
> Orothodox mystic spiritual marriage
> with God
> ....
> *Unitive mysticism* "complete fusion of
>   soul with the divine"
> ....
> epithalamic mysticism
> ....
> Soul cannot partake of God, but only
> resemble God.—Ruysbroeck (33 #17)

These notations, recorded in 1939, are sketchy, but subsequent entries are more explicit. For example, in a 1942 notebook (33 #31) Roethke presents thorough summaries of the discussions of mysticism found in Denis De Rougemont's *Love in the Western World*. His notes reveal a familiarity with such well-known mystics as Meister Eckhart, Saint Francis, and Saint Theresa and preserve comments from their writings that Roethke apparently found significant: "True mystics are [the] essence of prudence, rigor & clear-sighted obedience" and "All mystics have complained of a want of new words."

Were it necessary to compile one, quite a long list of Roethke's notes on mysticism could be presented. And the list could be tripled or quadrupled if original lines that obviously are derived from Roethke's readings in mysticism were included. But it seems unnecessary to go to such lengths to make a simple point emphatic: Mysticism was one of Roethke's abiding interests, from the beginning to the end of his poetic career. In addition to the abundance of references scattered throughout the notebooks, lengthy notes on mysticism can be found elsewhere in the Roethke manuscripts. These are sometimes entered on loose-leaf paper, sometimes in spiral notebooks, and, at least in one instance, in a tablet of typing paper.

These writings appear to be notes for teaching, but in many instances it is apparent that Roethke was writing as much for himself as for his students. For example, on one page beneath the heading "Mysticism" the following remarks appear:

> The business is Love. A total dedication of the Will.
> For silence is not God, nor speaking is not God, etc. . . . . But he is hid between them.
> Such a blind shot with the sharp dart of longing may never fail of the prick, the which is God.   —The Cloud of Unknowing
> Come out of the theological tree. Intelligence must rest without. (65 #12)

These entries seem designed primarily to jog the memory. If they were used in class, no doubt Roethke had pages of extemporaneous commentary to offer on each statement, and perhaps the last remarks functioned as an exhortation to his students: "Come out of the theological tree. Intelligence must rest without." But in many ways, these notes on mysticism resemble those found in the notebooks, and I am led to believe that they were more valuable to Roethke than to his students. It seems probable that if Roethke introduced his students to the arcane study of mysticism at all, it was because of his own fascination with the material.

Roethke's reading in mysticism intensified during the last ten years of his life, as did his interest in philosophy in general, but it seems clear that he read steadily and broadly in mystical literature from the late 1930s and early 1940s onward. And his reading was more than merely casual, as the following note found inside the cover of his copy of *The Soul Afire: Revelations of the Mystics*, edited by J. A. Reinhold, indicates: "Nowadays those who are near God must keep quiet. An extraordinary book: praised by nobody." This inscription indicates that Roethke not only read the book and read it thoroughly but also took it to heart, found something of value within its covers.

I do not propose to give an exhaustive listing of Roethke's readings in mysticism, but it is important to offer a representative selection of the things he read in that area. Following, then, is a short list of some of the titles of books on mysticism found in Roethke's private collection as well as some known to have been checked out of the University of Washington Library by him. In many cases, the books charged to his name by the library were kept well beyond their due dates and renewed several times: *On the Mystical Poetry of Henry Vaughan*, R. A. Durr; *The Cloud of Unknowing*, translated by Ira Progoff; *The Mystic Will: Based on a Study of the Philosophy of Jacob Boehme*, Howard H. Brinton; *Mysticism and Poetry: On a Basis of Experience*, A. Allen Brockington; *In Search of the Miraculous: Fragments of an Unknown Teaching*, P. D. Ouspensky; *Illumination on Jacob Boehme; The Work of Dionysius Andreas Freher*, Charles A. Muses; *Ruysbroeck*, Evelyn Underhill; *Dionysius the Aeropagite on the Divine Names and the Mystical Theology*, C. E. Rolt; *Practical Mysticism: A Little Book for Normal People*, Evelyn Underhill; *The Mystic Way: A Psychological Study in Christian Origins*, Evelyn Underhill; *The Soul Afire: Revelations of the Mystics*, edited by H. A. Reinhold; *Mysticism*, Evelyn Underhill; *Signature Of All Things, With Other Writings*, Jacob Boehme; *Mysticism, Sacred and Profane*, R. C. Zaehner.

This evidence substantiates Roethke's familiarity with mysticism. Even more than that, it emphasizes that his interest in the subject did not come late in life, as has often been supposed, but is traceable from the earliest phases of his career, long before the publication of *Open House* in 1941. Thus, in a 1935 notebook we discover the following entry, attributed to Saroyan: "For an eternal moment he was all things at once: the bird, the fish, the rodent, the reptile, and man" (32 #7). This comment is, in many ways, peculiarly Roethkean because it describes the mystical sense of unity often encountered in Roethke's poetry—in the later poetry, however, from *The Lost Son* on, not in the poems of *Open House*. Similarly, the following entry, found in the same notebook, connects more directly with the poems of a later period:

> What a sweet ineffable aura lay upon all experience at that time, when the merest act, the lifted finger, the barest lift of the brow, was suffused with tenderness. (32 #7)

These entries are striking for several reasons. First, as will become apparent through subsequent discussion, both describe in rather standard language what has been identified throughout the centuries as the mystical experience. I say the language is standard because mystics usually emphasize the paradoxical ("an eternal moment") and ineffable nature ("a sweet ineffable aura") of their perception. Second, as I have already indicated, both comments seem to have more in common with Roethke's later poetry than with anything he was writing in 1935. In fact, while they tell us little about the *Open House* poems, they may serve as a gloss for most of the poems in "The Lost Son" sequence ("A Field of Light," for example, or "Praise to the End!"). The explanation for this is relatively simple: Roethke's experience (as recorded in the notebooks) was running considerably ahead of his poetry. Time would be needed to assimilate what he had felt, that he had "Stood on the threshold of a mystic experience." (32 #7)

It is not merely coincidental that the entries that reveal something of mystical awareness appear in the same notebook in which Roethke recorded certain observations about his first mental breakdown. In fact, it seems obvious that whatever unusual perception Roethke may have had was a direct product of his collapse. It is interesting to note that Roethke himself described his breakdown as a mystical experience. According to Roethke's biographer, Allan Seager, Roethke told Peter De Vries that "he had a mystical experience with a tree and he learned there the 'secret of Nijinsky.'"[8] It is, of course, impossible to say exactly what Roethke meant by this, but I find Seager's speculations to be reasonable: that Nijinsky's encounter with the tree (described in his *Diary*) emphasized "the primacy of emotion over reason," an ordering Roethke himself believed in.[9] Whatever Roethke meant, it is clear that he felt he had encountered some transcendent truth during his manic excursion into the Michigan woods that cold November night. Some nine years later, he would remember it this way:

> For no reason I started to feel very good. Suddenly I knew how to enter into the life of everything around me. I knew how it felt to be a tree, a blade of grass, even a rabbit. I didn't sleep much. I just walked around with this wonderful feeling.[10]

This feeling of euphoria and unity is equivalent to the mystical experience, in which "the self perceives an added significance

and reality in all natural things: is often convinced that it
knows at last 'the secret of the world.' "[11] If the episode was in
some ways terrifying for Roethke and bore terrible consequences for him at Michigan State (where his job hung in the
balance), it was also a revelation for him. In a 1946 notebook,
he wrote of the experience, "Break-down, hell, that was a
break-up" (47 #10).

A fairly long account of the episode given by him during the
last year of his life illustrates just how profound the experience
was for Roethke. This commentary, part of the original interview transcript made in conjunction with the film *In a Dark
Time*, was not included in the sound-track recording and, to
my knowledge, has never before been published. I offer it
here, with a minimum of editorial changes, as evidence of how
vividly the experience remained with Roethke even after the
passage of some twenty-eight years. His remarks, which run
in almost stream-of-consciousness fashion, reveal an intensity
and excitement that underscore the significance of the event
in his life:

> There was the one time I played the Rimbaud business of really
> driving myself, seeing . . . you could really derange the senses,
> and it can be done, and let me tell you, I did it. I mean, I got in
> such good condition, I wasn't drinking at all. I was twenty–
> seven. This was in East Lansing, Michigan. I was running on
> those cinder pads four, five miles a day. Jesus, and teaching, too.
> But you know I got in this real strange state. I got in the woods
> and started a circular kind of dance, and I've never put this down
> very . . . I refer to it in "I tried to fling my shadow at the moon."
> I kept going around and just shedding clothes. Sounds Freudian
> as hell, but in the end, I had sort of a circle—as if, I think, I
> understood intuitively what the frenzy is. That is, you go way
> beyond yourself, and . . . this is not sheer exhaustion but this
> strange sort of a . . . not illumination . . . but a sense of being
> again a part of the whole universe. I mean, anything but quiet. I
> mean, in a sense everything is symbolical. In one of the Old
> Woman poems I just sort of put it in there, because I know if you
> put this down in prose, for God's sake [people will say,] "Oh,
> this is merely clinical"—I mean, "Obviously, he is crazy" and so
> forth. But it was one of the deepest and [most] profound experi-
> ences I ever had. And accompanying it was a real sexual excite-

ment also . . . and this tremendous feeling of actual power. But finally, when coming back, I was just so exhausted that I could hardly walk, in as good condition as I was.

What happened to me eventually . . . well, one thing, you have this curious sense that you're actually being transformed literally into an animal. You start getting fantasies—I mean, of power, lion–like power. But the next night was much tougher, in a sense—I really thought my features were changing. Of course, this was madness, you see, but the relationship between the ecstasy and madness is so . . . well, one of the things that the head-shrinkers know, or the good ones, that if these descents are too rapid [they] can be chaotic, and I mean, you knock. In other words, something could happen to you; you could get lost back there, because what you're doing is going right back into the history of the goddamn race. I mean, you're down to the animal, dog, and so forth, down to snake. It sounds nuts, but, well . . . fight your way out of that. What happened to me there, I simply blacked out, eventually. I knew I was teaching in real manic frenzy. Well, I woke up on the morning, somewhat like this, with very little sleep, and decided I wanted to get to his office. I took a little walk on the edge of the city. There I got so cold I lay down and took off a shoe, and there I had . . . this is again real loony, and goes beyond—there was a curious crabhole, and I lay there and started whistling to this thing, as if you were really trying to call it out of the earth. Well, I knew what I was doing, that this was not a snakehole, and so on and so on, but . . . and I put this down in one of those pieces, in one of those running ones. Then I got scared; it started getting cold; it was November, and I started to run with only one shoe on. Jesus Christ, here you are, and I was barefoot . . . well, symbolically, yet. I got into a gas station. There was a guy—I again—I just associated with my father. I was out on my feet, see, just punchy from . . . you know, I hadn't slept for five nights, and I said, "Can . . . get me, drive me," and he said, "Sure." He drove me to the campus, and I came in, you know, just like someone who had been beaten for five rounds. I sat down in that goddamn office and I thought, "Jesus Christ, you're going to have to adlib now." But the trouble in these high states of consciousness is that *everything* gets heightened, so that sound particularly . . . somebody walking overhead . . . it just sounds like a concatenation. Well, I finally said, "Just bring me a coach and I'll try to explain on what happened to me physically." I was just going to say, "I'm not nuts.

I'm just out on my feet because I've been working." I finally
thought I'd died. There was a profound and beautiful experience,
as if you . . . and you can hear the thing going, but you just die
right then.

The *real* point is that this business of the dance accompanies ex-
altation of the highest, the human thing, and it also goes into the
Dionysian frenzy, which in modern life hardly anyone even
speaks of anymore. But the real profundity of that experience, I
mean, in the sense of the mood itself, seemed to be, you know,
the whole Islamic world. All the cultures were with you. This is
exactly what they felt when they were rolling in the circular, you
know, frenzy thing. And your perceptions, as I say, both in sight
and particularly sound *and* smell, and frequently also . . . another is that you get the transfer of senses. Sometimes that comes
even with memory. You know, Hopkins says in one of his . . .
when he said, "I tasted brass in my mouth" . . . well, that's the
very essence, it seems to me, of metaphysical thinking. That is
when the body itself . . . when Vaughan says, "When felt
through all my fleshy dress, / Ripe shoots of everlastingness,"
well, *that's* the feeling. You feel one way that you are eternal, or
immortal, and it doesn't seem to be a cheap thing either. And
furthermore, death becomes, as it were, an absurdity, of no consequence. And also the notion, conception, of time is completely
subjective, and I've often thought sometimes that [when] the sui-
cidal leaps from the window, when he hits that pavement and is
just a blob, who knows, maybe he explodes into a million uni-
verses and he is happy. Who knows? That's behind, you know,
the nuttier aspects of certain Hindu religions, when they'd start
dancing and singing and finally in this ecstasy run right into the
goddamn sea when they know that all those sharks are there.
Nothing could stop 'em. I mean, we can say that this is collective
madness. It is, but it's part of the human psyche; it's there. (140)

This account goes far beyond Seager's, which describes only
what could be seen by an observer or a biographer not caught
up in the experience: Roethke's frenzied walk in the cold, in
the middle of the night, with only one shoe on. Such behavior
looks like purest madness, and that is the way it was viewed
by the administrators at Michigan State who chose not to rein-
state Roethke after his release from Mercywood Sanitarium.

But from Roethke's perspective, the episode went beyond madness to ecstasy, to the point that he could feel "a sense of being again a part of the whole universe." This sensation is identical to the mystic's sense of unity. No wonder, then, that the experience overwhelmed him and remained imprinted upon his memory, for one of the chief characteristics of the mystical insight is its indelibility. What Roethke saw and felt during his manic flight into the countryside was transcendent truth, a reality beyond what we normally regard as real. His perception marked a kind of initiation, an awakening, which inevitably modified everything.

To what extent Roethke willed his mental collapse is difficult to determine. Seager, who is willing to accept Roethke's claim that he induced the episode at Michigan State, cites Roethke's drinking, pill taking, and going without sleep as possible causes. But he also observes that manic-depressives characteristically insist that they bring on their attacks themselves.[12] Perhaps Roethke was trying to achieve a "break-up"; perhaps he was pushing toward something like Rimbaud's "*dereglement de tous les sens.*" An entry in a 1934 notebook reveals quite clearly that Roethke felt the need to make some changes in his life for the good of his poetry:

> I think God has sterilized me so I can't have any more poems. Maybe I had some poetic Spanish fly—some nightingale guano? Perhaps I've written all I can write in my present state of physical & moral development. Perhaps I should become a homosexual? (32 #6)

This passage, written approximately sixteen months before the first breakdown, lends credence to Roethke's claim that he induced his first episode "to reach a new level of reality." It is not improbable that Roethke became so disenchanted with his work that he determined to alter his "state of physical and moral development." Certainly, no one would doubt that the abusive way he treated himself during the time immediately preceding his collapse was at the least a contributing factor to his first episode. However, it is not my intent to discover the ultimate cause of Roethke's first breakdown, only to establish that he invited the episode, felt that he had induced it himself, and seemed convinced that it was in some way related to the production of his art.

That Roethke saw a positive relationship between his mental disorder and his poetry is revealed in a number of places in the notebooks. For example, in a draft of his contribution to the Ostroff-edited symposium on "In a Dark Time," Roethke makes the following observation:

> A "descent" can be willed—or at least the will—the human will— can be a factor. The real danger lies in the preceding euphoria, in the exhilaration getting out of hand. My first "breakdown" was in a very real sense deliberate. I not only asked for, I prayed that it would happen. True, I had used a tough resilient athlete's body as if it were rubber: had gone without any sleep at all for months. etc., etc. (42 #194)

Perhaps he had "prayed" for the breakdown because he was determined to escape from what he perceived to be stagnation in any way he could, even at great risk to his own well-being. As he writes in another notebook during the same year:

> All I care about is achievement: but it must be real achievement in its absolutely final terms: how achieved—at least in terms of the cost to the self—I do not care. (42 #193)

And in an earlier notebook he enters a similar remark in dialogue:

> "I can't go flying apart just for those who want the benefit of a few verbal kicks. My God, do you know what poems like that *cost*? They're not written vicariously: they come out of actual suffering; *real* madness."
> "I've got to go beyond. That's all there is to it."
> "Beyond what?"
> "The human, you fool. Don't you see what I've done: I've come this far and now I can't stop. It's too late, baby, it's too late."[13]

Roethke knew what he was doing, realized that his personal risks could be translated into poetic accomplishments, and he was even prepared to induce the manic-depressive cycle himself. He took the risk because the manic stages were periods of heightened activity and awareness during which he participated in the mystical feeling of "oneness," a feeling he claimed to have experienced "so many times, in so many varying circumstances, that I cannot suspect its validity."[14] The overall result of Roethke's self-exploitation, his daring risk taking, is a poetry that is richly mystical. His manic-depressiveness afforded him a perception that was parallel to mystical apprehension, and he utilized that perception to its fullest in his search for identity. He was not about to let the opportunity pass. As he comments in the middle of one notebook entry about mysticism: "Blake, too, was not of the type to let slip what he had learned." (36 #84)

The claim of a relationship between Roethke's manic-depression and his mystical temperament is more than justified by Roethke's own apparent recognition of their similarities and by certain observable elements common to both the manic and the mystic experiences. I wish to emphasize, first of all, that I feel certain Roethke's interest in mysticism was stimulated by his initial breakdown. Something both terrible and wonderful had happened to him; his perception of things had been radically altered, and he was eager to explain the experience. The most ready parallel, of which he was either already aware or which he discovered fortuitously, was the mystical experience. Certainly, the mystics afforded him perceptions that looked strikingly like his own.

I do not wish to imply, however, that mystics and manic-depressives are necessarily the same. Perhaps the most sensitive area for critics interested in Roethke's mysticism is dealing with the mystical elements in his poetry without bringing in all the religious elements conventionally associated with mysticism. Certainly, Roethke was not a religious man, at least not in any orthodox sense. The way out of the dilemma most likely lies in a careful description of the manic and mystic experiences for the purpose of making comparisons.

According to Seager, Roethke was diagnosed variously as a "manic-depressive neurotic, but not typical," a "manic-depressive psychotic, but not typical," and as a "paranoid schizophrenic."[15] The consensus was that Roethke was a manic-depressive, though the type was in dispute, and Roethke himself seems to have accepted that diagnosis. Certainly, the following textbook description of manic-depression seems to apply directly to Roethke's behavior during his manic episodes:

> The characteristic manifestations are psychomotor overactivity, elation of mood, distractibility and delusions with an omnipotent and omniscient content. The psychomotor overactivity is to be observed in the rapid speech, the pressure of talk, the continuous movement and the distractibility. As far as the mood state is concerned, the patient is not continually elated for there are occasions when there is depression with a lowering of self-esteem and self-criticism. When frustrated in his intentions the patient may become aggressive in word and action.[16]

There are many echoes here of Roethke's behavior: his insistence that he "started to feel very good" for no reason at all at the outset of his first breakdown, his grandiose business schemes (primarily those involving J. Robert Crouse and the utopian Hartland Area Project), his delusions about the Mafia, and his aggressive attitude toward various authority figures (for example, Dean Lloyd Emmons at Michigan State, whom he called a "Harvard son-of-a-bitch"), among other behavior characteristics cited by Seager in the biography. But perhaps the most significant element of the description concerns the mood state: the psychosis is characterized by movements from states of mania to states of depression. For Roethke, the depressed states were apparently not so long or so terrible, but then he always remained in a hospital where his depression was somewhat controlled by treatment and medication. Still, he did vacillate between these up and down phases, and that vacillation is significant because it is very similar to the swing from heightened states of awareness to deep troughs of despondency ordinarily associated with the mystic temperament. The "typical mystic seems to move toward his goal through a series of strongly marked oscillations between 'states of pleasure' and 'states of pain.' "[17]

Another element common to both manic-depression and mysticism is the "merging phenomenon." The manic-depressive may sometimes identify so strongly with other people or objects around him that he loses his identity and sense of self.

In this condition, "he no longer regards himself as an entity distinct from other entities."[18] This aspect of the disorder is seen in Roethke's claim that he "knew how it felt to be a tree, a blade of grass, even a rabbit."[19] And perhaps this, too, is the secret of Nijinsky and the explanation for Roethke's mystical encounter with the tree. Certainly, this phenomenon appears throughout the poetry, as in "A Field of Light"—"I moved with the morning," or in "Praise to the End!"—"Many astounds before, I lost my identity to a pebble." The mystic, too, senses this merging, for he is acutely aware of the unity of all things. His perception of the oneness of creation causes him to strive to give up his ego in favor of merging with the singleness he perceives. In fact, as we shall see in subsequent discussion, the determined movement of the mystic is toward a blending with what he views as the One, the Ultimate, or the Absolute.

The relationship between mysticism and various psychotic states has been observed before, and so I am offering no radical opinions here. However, I prefer not to attempt a resolution of the dispute that psychologists and psychoanalysts have been unable to settle themselves—whether the mystical experience is merely another kind of psychotic state or a truly higher level of consciousness. Certainly, there is much to be said for the theory that mystical states are essentially periods of regression, returning to the infantile condition where "the self and the world have not yet been separated from one another."[20] This notion brings mysticism and manic-depression into even closer proximity since the latter is also characterized by a return to infancy:

> The manic patient returns to a stage in which his impulses had not succumbed to repression, in which he foresaw nothing of the approaching conflict. It is characteristic that such patients often say that they feel themselves "as though new-born."[21]

Significantly, the mystic also speaks of rebirth, of starting over again in a completely new world. Obviously, this notion of regression to infancy bears directly upon Roethke's work, especially "The Lost Son" poems, where the protagonist is followed not only from infancy but from the womb. That Roethke himself was aware of some of the psychological views of mysticism is revealed in the following comment found in a 1942 notebook: "Material psychologists from Voltaire to Freud have said mystics are victims of sexual aberration" (33 #31).

It is not my intention to create confusion about the relationship between manic-depression (and other psychotic states) and mysticism but to show that a considerable amount of discussion about that relationship has been generated through the years. The very existence of such discussion substantiates the similarities. Choosing sides in the ongoing dispute for the purpose of labeling mysticism a psychosis or a higher condition of consciousness is not relevant to this study. Certainly, it is more important simply to acknowledge that the mystic and the manic-depressive have much in common. Parini obliquely broaches this issue when he says, "It would be easy to mistake certain phases of the manic-depressive syndrome for mystical apprehension of the Abolute, or surely, the Dark Night of the Soul."[22] However, he chooses to distinguish between the two conditions rather than to accept their similarities as something more than coincidence. If it is a mistake to relate the manic-depressive symptoms to the mystic's perceptions, then it is a mistake Roethke himself made.

Roethke's first breakdown, whether he willed it or not, was a welcome disruption, a stimulating disarrangement of his senses. It provided him with a new perspective on the world, which revealed itself to him during the episode as inherently harmonious and unified. The resulting insights were of the type that can change a life, and they changed Roethke's. Whether the experience was of a psychotic or mystical nature is beyond our ability to determine. What is apparent is that Roethke himself, judging from many of the notebook entries and his stimulated interest in mystical reading material immediately following the first breakdown, saw a clear relationship between his episode and the mystical experience. Accepting the standard diagnosis that Roethke was a manic-depressive in no way alters the nature of his experience. Ultimately, it is impossible to say with any certainty that Roethke was a mystic, but such a claim does not have to be made. However, it is possible, perhaps inevitable, that we acknowledge the mystical elements in Roethke's poetry, which are derived from his unusual experiences, whatever label we give them. Consequently, we find ourselves in the peculiar, but not improper position, of maintaining that, while Roethke may not have been a mystic, his poetry is unquestionably mystical.

Perhaps the most immediate and significant change brought about in Roethke's poetry by his manic (or mystical) experience involved the way he discovered material. After the episode, he determined "to probe a deeper (richer) level of the mind" (33 #13) and expressed a desire to "live on a higher, a nobler level" (33 #28). Instinctively, it seems, he turned to contemplation, or perhaps he took his cue from Rilke, whom he was reading quite devotedly during the latter part of the 1930s. Whatever the source of his interest, he obviously decided that contemplation could help him reach the desired state, as the following fragmentary line from a 1937 notebook indicates: "There is a level of the mind that none but those who contemplate. . . " (33 #13). Even though the sentence is incomplete, the sense is clear: only those who contemplate can attain a certain perception, a desired level of the mind. Roethke applied himself to the business of contemplation so assiduously that it appears he almost destroyed his interest in it at the outset. An early version of "Lines upon Leaving a Sanitarium," found in rough-draft form in a 1936 notebook, reveals a frustrated contemplative:

> The navel is no proper goal
> For eyes that represent the Soul;
> And brooding leads to blank despair
>
> My friends are often friends, I know,
>
> The mirror yields some truth, but not
> Enough to merit constant thought
>
> The hours spent gazing at the ceiling
> Are often very self-revealing
> Recumbency is unrefined
> Produces terror in the mind
> Dissection is a virtue when
> It operates on other men.
> And contemplation can produce

A great deal that's of little use.

He who inspects himself soon grows
Adept at playing with his toes
This introspection's bound to kill
All hope, and enervate the will. (32A #11)

What we see in this faltering but amusing poem is an apprentice contemplative who is nearly ready to abandon the practice. Although gazing at the ceiling for hours may be "very self-revealing," most of the speaker's efforts seem to be wasted, for he is apparently unable to find anything worthy of contemplation. Consequently, his introspection produces a considerable amount of useless information and serves only to depress him. Obviously, what Roethke sought is what he describes in "On 'Identity' ":

> To look at a thing so long that you are a part of it and it is a part of you—Rilke gazing at his tiger for eight hours, for instance. If you can effect this, then you are by way of getting somewhere: knowing you will break from self-involvement, from I to Otherwise, or maybe even to Thee.[23]

This kind of intense looking can lead to what Roethke describes elsewhere in the "Identity" essay as "the 'oneness,' . . . the first stage in mystical illumination, . . . the sense that all is one and one is all."[24] But for the moment, in those frustrating days of 1936, no such revelation was in the offing. Clearly, the problem here is the lack of an appropriate object of contemplation. Preoccupation with the self allows no opportunity to move beyond the self but leads instead to what Roethke described in "The Return" as "That self-infected lair" (CP, 47). Apparently, however, Roethke did not give up, and by 1942 he could say, "There are sources of life we must reach: we *must*. I hope I have [shown] to you the necessity, the inevitability of contemplation" (33 #28).

Roethke's attempts to find a "deeper level of the mind" through contemplation were prompted by his breakdown. He wanted to be able to regain something of the awareness he had experienced during his manic period; wanted, in other words, to re-create the mystical perception.

Roethke's recognition of a relationship between his mania

and the perspective that can be produced through contemplation is revealed in this 1962 notebook entry:

> Manic: a limitless expanding of the ego with no controlling
> princi [*sic*]
>   (1) an intense communion with nature in which subject and
>   object seem identical
>   (2) abdication of the ego is to another centre the 'self' of
>   . . . (43 #206)

The personal risk involved in courting the manic phase,
though considerable, was worth taking because of the inherent poetic possibilities. At this early stage in his career,
Roethke was ready to embark upon the road to contemplation,
which leads directly to mystical vision, for "*Contemplation* is
the mystic's medium."[25]

I have emphasized contemplation because of the role it plays
in mystical perception and, of course, because of its importance in Roethke's poetry. Contemplation was the process
whereby Roethke attempted to find that "deeper level of the
mind," and it led away from the neat verses of *Open House* into
the freer, more associative poetry of *The Lost Son* and subsequent volumes. As he recorded in a 1937 notebook, "The
method is to use the mind in a state of dissociation: rush of
images, with a condensation of meaning" (33 #12). Ultimately,
process and poem were, for Roethke, virtually indistinguishable. The contemplation he employed to discover poetic material seems to have become the poetry itself. This blurring of
the boundary between artifice and art is the product of
Roethke's well-known obsession with poetry. As David Wagoner says of him in his introduction to *Straw for the Fire*,
Roethke demonstrated "the most wholehearted, energetic,
even uncanny devotion to poetry I have known of, an apparently almost total commitment of time and attention."[26] For
Roethke, the objective in life was to reach that other level of
mind, the one his first breakdown had made him aware of,
and that was also the central concern of his poetry. Not surprisingly, then, the struggle and the poetic account of that
struggle fused; became the same thing: an arduous journey on
the mystic way, the road to ultimate reality.

2.

A Definition of Mysticism

"The mystic says life, not knowledge is the aim; eternal life
in the midst of time."—Roethke Notebooks (36 #86)

The comments made thus far about mysticism reveal, if
nothing else, the difficulty of categorizing it. But the question
of whether the mystical experience is a psychotic state or not
is only a small part of the problem. A much greater and more
fundamental difficulty involves presenting a workable definition. The degree of difficulty is indicated in the first few statements of virtually all definitions of mysticism, which generally
acknowledge the mystical experience to be *ineffable*, and therefore difficult to express verbally. Nevertheless, I shall attempt
a definition that, even if only moderately successful, should
serve as an adequate foundation for my analysis of the mystical elements in Roethke's poetry.

In its broadest and loosest usage, the term *mysticism* is applied to every kind of experience from vague premonitions of
what tomorrow's weather will be to mixed feelings of awe and
reverence before the altar on Sunday morning. In other words,
any insight or intuition that cannot be explained logically is
quite likely to be placed under the rubric of *mysticism*. Obviously, this wide range of application creates difficulties for
anyone who wishes to use the term in a more restricted way.
Even so, a certain consistency can be seen in the usage: mystical experience transcends logic or reason. In its broadest
sense, then, *mysticism* can be defined as "a theory or doctrine,
or view that considers reason to be incapable of discovering or
realising the nature of ultimate truth, but at the same time believes in the certitude of some other means of arriving at it."[1]

This brings us immediately to a fundamental division that is
always made in mysticism and that is also established in much
of Roethke's poetry: the separation of intuition and the logical
thought processes. The mystic, from the very beginning of his

quest for the Absolute, regards as unreliable the senses and the logical mind they inform. Something (which for want of a better word, I shall call intuition) tells him there is more to be known than is communicated to him through his senses, more than his analytical mind can comprehend. It is this aspect of the mystical experience that renders it ineffable, "beyond the reaches of discursive thought—but it is non-rational, not irrational."[2] The experience *can* be understood, though not through the usual channels or in the way we normally understand things.

The ineffable, transcendent quality of the experience has led many people to assume that mysticism is simply an extension of organized religion; another manifestation of Roman Catholic devotion, for example. Not surprisingly, a significant number of mystics have been devout followers of certain religions, particularly Catholicism. But this does not at all imply that mysticism can be subsumed under one, or even several, of the world's great religions, for it is much too universal to be restricted to so narrow a realm. Mysticism is, by its very nature, religious, because the mystic's final goal is knowledge of and union with God, ultimate reality, or the One. But it is "the essential religious experience of man," "the expression of the innate tendency of the human spirit towards complete harmony with the transcendental order; whatever be the theological formula under which that order is understood."[3] It is not inaccurate, then, to view mysticism as the fundamental religious impulse containing and surpassing all individual religions.

Despite the universality of the mystical experience, a distinction is usually made between Christian and oriental mysticism. Many Christian scholars point out that oriental mysticism is pantheistic, whereas Christian mysticism is not, but this is a distinction that arises from religious dogma, and it loses its validity when one notes the many Christian mystics who see God shining forth from every leaf and blade of grass. A more useful distinction is that which takes into account the effect of the mystic quest upon the mystic himself. The Christian is ordinarily energized by his perception of ultimate reality, and his attainment of union usually results in an active life of good works. The oriental mystic, on the other hand, believes in the annihilation of the individual soul in ultimate reality, and he ordinarily tends toward the passive life. Nevertheless, the Christian and the oriental mystic are surprisingly similar despite their cultural and religious differences, and this lends validity to the contention that mysticism is too broad to be contained within the confines of any one religious system. The objective of the mystic's quest, whether he defines it as God, Nirvana, or Brahma, is virtually the same thing: ultimate truth or reality. And whether the mystic is Christian, Buddhist, or Hindu, he must travel essentially the same road to reach his objective.

No attempt will be made in this study to label Roethke's mysticism Christian or oriental, because it is doubtful that such a distinction could be made or that it would be of any value. The essential matter is to substantiate Roethke's mystic quest, and because both the Christian and the oriental mystic travel in the same direction, distinctions of East and West seem unimportant. Moreover, Roethke himself did not have a very extensive knowledge of Eastern mysticism. Most of his information about the subject was obtained from general works such as De Rougemont's *Love in the Western World* and Evelyn Underhill's *Mysticism*. And although his notes on mysticism focus considerably more on the Western (specifically Catholic) mystics, the division between East and West was not meaningful for Roethke in terms of his own experience.

Thus far, I have established only very broad boundaries for mysticism and have in the process counteracted some common misapprehensions. Before moving on to a more specific definition, it would be useful to distinguish between mysticism and occultism, since it has become fashionable in recent years to employ the term *occultism* and reject the term *mysticism* when talking about man's pursuit of ultimate reality. This substitution is usually made in an attempt to escape the religious (specifically Christian) connotations that are attached to *mysticism*, but one would expect the exchange to be invalidated by the voodoo, black magic connotations that cling to *occultism*. Those who have an aversion to both terms employ yet another word, *Hermeticism*, but that is merely occultism by another name.

John Senior, in his germinative book *The Way Down and Out*, maintains that "mysticism is the form occultism took in Christendom as yoga is the form it took in India."[4] Such a statement is possible only if one views mysticism and occultism as the same thing, or, as Senior does, as a part and its whole. Actually, the two, though they parallel one another, are quite different: occultism provides a way of acquiring something, usually knowledge or power, while mysticism provides a way of being. The occultist proceeds from three basic assumptions: "(1) the universe is animate; (2) there is an animating 'force'; (3) this force can be controlled through sympathy and contagion in various kinds of ritual and discipline."[5] The mystic proceeds from two similar but fundamentally different assumptions: (1) there is a higher truth or reality, and (2) one can know this truth or reality by bringing himself into a proper relation with it. The difference is obvious: the occultist exalts the will and attempts to gain control, whereas the mystic surrenders his will and allows himself to be absorbed into the truth he perceives. The dichotomy is as old as man himself, and to mistake the difference is to confuse two human impulses. Roethke's impulse, for example, is to discover his identity, his place in ultimate reality so that he can *be*, not so that he can control. In his own words, "Being, not doing, is my first joy."[6] Mysticism and occultism, then, proceed from the same kind of awareness, an intuition that there is something more than the reality that is normally perceived. But mysticism seeks knowledge leading to being, whereas occultism seeks knowledge leading to power.

Failure to make this distinction can lead to insurmountable problems, not the least of which are erroneous readings of the poetry. Occultism and Hermeticism may be relevant to a reading of much of Yeats, but they have no applicability to Roethke, whose movement was always toward "pure being," not toward any kind of control. The following entry in a 1946 notebook reveals that Roethke was himself aware of the distinction: "The mystic says *life, not knowledge*, is the aim" (36

#86). This, of course, is the fundamental philosophical differ-
ence between Roethke and his literary father W. B. Yeats. Regardless of whatever stylistic similarities there are in the poetry (and Roethke has been more than adequately criticized for
his poetic "borrowings" in this area), there is a significant difference in the attitude each of these poets holds toward what
Yeats called the Unity of Being. That difference is nowhere better expressed than in *A Vision*, Yeats's complex system. Whatever presences Roethke felt, those of Yeats or "the poets
dead,"[7] led directly to poetry, to a sustained effort to "rise from
flesh to spirit" (*CP*, 107), whereas Yeats received his "communicators" while busily copying down gyres and cones and
trying to detect the entrance of a confuser. One man strove to
be, in the absolute sense, while the other tried to accumulate
knowledge.

Having established these general boundaries, we can now
move on to a more specific definition of mysticism, with assistance from others who have struggled with the problem of defining the term. One of the most striking consistencies among
the various definitions, as I have already noted, is the claim
that mysticism is basically ineffable. Although it cannot be
easy to describe the indescribable, many writers have made
the attempt, and their descriptions are remarkably similar.
This leads me to believe that mysticism does have certain dis-
cernible characteristics in spite of the fact that it so stubbornly
resists description.

Bertrand Russell, in his book *Mysticism and Logic*, a work
known to Roethke perhaps as early as 1942, considers mysticism to be "little more than a certain intensity and depth of
feeling in regard to what is believed about the universe."[8]
While this is a less than satisfactory definition, it does contain
the significant word "feeling," which signals an important distinction between mysticism and logic. Russell then proceeds
to list four characteristics of mysticism: (1) "the belief in insight
as against discursive analytic knowledge," (2) the "belief in
unity," (3) "the denial of the reality of Time," (4) the "belief that
all evil is mere appearance."[9] These are characteristics that few
students of mysticism would reject, as they describe the illumination derived from insight rather than analysis, the sub-

sequent merging of the individual in the All, and the consequent loss of a sense of time and opposites in the embrace of the Absolute.

William James, in his well-known definition, also offers four characteristics of mysticism: (1) ineffability, (2) noetic quality, (3) transiency, and (4) passivity.[10] Essentially, James maintains that mysticism cannot be described directly but can only be sketched obliquely through the use of symbol or metaphor; that mystical insights are states of knowledge that are not gained through the discursive intellect; that mystical illumination cannot be sustained for long periods; and that the mystical state cannot be controlled by the will. These descriptive categories are accurate and true to the nature of mysticism, but they are not specific enough for many. The most significant thing here is that James also notes the nondiscursive quality of the mystical insight.

Other definitions range from the apparently simple—"Mysticism is an inward search for unity, whereby the narrow bonds of egotism are dissolved"[11]—to the psychologically complex:

> The mystical state can be described as regression to the earlier pre-infantile level of the collective unconscious which is the matrix of man, wherein lie the seeds of his creativity, his sense of being, his source of integrity and inner harmony, his identity with mankind, and his profound inner union with the integrating principle of the universe.[12]

Yet another definition that combines the simplicity and the complexity of both the preceding efforts in a rather straightforward way is that given by Aldous Huxley:

> The mystical experience, I think, may be defined in a rather simple way as the experience in which the subject–object relationship is transcended, in which there is a sense of complete solidarity of the subject with other human beings and with the universe in general.[13]

The striking thing about all these definitions is that beyond their differences in terminology they say essentially the same thing. Although one would not expect to find such agreement where the ineffable is concerned, most students of mysticism do agree on the basic aspects of mysticism. That harmony of opinion is derived directly from the fact that the characteristics of mystical experience are highly consistent. From individual to individual, across cultures, and even across the centuries, the mystical experience remains fundamentally the same. The individual, usually through no action of his own, becomes intensely aware of the unity of the universe and his place in it. He is made joyously awake to the meaning of life, to the "rightness" of everything. All opposites, including those of life and death, disappear, and all that is left is the single, unified Absolute with which the individual, however briefly, merges. As might be expected, the person who has had this experience feels that he has been vouchsafed a tremendous secret, and though he can never adequately communicate it to anyone else, he carries it with him always. This is the kind of feeling Roethke had in 1935 in East Lansing, Michigan, when he claimed to have had a mystical experience with a tree and learned Nijinksy's secret. It matters little whether we label the episode manic or mystic; the experience was the same: Roethke understood something profound, and it changed his life and his poetry.

Of all the examinations of mysticism that might be cited here, the one which is of most value to this study is Evelyn Underhill's monumental *Mysticism*. In her exhaustive study, Underhill presents a much more detailed picture than Russell, James, and most other scholars in the field, but most significantly, her book was one that Roethke apparently read several times. His copy, which is missing from the University of Washington Manuscript Collection, is nonetheless listed in the Roethke inventory there as one of his personal library books that was heavily annotated. But there is more concrete evidence to indicate that Roethke was thoroughly familiar with Underhill's study. In a 1946 notebook, on a page dated April 7, appears this entry:

> Go back to Evelyn Underhill's Mysticism: A Study in the Nature
> and Development of Man's Spiritual Consciousness. 1912
> 1) Awakening—to a sense of divine reality
> 2) Purgation of self, when it realizes its own imperfections

3) an enhanced return of a sense of the divine order, after the Self has achieved its detachment from the world.
4) Dark night of the Soul (36 #84)

This brief outline, which lists four of the five stages along what Underhill terms the Mystic Way, is copied nearly verbatim from pages 169 and 170 of *Mysticism*. It is the heart of Underhill's study because it establishes classifications and provides the organization for her analysis of the mystical experience. Why Roethke omitted the final stage, union, is not clear since he obviously was not reproducing the outline from memory but was transcribing it in shortened form from the book itself.

It is, of course, impossible to say how much Underhill's work may have influenced Roethke. Certainly, there were other works on mysticism in his personal library: *The Cloud of Unknowing*, Anonymous; *The Mystic Will: Based on a Study of the Philosophy of Jacob Boehme*, Howard H. Brinton; *Mysticism and Poetry: On a Basis of Experience*, A. Allen Brockington; and many others, including several more titles by Underhill. However, we can say with considerable assurance that Roethke obviously found *Mysticism* to be a worthwhile study since he directed himself to "go back" to it. Some critics, most notably William Heyen and Jay Parini, have maintained that Roethke was very strongly influenced by Underhill's study, and Heyen even goes so far as to claim that Roethke used the work as the basis for much of the poetry in *The Far Field*.[14] Rather than prove such an influence, I intend to make a broader claim: that mysticism informs Roethke's poetry from beginning to end and that Underhill's book, which was known to Roethke, is a useful source to help explain that element in his work. Roethke's interest in books on mysticism was prompted by a need to understand his manic experiences, and though these works may ultimately have influenced his poetry, especially toward the end, I doubt that they were ever exploited for poetic material. Rather, they were used simply as corroborative evidence, to confirm and explain Roethke's own experiences, to enable him to understand himself. Consequently, these works (in particular, Underhill's) can contribute significantly to our understanding of Roethke's poetry.

According to Underhill, the mystic is conscious of a higher plane of reality, a greater truth than that which is normally apprehended, and he dedicates himself to the attainment of that higher plane. His "one passion appears to be the prosecution of a certain spiritual and intangible quest: the finding of a 'way out' or a 'way back' to some desirable state."[15] This, then, constitutes the two basic assumptions from which mysticism proceeds: (1) that there is a higher truth or reality and (2) that one can know that truth or reality by bringing himself into a proper relation with it.

Invariably, the mystic perceives that higher truth either as transcendent or immanent. If transcendent, it is viewed as something outside man, something infinitely high and beyond the everyday world. In order to attain it, the mystic must go beyond himself, must make the arduous climb upward to the summit. If immanent, the higher truth is seen to reside within the individual. The universe is "charged with the grandeur of God," and the mystic must but realize that he possesses within himself the truth he seeks.

Regardless of whether the mystic perceives ultimate reality as transcendent or immanent his attempts to attain it will follow a fairly well defined process. Underhill calls this process the Mystic Way, and she presents it in five stages: (1) awakening, (2) purgation, (3) illumination, (4) dark night of the soul, and (5) union. These categories, of course, are not absolute or inviolable. In fact, the progress of the mystic toward his goal is essentially an alternation between states of pleasure and states of pain: illumination offset by *purgation* or *dark night of the soul*. Nevertheless, these five stages do provide a good idea of the general direction in which the mystic travels and should therefore be of considerable use to us as landmarks in our study of Roethke's mystic quest.

The *awakening* is an initial insight that causes the individual to realize there is a higher level of truth. This insight is not volitional but occurs automatically, beyond the control of the will (as in Roethke's first manic episode—although he felt he helped to bring it on). Most people have experienced moments in which they have felt inexplicably happy or sad, or when a perfectly ordinary sight, a wren on the fence, perhaps, has seemed charged with significance and meaning. Such flashes are similar to what the mystic experiences at the moment of awakening, except that he, unlike most of us, realizes the full import of that moment and acts to align himself with the truth he perceives.

Purgation is a period of "pain and effort." The mystic, after realizing that there is a higher truth and desiring to attain it, becomes aware of his own flaws and imperfections that hold him back. He realizes that he must cleanse himself if he is ever to attain the object of his desires. This is a period in which the body is abjured (and frequently abused) in an attempt to suppress the weak flesh and extend the spirit.

Illumination, as the word implies, is understanding, a time when the light shines through and the reality that was sensed at the moment of awakening and prepared for during purgation is seen completely. In Blake's terminology, the windows of perception have been cleansed. This is a period of joy, during which everything reveals its true meaning; the secret of the universe is understood. But the transcendent reality is only seen and understood, not attained. The mystic, at this point, can see the object of his quest at the end of the road, but he still has a considerable distance to travel.

The *dark night of the soul*, or mystic death, is the backward swing of the pendulum. The mystic, having experienced illumination and a complete sense of the reality he seeks, is now left in the darkness. The sense of despondency and loss is acute, for he can never be satisfied with anything less than the truth he has perceived. According to Underhill, this is a final stage of purgation in which the mystic is stripped of the last rags of selfhood, is taught that the pleasure of mystical vision is different from the reality of mystical life. "The Self now surrenders itself, its individuality, and its will, completely." [16]

The final stage of the Mystic Way is *union*. This is the mystic's ultimate destination, the object of his quest. The reality he sensed in the moment of awakening, saw fully in the period of illumination, and prepared himself for through purgation and the mystic death is finally attained. He and the transcendent reality are one.

These five stages, then, represent Underhill's pattern of the mystic quest. But, as indicated earlier, they are by no means absolute, for in the experience of various mystics some of these stages are merged or altogether absent. However, these stages do give a valuable picture of the road the typical mystic (insofar as it is possible to refer to any mystic as typical) travels. Ordinarily, his progress is accompanied by some slipping back: states of pleasure are offset by states of pain, but he invariably advances. Roethke expresses this aspect of the experience rather succinctly: "It is necessary to suffer in order to praise" (36 #84).

Because the mystic's experiences are of an ineffable nature, it is difficult for him to describe them to the uninitiated, but so convinced is he of the significance of his struggle and the insight he gains that he frequently makes the attempt. This invariably leads him into metaphor and symbolism, because it is only by telling what his experience is *like* that he can communicate it to those familiar only with the reality of the everyday world. Underhill maintains that the various symbols employed by the mystics can be subsumed under three major categories: symbols of (1) the journey, (2) growth or transmutation, and (3) the lovers.[17] Those who use the symbol of the journey are ordinarily, but not exclusively, mystics who perceive ultimate reality as something external to themselves, something above and beyond, toward which they must travel. Symbols of growth or transmutation are used primarily, but once again not exclusively, by those who perceive ultimate reality within themselves. For them, the process is one of internal change. The symbol of the lovers is employed by all mystics generally, as all mystics think in terms of love and are actively involved in the process of loving God (or ultimate reality). The symbolism a particular mystic uses to describe his experience is ordinarily reflective of the kind of experience he has, or rather, the way he perceives it. However, it is not uncommon to find those who employ all three major symbols in an exhaustive attempt to convey something of their ineffable experience to the uninitiated.

Roethke is one of those who uses all three kinds of symbols in an effort to communicate some sense of his manic or mystical perceptions. Furthermore, Roethke's collected poetry di-

vides rather naturally, according to symbolic type, into Underhill's three categories of symbolism: the journey, inward
growth, and the lovers. Moreover, within each of these divisions Roethke's search for identity closely follows the five
stage Mystic Way.

In addition to Underhill's three basic symbolic categories,
Roethke's last poems comprise a fourth category, which we
might call symbols of the infinite. It is in these last poems that
all of Roethke's previous searching merges into a final preparation for the union of death. The route is cyclical, and
Roethke is in many ways a "Perpetual beginner" (CP, 171),
searching outside himself, within himself, and in his relationship with another person for his identity, following each path
as far as he can, and then beginning again, but always passing
through the various stages of awakening, purgation, and illumination, occasionally experiencing the dark night and ultimately approaching union.

3.

The Mystical Tradition: Vaughan, Traherne, Blake, and Yeats

"A test of a writer is how he survives his influences."—Roethke Notebooks (33 #15)

Aside from the insights his own particular condition afforded him and those he obtained from the mystical texts he read more and more as the years passed, Roethke had another rich store of mystical perception available to him in the work of earlier poets. He was a voracious reader of poetry, not only of that produced by his contemporaries but of what we might call classical or traditional English poetry, and his notebooks reveal a broad acquaintance with the works of writers throughout history. David Wagoner remembers Roethke as one of the best read men he has ever met, with a brilliant mind, able to recite lengthy passages and whole poems on the moment to make a point in class or in conversation.[1] The fact that Roethke himself was apparently not impressed with his knowledge and ability in this area—viewing himself instead as a "grunt and groan" man, anything but an intellectual—reveals a good bit about his personal insecurities.

Many critics, in particular Malkoff, La Belle, and Parini, have already tracked down Roethke's sources, from Shakespeare to Auden. The definitive work in the area of Roethke's literary influences, and the place to turn for a thorough accounting of how Roethke's readings in poetry influenced his work, is La Belle's fine book, *The Echoing Wood of Theodore Roethke*. Rather than duplicate her effort, I will focus my comments on a select group of poets who had a profound and lifelong effect on Roethke. I agree with Malkoff that Roethke was influenced "by a tradition of poetry that included Vaughan, Traherne, Blake, and contemporaries whose verse contained a quasi-mystical view of reality."[2] However, I would modify his observation by eliminating "contemporaries" and substituting Yeats, whose

strong influence on Roethke has been adequately acknowledged but whose significance changes when he is viewed as
part of a mystical tradition. Although other poets who influenced Roethke, most notably Wordsworth and Whitman, are
also properly included in the mystical tradition, they are ex-
cluded from this discussion because they are poetical descend-
ents of Vaughan, Traherne, and Blake. My objective is to get
back to Roethke's primary ancestors.

According to La Belle, "Roethke went beyond responding to
a single poet and actually formed a tradition of poets" whose
themes and techniques were useful to him.[3] However, in the
area of mystical poetry, Roethke did not so much have to form
a tradition as to perceive the one that already existed, and his
own peculiar temperament made it easy for him to do just
that. Like most of us, Roethke was attracted to literature that
seemed to speak directly to him and to reflect something of his
own feelings and experiences. It was characteristic of him to
identify with the so-called "mad" poets, Christopher Smart,
John Clare, and William Blake, sensing a common bond between himself and them on the basis of his own "mad" experiences. Significantly, he turned to the mystical poets early
in his career and sustained a strong interest in them throughout his life because he felt a kinship with them. What he found
in their poetry, other than a reflection of his own unusual perceptions and validation of his manic experiences, was a ready-
made and altogether acceptable set of images and symbols for
his own writing. I am speaking not of individual borrowings,
which La Belle and others have adequately identified, but of
larger motifs, of images and symbols rooted so firmly in mystical experience that they can be called archetypal. Specifically,
Roethke found in mystical poetry the imagery and symbolism
of light, plants, and children, all central elements in his own
work. Had these images and symbols not been compatible
with his own perceptions, of course, Roethke would not have
been attracted to them, so there is some reason to speculate
that he discovered them on his own and merely found their
usefulness corroborated in mystical poetry. Whatever the sequence of events, we can say without qualification that
Roethke learned a great deal about the basic images and sym-

bols of mysticism from poets such as Vaughan, Traherne,
Blake, and Yeats, and that what he learned had an impact on
his poetry.

The following passage, taken from a 1962 notebook, identifies one of the mystical poets who most strongly influenced
Roethke and reveals Roethke in an uncharacteristically hum-
ble mood, freely acknowledging his debts:

> Teach me, sweet love, a way of being plain!
> My virtues are but vices in disguise.
> The little light I had was Henry Vaughan's.
> I hunted fire in ice: the soul's unease,
> In the loose rubble, the least glistening stone,
> And what I found was but one riddled bone:
> I move, unseeing, toward an absolute
> So bright within it darkens all I am. (42 #210)

Perhaps the self-effacement in these lines can best be understood in the context of the final poems of *The Far Field* in which
Roethke struggles to get beyond self and to achieve an acceptance of death. It is a process of humility, in mystical terms, of
finally getting rid of the cumbersome baggage of the individual identity and yielding one's self to the larger One. The
reference to Vaughan's light may be taken on two levels of
meaning: as a reference to Vaughan's insights, his own personal visions, or as an allusion to one of Vaughan's principal
symbols, which Roethke himself adopted. In the context of the
passage, both meanings seem to be functioning, and each is
an acknowledgment of the influence of Henry Vaughan. However, the second meaning is more valid since Roethke clearly
had his own unique illuminations, however much they may
have resembled Vaughan's. What he borrowed from Vaughan
was his symbol of light.

Roethke's early acquaintance with Vaughan's poetry is revealed in a paper written in 1930 while he was still a student
at Michigan. The essay, an examination of Vaughan's influence
on Wordsworth, contains the following significant remarks:

> But this sense of activity in nature—especially a divine activity—
> occurs with far greater frequency in Vaughan. He has been called
> "The Poet of Light," but light to Vaughan was only one kind of
> activity. It is almost impossible not to find in any of his poems

> some manifestation of this, either in the use of a single epithet or
> as a considerable part of a poem. Vaughan was literally over-
> whelmed by movement in the world, not merely as movement
> but as a manifestation of the divine. (60 #12)

It is interesting to observe Roethke's interest in the mystical
perception at this early date, five years before his own first
manic experience permanently altered his view of the world.
By identifying light with activity, this passage shows that he
implicitly understood the nature of mystical illumination, that
joyous perception in which all the world seems alive and filled
with significance. Certainly, in Roethke's later poetry, particularly in *The Lost Son*, he himself made this connection, and
light is always associated with great activity (as in "A Field of
Light"). However, at such an early stage Roethke could only
intuit the relationship because he lacked the experience to understand it.

To illustrate Roethke's initial lack of mastery over the symbol
he so admired in Vaughan, one needs only to look at "This
Various Light," which Roethke attributed to Vaughan's influence. The final stanza of the poem is representative of the
whole:

> This light is heaven's transcendent boon, a beam
> Of infinite calm; it will never cease;
> It will illuminate forever the aether–stream;
> This light will lead me to eventual peace.[4]

Although he described this poem in a 1934 letter as "one of the
best I've ever done"[5] and worked hard to get it published
(without success), he finally came to view the piece as a failure
and used it as an example of "pastiche" in his article "How to
Write Like Somebody Else." The problem, of course, is that the
poem is totally discursive and out of touch with any genuine
insight. Compared to the following passage from "Unfold! Unfold!," which takes its title from the first line of Vaughan's "The
Revival," the imagery in "This Various Light" is static and
mundane:

> A light song comes from the leaves.
> A slow sigh says yes. And light sighs;
> A low voice, summer-sad. (*CP*, 90)

Here, light is truly animate as it is in Vaughan, and it is clearly associated with illumination: "At first the visible obscures: / Go where light is" (*CP*, 90). Of course, the differences between the two poems have something to do with Roethke's growth and development as a poet between 1933 and 1949, but the differences are not entirely attributable to the normal maturing process. Certainly, Roethke's manic experiences had a great deal to do with his ability to understand the true significance of Vaughan's mystical verse, and they enabled him to use the symbol of light with conviction rather than as an attractive ornament. The change is basically from intellectual detachment to active participation in the brilliant unity of the world.

Aside from the symbol of light, Roethke may also have found Vaughan's images of plants and flowers influential. At least one such image, found in "The Retreate," invites comparison to Roethke: "felt through all this fleshly dresse / Bright *shootes* of everlastingness."[6] The similarity to "Cuttings (later)" is obvious: "I can hear, underground, that sucking and sobbing, / In my veins, in my bones I feel it,—" (*CP*, 37). Vaughan's images of flowers, trees, and the natural world in general may have appealed to Roethke as strongly as the symbol of light. Certainly, Roethke had the background to employ such symbolism, and from his first manic episode forward he must have found it irresistible.

Just as Vaughan opened Roethke's eyes to the symbols of light and plants, Thomas Traherne made him aware of the world of the child and its usefulness to poetry. Of course, Blake, too, was influential in this area, but it is Traherne to whom Roethke points in his letter to Babette Deutsch (subsequently published as "Open Letter") when naming the influences on "The Lost Son" sequence: "My real ancestors, such as they are, are the bible, Mother Goose, and Traherne."[7] From the Bible he took the simple but elegant English of King James and used it to construct aphorisms and questions: "Hath the rain a father?" (*CP*, 56); Mother Goose afforded him the pattern for the many skip-rope songs: "Gilliflower ha, / Gilliflower ho, / My love's locked in / The old silo" (*CP*, 60); Traherne's poetry suggested the general importance of the child's point of view in the search for ultimate reality. For Traherne, the mystical doctrine of regeneration or rebirth was translated literally into the need to recover the lost perceptions of childhood. Of the three influences cited by Roethke, Traherne is the most significant because what Roethke took from him was more than a stylistic effect: he took the basic premise that frames the entire "Lost Son" sequence.

Examples of Traherne's view of childhood abound in his poetry, but his attitude is nowhere better expressed than in "Wonder." I quote only the first stanza, which is sufficient to illustrate:

> How like an Angel came I down!
>   How bright are all things here!
> When first among His works I did appear
>   O how their Glory did me crown!
> The world resembled his *Eternity*,
>   In which my soul did walk;
>   And every thing that I did see
>   Did with me talk.[8]

For Traherne, the child is in communion with all of life. Having recently come from somewhere above, like an angel, he still carries a memory of his place of origin and so sees the world in terms of that "Eternity." Of course, this idea is also found in Blake and Wordsworth, both familiar to Roethke, but Traherne is the original source for him.

While "The Lost Son" sequence may represent, as Roethke maintained, "an effort to be born,"[9] it also describes, in the opposite direction, a regression to childhood. The objective is to obtain a lost innocence, to regain the lost world of the father, and the word *father* must be taken in both its familial and its cosmic sense. Like Traherne, Roethke turned to childhood for illumination, for a stronger sense of the unity that is more accessible to the child than to the adult. To be sure, Roethke's obsession with his father and the greenhouse world may have impelled him to turn to his own childhood for subject matter, quite apart from Traherne's influence. But Traherne's poetry stood as a clear example of the poetic insights available to the poet who can recapture something of the child's perception, and Roethke felt he was important enough to list him as one of the sources of his sequence.

When Roethke revised his letter to Babette Deutsch for publication, he placed the name of Blake alongside that of Traherne in his list of ancestors, indicating that Blake, too, was instrumental in the attempt to create the "as if" of the child's world. Traherne showed Roethke the value of the child's perspective from the adult's viewpoint, but Blake went even further and spoke directly from the child's perspective, as if he were a child. Breaking down the barrier between the adult's and the child's view of the world was an essential step in Roethke's effort to attain "a consciousness beyond the mundane,"[10] and Blake's work showed how effectively that step could be taken. Consequently, the progress in "The Lost Son" sequence from innocence to experience owes a good deal to Blake's influence. The protagonist in the sequence moves from the naive world of the child to the knowledgeable world of the young adult and beyond to a benign sense of unity which recaptures something of the child's original perception. This movement toward "a final innocence,"[11] as Roethke called it, bears a striking resemblance to Blake's concept of "organized innocence," in which the child's and adult's perceptions combine to produce a final and superior illumination. Blake's idea of *contraries* without which there is no progression is apparent in Roethke from the beginning in his opposition of body and spirit and subsequently in his pairings of child and adult, the male and female lovers, and finally, life and death. In the words of the lost son, "The depth calls to the Height" (*CP*, 97).

Blake was influential in other ways, too. We can see, for example, Roethke's attraction to the aphoristic style Blake employed in "The Marriage of Heaven and Hell." Interestingly, one of Roethke's unpublished poems, "Enough! Or Too Much," written in 1943 or 1944, takes its title from a line in Blake's poem and reveals that Roethke was probably reading Blake at the time he was beginning to work on "The Lost Son" sequence. Beyond such stylistic influences, Roethke felt a kinship with Blake as one of the mad poets, implicitly relating his own unusual perceptions during his manic episodes to Blake's visions. He undoubtedly felt that he and Blake, and poets like John Clare and Christopher Smart, shared comparable insights. Their madness was "nobility of soul/At odds with circumstance" (*CP*, 239). However, Roethke did not share Blake's prophetic voice or his desire to create a system out of his unique perceptions. Roethke's efforts were too personal to lead him in that direction. As he said in one of his notebook entries, "In crawling out of a swamp, or up what small rock-faces I try to essay, I don't need a system on my back."[12] The struggle was to bring the self to a realization of its true identity, and there were no time and energy left over for system building. In this connection, Roethke's final line in "The Abyss" takes on additional significance: "Being, not doing, is my first joy" (*CP*, 222).

Another great system builder and inheritor of the tradition handed down through Blake was W. B. Yeats, who had a significant impact on Roethke. During Roethke's own lifetime, the influence of Yeats on his poetry was discussed to such an extent that Roethke remarked, almost in exasperation, "I should like to think I have over-acknowledged, in one way or another, my debt to Yeats."[13] To be sure, Roethke learned a great deal from Yeats about the technicalities of verse, and his free use of Yeatsean cadences and diction has been the subject of much comment and criticism. However, it is interesting to note that Yeats's influence is strongest at both ends of Roethke's career. In *Open House*, in many respects an apprentice work, Roethke borrowed freely from Yeats and was accused of not successfully assimilating his influence. And, in his last decade, when Roethke was at the height of his powers, he once again turned to Yeats as a kind of literary or spiritual father. Standing between these two periods of Yeatsean influence is a large body of poetry, most notably *The Lost Son*, which has no connection with Yeats at all. In a very real sense, then, the importance of Yeats to Roethke's poetry has been somewhat overstated. As Sullivan says, "what makes Roethke seem more dependent on Yeats than he actually is, is that he sometimes borrowed Yeatsean conventions . . . and words."[14]

Roethke himself had some interesting things to say about Yeats in the 1963 interview with the students who were filming

In a Dark Time: "If you want to talk about ancestors, it's a mistake to set up Yeats as a central guy; for one reason, I resisted Yeats for a long time. I remember even saying to Bogan, 'I don't get him'" (140). Later in the same interview he remarked "I was much more grounded in Blake, say, than I ever was with Yeats and also with some of the people that affected Yeats" (140). These remarks may make Roethke sound as though he is protesting too much, but there is a fundamental truth here. As a modern poet seriously interested in the mystical philosophy, Yeats stood at the end of a long line of poets who were familiar to Roethke, particularly Vaughan, Traherne, and Blake, and as we have already seen, Roethke was indeed well grounded in those poets. The problem, then, is determining the source of the influence on Roethke's work. Undoubtedly, the Yeatsean style found its way into a number of Roethke's poems. However, the Yeatsean philosophy did not. In this regard, when Roethke downplays Yeats's significance as an ancestor, he is telling the truth.

The essential difference between the two poets is the difference between mysticism and occultism. Yeats's insights, with the possible exception of the one described in "Vacillation," were not spontaneous. Instead, his illuminations were derived from Irish history and mythology and from his pursuit of occultism. Roethke, speaking once again in the context of the 1963 interview, put it this way: "The difference is that I can dance, and Yeats can't . . . and I can say this without batting an eye, that I know, in the final term, something and perhaps a good deal more than I realize about mystic experience. Yeats didn't" (140). This is a curious comment to come from someone who wrote a poem titled "The Dance" and acknowledged Yeats as its principal source. However, the validity of the remark becomes clear when we realize Roethke was equating the dance with mystic experience. Yeats may have had some lilting cadences, but in the final analysis he himself did not know how to dance. *Dancing* in this sense implies letting go and giving oneself up to the vision of a larger self. Clearly, Yeats could never relinquish control, and *A Vision*, that marvelously incomprehensible system, stands as a monument to his desire not only to know but to exercise some control over what he knew. While Roethke was "dancing mad" and giving himself over to the brilliance of illumination, Yeats was taking hurried notes, in the best intellectual fashion, from his "communicators."

Yeats's inability to dance explains why he was not influential in "The Lost Son" sequence. The object there is to regain a lost innocence, and this implies giving up knowing, allowing oneself to be swept into the swirling dance beyond rational thought. Roethke obviously understood that Yeats could not assist him in this effort because it required a mystical and not an occult temperament. The occultist never abandons knowing, since he ultimately wishes to exert control over whatever illuminations he has. Ironically, this may explain why Roethke, in his final years, once again turned to Yeats, to see how the Irishman came to terms with his approaching death and the inevitable relinquishing of control. Having turned to Yeats as a model when first setting out, in *Open House*, he came back to him at the end, not as the novice poet but as the novice at dying.

It is important to note that the Yeats who presented himself most forcefully to Roethke was the old Yeats, the "sixty-year-old smiling public man"[15] who confronted eternity in poems like "Sailing to Byzantium" and his own declining powers in "The Circus Animals' Desertion." For at least a decade before his death in 1939, two years before the publication of *Open House*, Yeats had presented to the world the image of the old man awaiting his end, "Dreading and hoping all."[16] Certainly, that is the picture Roethke conjures up in "The Dying Man," the poem he dedicated to Yeats. More and more during the last decade of his own life, Roethke came to identify with Yeats, becoming himself "An old man with his feet before the fire,/In robes of green, in garments of adieu" (*CP*, 201). Having explored the depths of his own psyche and the reaches of the love relationship, he began considering "Death's possibilities" (*CP*, 153). In this final push toward illumination and union, Roethke employed Yeats as a symbol of how the poet confronts death's vast abyss, of how he stops being a bird but continues to beat his wings "Against the immense immeasurable emptiness of things" (*CP*, 156).

William Meredith has said of Roethke's interest in Yeats, "It is hard to think of another instance where a first-rate poet engaged so personally and in maturity a talent greater than his own."[17] While Roethke's interest in Yeats may be attributed to his characteristic bravado, his desire to best the master at his own game, he also may have turned to Yeats because Yeats afforded the most exact parallel to his own condition. Surely Roethke could not have been unaware of the risks, but whatever risks were involved must, to Roethke's mind, have been outweighed by the poetic advantages. Just as he learned about light from Vaughan and the value of the child's perception from Traherne and Blake, Roethke learned a great deal about the dying man from Yeats. In each case, Roethke was attracted to something that paralleled his own experiences, and the poetry of his literary ancestors was used not to fill gaps in his own work but to augment themes and symbols he had already derived from his own intense perceptions. Roethke's accurate premonitions of his death, expressed so poignantly in the poems of *The Far Field*, are among the most intriguing aspects of his poetry. Somehow, barely fifty years old, Roethke sensed that his own death was approaching, and he turned to Yeats as to a counselor or guide.

A final word must be said about Yeats in the context of the mystical tradition. In the sense that Yeats is the literary descendent of Blake, he represents an extension of the mystical tradition into the twentieth century. But Yeats presents something of a problem in this area because his work cannot properly be called mystical, at least not in the same sense as that of Vaughan and Blake. Even if we substitute the term "visionary" (which Northrop Frye prefers for Blake) for "mystical," Yeats still does not resemble his literary predecessors closely enough to qualify. Yeats labored after his visions, went in search of them in Irish folklore, spiritualism, Rosicrucianism, and theosophy. He was, by strict definition, an occultist, eager to conjure an illumination and hungry for the knowledge it could bring. This approach clearly separates him from Vaughan, Traherne, and Blake, whose periods of illumination were not manufactured by the intellect in search of knowledge but experienced spontaneously by the intuitive faculties. Even if we accept Roethke's claim that he willed his first manic episode, that does not change the fact that his experience was fundamentally different from Yeats's insights. Roethke strove continually to escape the boundaries of the phenomenal world while Yeats, in customary occultist fashion, labored to extend them.[18] More than a definitional quibble, this distinction is fundamental to an understanding of the mystical tradition and Roethke's place in it. A logical extension of this discussion brings up the issue of whether it is possible to be both a poet and a mystic, but that matter will be reserved for discussion in a later section. At this point, the concept of a mystical tradition and the mystical qualities inherent in Roethke's poetry and the poetry of his literary ancestors are separate and more immediate concerns.

It is ironic that the poets who influenced Roethke can be seen most clearly in what is considered his most original poetry, "The Lost Son" sequence. Roethke's claim that the sequence does not depend on allusion may be true in the narrow sense, although La Belle and others have presented evidence to the contrary. However, in the broader sense the sequence not only alludes to, but derives from the mystical tradition, as does most of Roethke's poetry. This is not to say that Roethke engaged in wholesale borrowing, but that he was drawn to and influenced by those poets whose views and experiences matched his own. Determining the extent of their influence on his poetry is perhaps impossible, but it seems likely that Roethke found in the work of poets like Vaughan and Blake models for his own innate longing for an ultimate reality. At the outset, particularly after his first manic episode in 1935, Roethke's experiences and perceptions were unconnected; they were aberrant. Putting them into their proper context involved reading poetry, where he found not only reassurance but a clear indication of the path he was to take in his own writing.

II. The Outward Journey

4.

The Arrival of Awareness

"The theory that there are many other worlds, even greater, many other forms of life, perhaps higher, should not depress us, but call us to greater endeavor."—Roethke Notebooks (35 #66)

In 1955 Theodore Roethke wrote of *Open House*: "It took me ten years to complete one little book, and now some of the things in it seem to creak. Still, I like about ten pieces in it."[1] In less positive terms, Roethke did not like approximately three-fourths of his book. Though we may detect in his remark the artist's familiar disenchantment with his early work, we are likely to agree that *Open House* contains much weak verse. Roethke himself felt that most of the poems were "over-neat, mere Jacobean doo-dads."[2] And indeed some are neat to the point of triteness. For example, "The Favorite" tells of a lucky "knave" who became so jaded by his easy successes that he began to long for failure, a paradox that seems as contrived as the sonnet format that contains it. Similarly, "Death Piece" and "No Bird," though they have a fine epigrammatic terseness, lose some of their impact when looked at side by side, for they are essentially two versions of the same poem.

In many ways, the form in Roethke's early poetry seems to take precedence over the content, and the meter and rhyme frequently force him into awkward constructions, as in the final couplet of " 'Long Live the Weeds' " (*CP*, 18): "Hope, love, create, or drink and die:/These shape the creature that is I." Even in 1936 when Harriet Monroe printed this poem in *Poetry*, the inversion must have seemed a bit artificial.

Richard Allen Blessing is correct when he says that Roethke in the early part of his career relied on the restrictive forms because they stimulated his imagination, prompted him to think of things he might not otherwise have thought of.[3] But too often Roethke seems to have gone straight for the "poetic" subject, the grand theme. Consequently, we might say that the most significant breakthrough during the mid-1940s was not so much Roethke's development of a new style as his discovery of his true subject; the form then followed naturally. In the years between *Open House* and *The Lost Son*, Roethke was able to resolve the form/content question this way: "Do you invent your own patterns or go back to the past? The poem invents the form; it insists on the form" (33 #22). But throughout the 1930s, the opposite seems often to have been true.

The importance Roethke placed on form can best be illustrated by presenting three short poems that have obvious things in common. The first, "Death Piece" (*CP*, 4), is a concentrated little poem that achieves its effect through the compressed style and vivid metaphors it employs:

> Invention sleeps within a skull
> No longer quick with light,
> The hive that hummed in every cell
> Is now sealed honey-tight.
>
> His thought is tied, the curving prow
> Of motion moored to rock;
> And minutes burst upon a brow
> Insentient to shock.

I have already mentioned that this poem is strikingly similar to "No Bird," but consider it in relation to the following poem, "There Is No Word" (33 #20), found among the notebooks:

> There is no word that can be said
> In this imperial peace.
> The quiet wrapped about his head
> Bespeaks the mind's surcease.
>
> His shadow is dispersed, its size
> Is lost in rolling shade.
> Withhold the anguishment of eyes
> For tongueless accolade.

Still another poem, "Genius" (20 #6), found among the unpublished poetry manuscripts, displays essentially the same flourishes:

> His strength is coiled about a core,
> A central spot of mind;

One continent, one endless shore
By single sea confined.

A meaning laid upon a shelf,
A secret cooped and furled—
Or sea that breaks upon itself
Yet shakes a sodden world?

All three of these poems were apparently composed in 1934,
and I speculate, they were written within the span of only a
few days. ("Death Piece" appeared in the *Nation* and "Genius"
in the *Atlantic Monthly*, both in May.) They are essentially practice pieces, identical in meter and rhyme pattern and strikingly
similar in content. In fact, they are all fundamentally the same
poem. But, what seems paramount to each is the form; the
content is merely something poured into the mold.

Between the publication of *Open House* in 1941 and *The Lost
Son* in 1948, Roethke's poetry underwent a remarkable transformation, particularly in the area of form. While we might
speculate with Malkoff that the change was inevitable and
merely reflective of Roethke's maturation as an artist,[4] I suggest it grew out of his breakdown in 1935. After that experience, Roethke's focus gradually shifted away from the traditional poetic topics and onto himself, away from the standard
rhetoric and neat syntactic packages of his early years and into
a more organic style reflective of his expanded consciousness.
He no longer needed the forms to stimulate him; he had his
own extraordinary perceptions to explore. At the same time,
there is continuity between *Open House* and *The Lost Son*. That
first volume of poems contained the seed, however deeply
buried, of what grew vigorously in the greenhouse world of
The Lost Son.

Open House is constructed on two related dichotomies: (1)
analysis and intuition, (2) flesh and spirit. These divisions are
at the very center of the mystical experience. The mystic believes that he can arrive at ultimate truth or reality only by
rejecting logic and analytical reasoning, because they are the
basis for the reality normally perceived and are therefore of no
use to anyone who wishes to perceive *true* reality. He realizes
that he must somehow transcend them if he is to apprehend

things as they truly are, and he does this through the only means available to him, his intuition. Likewise, the mystic invariably perceives a tension between flesh and spirit. A close relationship is seen between the analytical mind and the flesh, which are undesirable because restrictive, and between intuition and the spirit, which can lead to new perceptions. The mystic realizes that the flesh and its unreliable senses, which inform the analytical mind, must be subdued and the spirit extended if he is to approach the reality he desires. He accomplishes this task through mortification and denial of bodily comforts, whereby the flesh is abused and rejected, and through contemplation that allows him to step outside his body and participate in the reality of the thing he is focused upon. The movement from logic and flesh to intuition and spirit corresponds closely to the mystical stages of awakening and purgation, and the process is often symbolized, as in *Open House*, by a journey.

The best place to begin an examination of Roethke's outward journey is with his awakening, his realization that there is something beyond his normal range of awareness, and his subsequent understanding that analytical thought and the senses of the body are incapable of approaching the ultimate truth he intuits. Sometimes, for no apparent reason, another reality reveals itself, but only momentarily. Consider, for example, "The Signals" (*CP*, 8):

> Often I meet, on walking from a door,
> A flash of objects never seen before.
>
> As known particulars come wheeling by,
> They dart across a corner of the eye.
>
> They flicker faster than a blue-tailed swift,
> Or when dark follows dark in lightning rift.
>
> They slip between the fingers of my sight.
> I cannot put my glance upon them tight.
>
> Sometimes the blood is privileged to guess
> The things the eye or hand cannot possess.

Here, it is interesting to note Roethke's description of the perception: He *meets* "A flash of objects never seen before." The word *meet* is significant because it appears where we might expect to find *see*. The strange objects are not seen, at least not in the usual sense. Rather, they are met or experienced. In fact, the perception is more a function of the blood than of the eye, and thus we have a clear division between the senses and the intuition. Still, the experience is described in terms of vision: "A flash of objects," a "blue-tailed swift," a rift of lightning. This is characteristic of descriptions of mystical perceptions, that, finally, can be described only in terms of the senses, even though the experience itself transcends them. The most significant thing here is that Roethke describes his perception in a way familiar to every student of mysticism, as a "flash," a brilliant light amid the surrounding darkness, a moment of illumination. Roethke senses what all mystics sense during the stage of awakening, that there is something more than the normal, everyday world in which we conduct our routine lives, and this awareness is expressed even more directly in a 1946 notebook entry that can serve as a gloss for "The Signals":

> The feeling that one is on the edge of many things: that there are many worlds from which we are separated by only a film; that a flick of the wrist, a turn of the body another way will bring us to a new world. It is more than a perpetual expectation: Yet sometimes the sense of richness is haunting: it is richness and yet denial this living a half a step, as it were, from what one should be. (36 #86)

This feeling was one that stayed with Roethke and that he tried in various ways to communicate. In "Open Letter" he discusses "The Lost Son," emphasizing the intuitive or nonrational experiences of the protagonist who sees what are "almost tail-flicks, from another world, seen out of the corner of the eye." In Roethke's words, the protagonist "goes in and out of rationality."[5]

A poem that illustrates the inadequacy of the analytical mind and functions as a kind of companion piece for "The Signals" is "The Adamant" (*CP*, 9):

> Thought does not crush to stone.
> The great sledge drops in vain.
> Truth never is undone;
> Its shafts remain.

The teeth of knitted gears
Turn slowly through the night,
But the true substance bears
The hammer's weight.

Compression cannot break
A center so congealed;
The tool can chip no flake:
The core lies sealed.

The success of this poem depends largely on the tension that exists between structure and content. Even as the speaker asserts that thought can never get at the core of truth, the poem moves forward with the precision of "knitted gears." Each stanza is constructed of three lines of iambic trimeter followed by one shortened line of iambic dimeter, which produces the effect of a machine building up enough power to drop its hammer or working steadily at compressing an adamant object, but finally stalling. Roethke achieved this effect by deleting an adjective from the final line of each stanza of the original draft: "Its *jagged* shafts remain," "The hammer's *heavy* weight," and "The core lies *unrevealed*" (18 #4). The poem's meaning is clear: No matter how persistent one may be, he can never get at the essence of truth through logical analysis; the machine breaks down. Interestingly, the gears turn through the *night*, as if trying to compress some light, some brief flash from the adamant.

A passage from Underhill touches on the same issue:

> We, deliberately seeking for that which we suppose to be spiritual, too often overlook that which alone is Real. The true mysteries of life accomplish themselves so softly, with so easy and assured a grace, so frank an acceptance of our breeding, striving, dying and unresting world, that the unimaginative man—all agog for the marvellous—is hardly startled by their daily and radiant revelation of infinite wisdom and love. Yet this revelation presses incessantly upon us. Only the hard crust of surface-consciousness conceals it from our normal sight. In some least expected moment, the common activities of life in progress, that Reality in Whom the mystics dwell slips through our closed doors, and suddenly we see It at our side.[6]

The deliberate attempt to crack open the core of truth is unsuccessful, but sometimes, when least expected, truth opens itself and moves along the periphery of vision, just beyond the focus of the eyes. In Roethke's words, "A mind too active is no mind at all" (43 #202); another way to perception must be found. It is this tantalizing glimpse of ultimate reality, which is nothing more than an intuition, a guess made by the blood, that sets a person upon the road of the mystic quest.

Another early poem dealing with the theme of analysis versus intuition is "Dream" (19 #16), which was included in an early draft of *Open House* but cut from the final version[7]:

> A tangle of disorder vexed my sight
> That strained to follow one consistent thread,
> The strand that tied me to the tethered dead.
> Patient, I picked beneath a dimming light.
>
> My finger-ends grew calloused at the task
> Of loosening what bound the corded brain.
> I yanked and swore, but effort was in vain:
> Each ravelled end was tougher than a tusk.
>
> I fell back faint, with no will to resist;
> The coils slid off and swayed like beckoning fronds.
> As I shook free from those uncleanly bonds,
> One hairy rope struck like a fang, and missed.

As in "The Adamant," analysis is ineffectual. The eyes strain beneath the "dimming light," and the fingers grow calloused and clumsy. In other words, the senses are useless in trying to untangle what binds "the corded brain." What binds it is analysis as well as the accompanying confidence in the brain's analytical powers. The mind, set upon the task of understanding itself, is too active and therefore is "no mind at all." Only when the speaker gives up, abandons his will, does he begin to get somewhere. This is the expression of one of mysticism's central paradoxes: one must lose himself before he can truly find himself. In the words of Dionysius the Areopagite: "Attainment comes only by means of this sincere, spontaneous, and entire surrender of yourself and all things."[8] Only by giving up can you hope to succeed.

In many ways, the activity described in "Dream" is analogous to what happens in Eastern mysticism when an initiate contemplates a koan: The mind opens to a perception of higher consciousness. A koan is a kind of puzzle designed deliberately to thwart the analytical mind: for example, "What is the sound of one hand clapping?" By asking such a question, which has no logical answer, and then focusing the mind upon it, the contemplative can jam the analytical processes, thereby permitting the intuition to take charge. This is apparently what happens in "Dream," if we take the knotted cord as the koan. The speaker applies himself to the task of unraveling the cord (answering the riddle) until he becomes frustrated. At this point, he gives up (his analytical mind having been blocked out), and everything becomes clear.

Roethke is even more direct in stating his views of the analytical in an unpublished poem titled "Essay" (19 #30), aptly named for its discursive qualities. Here are three of the nine couplets, including the final one:

> Those celebrators of the brain confined
> To avid circumspection of the mind,
>
> By devious ways would pry the breast apart,
> Turn analytic eyes upon the heart.
> ....
> No life more perilous and strange than this
> Self-consecration to analysis.

The ironic thing here, of course, as in all the poems that speak out against analysis during these early years, is that the form is itself analytical. What we have is a clear indication that Roethke knew the correct way to go, though he was not yet able to set out. These poems, then, represent a time of struggle, of preparation, what Blessing has aptly called Roethke's years of "tiny poems and enormous rages."[9]

"Verse with Allusions" (*CP*, 25) deals with those people who stand at the analytical extreme. They are not concerned with pursuing ultimate truth through abstract thinking or by focusing on tail flicks from another world but are interested only in what they can grasp in their hands:

> Thrice happy they whose world is spanned
> By the circumference of Hand,
>
> Who want no more than Fingers seize,
> And scorn the Abstract Entities.

> The Higher Things in Life do not
> Invade their privacy of Thought.
>
> Their only notion of the Good
> Is Human Nature's Daily Food.
>
> They feed the Sense, deny the Soul,
> But view things steadily and whole.
>
> I, starveling yearner, seem to see
> Much logic in their Gluttony.

Such people as these are absolute realists, or, in the root sense of the word, sensualists. They are, in fact, the most basic and primitive kind of analysts, believing only what they can touch. Matters of the invisible soul or spirit do not concern them. Significantly, no reference is made to their seeing, for they lack the sense of vision. The "view" of line 10 is more an attitude than a perception. In the concluding couplet, the speaker realizes how much easier life would be if he were to give up the pursuit of "Higher Things" and dedicate himself solely to their world of senses. At least then he would not be troubled by "things the eye or hand cannot possess." Yet, even as he envies those who are loyal only to the senses, he realizes that there is "logic in their Gluttony." Here the word *logic* is tinged with more than a little irony. Theirs is a pragmatism that, though attractive, is nothing more than fundamental logic—belief only in what can be perceived through the senses—and he knows that logic can never crack open the truth for him. It is this realization that prevents him from joining the ranks of the "gluttons." The logic he sees in their actions does not recommend their approach to him but puts him off, despite the fact that he may momentarily envy them their facile resolution of life's mysteries.

"Second Version" (23 #30) more clearly describes the relationship between the senses (or the flesh) and the analytical mind:

> To measure love by love's machine,
> I fashioned out of bone and skin
>
> A sensitized receptacle
> Of all that could be beautiful,

Strung nerves more fitly to receive
A love the mind could not believe.

No cosmic attribute, no brain
To arch above the body's pain,

Only the flesh, perceptive sense
Interpreting love's violence,

Made up this miracle of blood,
The engine of my fortitude.

I set the delicate instrument,—
My bright upstanding body bent
Recording passion's element.

But fleshless substance still prevailed,—
The instrument of sense had failed!

Infinite terror pierced my side,
The single flesh had been denied!

The mind imposed a separate gauge
To measure love's incarnate rage,

Arranged a schedule thereupon
For pleasures of my skeleton,

Directed by a sheer control
The finite flesh, the infinite soul!

The flesh cannot operate without the direction of the mind that measures and organizes its sensual activities. Flesh and mind together form the basis for analysis, since the flesh receives information that is interpreted by the brain. It is a feedback system in which the two must function together. Also of significance here is the comment that the mind directs the soul as well as the flesh. In other words, the analytical mind restricts "the infinite soul," prevents it, like the fleshly instrument, from experiencing love beyond measurement.

While Roethke's division of logic and intuition began as a poetic nicety, it became a private necessity. Consequently, the early poems reveal a basic tension between the conventional and the personal. Before the fall of 1935, Roethke was perhaps only toying with intellectual dichotomies, but after his manic episode he had first-hand evidence of what can happen when the logical mind is usurped.

Though the senses are generally held to be unreliable, the sense of sight is considered to be of value in the pursuit of truth, because of its relationship to vision. The mystic generally describes his experience as a perception, as something "seen." In "Prayer" (*CP*, 8) the speaker maintains that though his other senses may be corrupt, the "Eye's the abettor of / The holiest platonic love." He expresses his readiness to give up all his other senses if he can but keep his sight: "Take Tongue and Ear—all else I have— / Let Light attend me to the grave!" Throughout the poem the senses are not mentioned—only the organs with which they are associated: *tongue, nose, ears, hand,* and *eye*. But in the final line the metonym *light* takes the place of *eyes*, and in the absence of any other senses, it strikes most forcefully. *Light*, of course, represents more than mere sight; it connotes knowledge, even insight. In the later poetry, light is representative of mystical illumination, but here it is enough to say that it represents a kind of seeing that transcends normal sight. And so what the speaker prays for is not simply his eyes, but the ability to see things truly.

Karl Malkoff, in his *Introduction to the Poetry*, makes much of Roethke's "epic of the eyes" by maintaining that in *Open House* "the actual movement of the poet's emphasis is from 'I' to 'eye.' "[10] Certainly, we can agree with Malkoff that the "eye" is of considerable importance, for the poetry is consistently concerned with seeing.[11] The attempt to split open the core of truth is motivated by a desire to "see," and the signals received at the edge of the field of vision are encouraging signs that there is something to be seen, if one can but focus in on it. Obviously, such seeing involves more than mere sight, for sight is but one of the body's senses, a process of data collecting, of supplying the analytical mind with information. True seeing, as we have already noted in several poems, is intuitive.

"The Premonition" (*CP*, 6) describes the act of seeing on both the sensuous and intuitive levels:

> Walking this field I remember
> Days of another summer.

Oh that was long ago! I kept
Close to the heels of my father,
Matching his stride with half-steps
Until we came to a river.
He dipped his hand in the shallow:
Water ran over and under
Hair on a narrow wrist bone;
His image kept following after,—
Flashed with the sun in the ripple.
But when he stood up, that face
Was lost in a maze of water.

There is nothing at all unusual in the actions described here, and yet, because we are invited by the title to regard this experience as a premonition, we sense a deeper meaning. In order to get at that deeper meaning, we must see not only with our eyes but with our intuition, just as the speaker himself does. In effect, then, by not telling us the significance of the event he describes, the speaker enables us to utilize our own powers of "seeing"; he takes us through the discursive to the nondiscursive, or, to use our previous terminology, through the analytical to the intuitive. We sense, with the speaker, that the event he describes was a foreshadowing of his father's death. This sense is reinforced by the "flashing" image of the father, which recalls the flash of strange objects in "The Signals." Perhaps the finest line in the poem is "Hair on a narrow wrist bone," which subtly conveys the premonition of death by alluding to a similar image in Donne's "The Relic": "A bracelet of bright hair about the bone."[12] This image, in combination with the final two lines, comprises the premonition. It should be noted that in the last two lines death is viewed as a kind of absorption, or a blurring out of focus, and not as an obliteration. This premonition of death as mergence parallels the mystic's view of death as a return to the One, an idea that Roethke treats more fully in later poems.

"The Bat" (*CP*, 16) affords a similar instance of intuition, when the speaker realizes that "mice with wings can wear a human face." The embodiment of three different animals in one form bespeaks a close relationship among apparently unrelated things, a kind of universal kinship that is central to much of Roethke's later poetry, in which he sees himself reflected in a variety of beings. For the present, the intuition is unassimilated, and the speaker feels simply that "something is amiss or out of place."

The same kind of correspondence is dealt with on a more personal level in "My Dim-Wit Cousin" (*CP*, 25) when the speaker, in the process of privately maligning his cousin, is shocked to hear that cousin's laughter rumble in his own belly. As the speaker in "The Bat" is startled by the sudden realization that bats are a little like humans, the speaker in this poem "jerked back in sudden terror" at the realization that he is a little like his dim-wit cousin. Once again, apparently disparate things are brought into close relation with each other, but here, as in "The Bat," the full significance of that relationship is not understood, although in this instance the speaker is less detached, more personally involved in the intuition.

The process of awakening takes Roethke very near to the edge of illumination, but he is not yet able to see things clearly. His flashes of insight are only vaguely perceived and incompletely understood, but they are enough to convince him that there is a higher truth. This, as noted in the preceding chapter, is the first of the mystic's two basic assumptions. As Roethke remarked during the last year of his life, "I believe that one can suddenly become aware of another consciousness, a consciousness other than [the] immediate; and sometimes that may happen [to] be [caused by] a very trivial thing."[13] The second assumption made by the mystic is that the higher truth that is sensed obliquely can be viewed clearly if the individual can but bring himself into a proper relation with it. Roethke begins the process of aligning himself by rejecting analysis in favor of intuition. The next step is to reject the body and its senses, which are the source of analytical thought, and he is led to this naturally enough because of the connection that exists between analysis and the senses. Rejection of one implies rejection of the other. This rejection is the second stage in the mystic quest: *purgation*.

5.

The Start of the Struggle

"Great poets are insurgents. They are in revolt against
the limitations of reason and logic."—Roethke Notebooks (43 #202)

As a result of awakening, the self realizes "the horrible contrast between its clouded contours and the pure sharp radiance of the Real; between its muddled faulty life, its perverse
self-centered drifting, and the clear onward sweep of that Becoming in which it is immersed."[1] This realization initiates the
period of purgation, in which the body is abjured in an effort
to elevate the spirit. It is a cleansing process undertaken by the
individual in the attempt to make himself worthy of the vision
of ultimate truth. The operating assumption is that the spirit is
capable of apprehending true reality but is held back by the
flesh. This tension between flesh and spirit is implicit in
Roethke from the very beginning, in the title poem of *Open
House* (*CP*, 3):

> My secrets cry aloud,
> I have no need for tongue.
> My heart keeps open house,
> My doors are widely swung.
> An epic of the eyes
> My love, with no disguise.
>
> My truths are all foreknown,
> This anguish self-revealed.
> I'm naked to the bone,
> With nakedness my shield.
> Myself is what I wear:
> I keep the spirit spare.
>
> The anger will endure,
> The deed will speak the truth
> In language strict and pure.
> I stop the lying mouth:
> Rage warps my clearest cry
> To witless agony.

Ralph Mills has stated, "The art proposed in these stanzas is peculiarly autobiographical, 'naked to the bone,' . . . which traces the path of a sensitive mind from bondage into the freedom of the open air."[2] But, to speak more accurately, it is the spirit that is bound, not the mind. The speaker compares himself to an open house, doors flung wide allowing us to enter, and what we find inside is a "spare" spirit. Roethke explained that he was "not speaking of the empirical self, the flesh-bound ego; it's a single word: *myself*, the aggregate of the several selves, if you will. The spirit or soul—should we say the self, once perceived, *becomes* the soul?—this I was keeping spare in my desire for the essential."[3] This is the secret we discover upon entering the house, a gaunt prisoner who has been rationed just enough food to sustain him—or perhaps he is a cloistered monk who has denied himself in the pursuit of the "essential." Whichever he is, the real invitation of the open house is to meet this "self," this spirit that dwells within, for he becomes the focal point of much of the poetry as he attempts to step out of the house, to begin the journey toward the "essential" that he desires.

Of course, the abandonment of the house and its contents in order to set out on the good but difficult road is a stock metaphor that finds its most complete expression in Christianity. However, the distinction Roethke makes between the "flesh-bound ego" and the "self" is one that mystics have traditionally made. "In the mystic experience the center of gravity is transferred from the ego, which is the center of consciousness, to the self, which is the center of the whole psyche, and therefore of the person."[4] Roethke goes one step further and identifies the self as the soul, the part that must be freed from the restrictions of the house, the ego, if it is to progress toward ultimate truth.

Two other poems found among the manuscripts greatly resemble "Open House" in form and content. The earlier one, "The Conqueror" (18 #52), was written in 1931, and it provides an interesting counterpoint to "Open House":

Be proud to live alone.
Be murdered and undone,

But do not seek escape,
In visionary shape.

Be brave, and do not keep
A guardian for your sleep.

Preserve your promised word
Brighter than a sword,

Your lively mirrors chaste,
Uncheckered to the last.

Erase the shape of doom
From the walls of your room;

Constrain the willing blood
To virtue's platitude.

Beneath a sturdy roof
Live unconfused, aloof,

The dreaming heart, the sense
Remote from all pretense.

O fear no little death,
But live by truer faith

And find through pure control
The measure of your soul!

This poem, which was among those praised by Robert Hillyer, is very much in Roethke's early didactic vein.[5] It is ostensibly addressed to the reader, but is actually nothing more than the poet talking to himself in a rather high-flown fashion. Truly, the poem is one of "pure control" in which the poet exhorts himself to be proud, realistic, brave, honorable, chaste, optimistic, virtuous, calm and detached, unpretentious, faithful, and in command of himself. The speaker, who begins to sound like Polonius, advocates the old values and a stiff spine. Clearly, while the theme is the same, his approach is nothing like that of the speaker in "Open House," who is capable of crying out in rage and agony. "The Conqueror's" speaker is too proud, too much under control to allow himself such liberties.

These two poems, looked at alongside one another, reveal a great deal about the change that took place in Roethke's verse between 1931 and 1936. In only five years, he moved from a firm determination to live beneath "a sturdy roof" to an impulse to abandon the house altogether. A great deal of loosening up was taking place, but of course, Roethke was to get considerably looser. At this point, his desire to escape the house of his flesh was not matched by an effort to escape the formal house of his verse. But he was moving in that direction.

"Statement" (24 #2), the second manuscript poem that resembles "Open House," was written in 1937:

> My former self goes out;
> The flesh is purified.
> The past will be my foil
> Against corrosive doubt.
> Discord shall not prevail
> While blood beats in my side.
>
> The body learned its length
> And breadth; my darkest mood
> Was written with my name.
> Now I declare my strength
> And find a proper theme:
> My vigor is renewed.
>
> I drop my foolish ways
> For wisdom dearly bought,
> And salvage what I can
> Out of my wasted days.
> The present is my span:
> I move to richer thought.

The metrical similarities to "Open House" are obvious, and there are also significant correspondences on the thematic level. Here, too, the speaker is engaged in an effort to purify himself, to "move to richer thought." This involves purging the "former self" and abandoning the "foolish ways" and "wasted days" of the past. As in "The Conqueror," the speaker consolidates his strength, but in this case it is not the strength to maintain the status quo of his old values but to learn from the past and move forward from the present. The movement is outward, away from the "former self" toward new perceptions. As Roethke remarked in a notebook entry, "I only know that I am moving toward, or I should be moving toward, a richer experience. The best that I have done should be but hints" (33 #28).

The house metaphor is continued in "The Auction" (*CP*, 21), but in this poem the speaker is more explicit about some of the contents of the house:

> Once on returning home, purse-proud and hale,
> I found my choice possessions on the lawn.
> An auctioneer was whipping up a sale.
> I did not move to claim what was my own.
>
> "One coat of pride, perhaps a bit threadbare;
> Illusion's trinkets, splendid for the young;
> Some items, miscellaneous, marked 'Fear';
> The chair of honor, with a missing rung."
>
> The spiel ran on; the sale was brief and brisk;
> The bargains fell to bidders, one by one.
> Hope flushed my cheekbones with a scarlet disk.
> Old neighbors nudged each other at the fun.
>
> My spirits rose each time the hammer fell,
> The heart beat faster as the fat words rolled.
> I left my home with unencumbered will
> And all the rubbish of confusion sold.

The items, initially viewed as "choice possessions," are ultimately seen as "the rubbish of confusion," and so the owner makes no attempt to intervene in the sale because he is happy to get rid of his junk, specifically, his pride, illusions, fear, and honor. These are all things that distort one's vision or turn it in upon the ego, thereby preventing a view of ultimate truth. According to Underhill, he who would see clearly must "accept poverty, . . . demolish ownership, the verb 'to have' in every mood and tense."[6] This applies not so much to tangible possessions as to the frills and embellishments of the ego, such superfluities as pride and honor and the illusions and fear that feed on them. These are things of the flesh, and if the spirit is to be freed, it must be unburdened of such weights. It is significant that the auctioneer is "whipping" up a sale; he is, in effect, mortifying the body, driving out the weaknesses of the flesh. When the speaker says, "My spirits rose each time the hammer fell," he is speaking not only of a feeling of excitement, but of an actual unburdening of the spirit that allows it to rise from the rubbish-filled house. This is the act of purgation, the "setting of [the] house in order, an orientation of the mind to truth . . . the getting rid, first of self-love; and secondly of all those foolish interests in which the surface-consciousness is steeped."[7]

Underhill cites a passage from a fourteenth-century book by Walter Hilton, *The Scale of Perfection*, which functions as a surprisingly useful gloss for both "The Auction" and "Open House." Hilton says that anyone who wishes to undertake the journey to ultimate truth "leaveth behind him house and land, wife and child, and maketh himself bare from all that he hath, that he may go lightly without letting: right so, if thou wilt be a ghostly pilgrim, thou shalt make thyself naked from all that thou hast."[8] This passage recalls the abandonment of the "rubbish of confusion" and the setting out from home with "unencumbered will" in "The Auction," but perhaps even more striking is the similarity between the traveler who is made naked of all his possessions and the speaker's nakedness in "Open House": "naked to the bone, / With nakedness my shield. / Myself is what I wear: / I keep the spirit spare." These similarities, surprising though they may be, are attributable to a common ground shared by all mystics. Those who view ultimate reality as something external to themselves invariably describe their attempts to attain that reality as a going forth, a journey. And when the metaphor is extended, it usually includes a house filled with unessential possessions at one end of the road, with ultimate truth or reality at the other end. He who would travel the road must leave his house behind, must, in effect, strip himself bare.[9]

Another phrase in the Hilton passage, "ghostly pilgrim," may have some applicability to the unusual ghost in "Epidermal Macabre" (*CP*, 19):

> Indelicate is he who loathes
> The aspect of his fleshy clothes,—
> The flying fabric stitched on bone,
> The vesture of the skeleton,
> The garment neither fur nor hair,

The cloak of evil and despair,
The veil long violated by
Caresses of the hand and eye.
Yet such is my unseemliness:
I hate my epidermal dress,
The savage blood's obscenity,
The rags of my anatomy,
And willingly would I dispense
With false accouterments of sense,
To sleep immodestly, a most
Incarnadine and carnal ghost.

Roethke described this as "a violent little poem" showing "an acute sense of defilement, a hatred of the body" and a "desire for a reality of the spirit."[10] But it is paradoxical that the speaker "wishes his body away in favor of a spirit remorselessly sensual."[11] He wants to be a ghost, but a bloody, fleshy one. As the speaker in "The Auction" was rid of the "rubbish of confusion," the speaker here would be rid of his "false accouterments of sense." The key word is "false," for the senses, as we saw earlier, are unreliable and of no use to anyone who desires a "reality of the spirit." Therefore, the speaker would like to peel away his skin, and with it his senses, so that he might be better able to apprehend ultimate truth, but still be essentially himself. The image is more grotesque, but not unlike Hilton's image of the "ghostly pilgrim" who has shed his unnecessary possessions to set out on the road of the mystic quest. What the speaker really desires, however, very much like the speaker in "Second Version," is, to use Roethke's phrase, a "rampant fleshly mysticism."[12] But such a combination, as we have already seen, is impossible.

"Prayer Before Study" (CP, 24) closely parallels "Epidermal Macabre" in theme and imagery:

Constricted by my tortured thought,
I am too centred on this spot.

So caged and cadged, so close within
A coat of unessential skin,

I would put off myself and flee
My inaccessibility.

A fool can play at being solemn
Revolving on his spinal column.

Deliver me, O Lord, from all
Activity centripetal.

The speaker feels himself trapped inside a "coat of unessential skin," and, like his counterpart in "Epidermal Macabre," he wishes to be rid of his confining garment: "I would put off myself and flee / My inaccessibility" is remarkably similar to "And willingly would I dispense / With false accouterments of sense," not simply because of the tetrameter couplets, but because of the sentiment expressed. The urge is to get outside the skin somehow, to leave behind the false senses that render one inaccessible to true knowledge. The imagery of the flesh as a garment that would be taken off, were it possible, is central to "Epidermal Macabre" and is sustained through a variety of synonyms for clothing: "clothes," "fabric," "vesture," "garment," "cloak," "veil," "dress," "rags," and "accouterments." This imagery also occupies an important place in "Prayer Before Study," though only one clothing noun, "coat," appears in the entire poem: "So caged and cadged, so close within / A coat of unessential skin." But also contained in this couplet is the verb "cadged," that, in addition to rhyming rather cleverly with "caged," contributes to the central clothing metaphor. In current usage, "to cadge" means to obtain by begging, a sense that obviously is not operable in the poem. However, the verb was at one time associated with tailoring, meaning, in that context, to bind the edges of a garment. It is this archaic sense that functions in the poem. The speaker feels as though he is sewn up inside his coat of skin, and he wishes to "put off" the restricting garment. This loathing of the flesh closely parallels the hatred expressed in "Epidermal Macabre," but also present here is the rejection of analytical thought. Significantly, flesh and analysis are yoked, revealing the close relationship between these two halves of the flesh / spirit and analysis / intuition dichotomies. It is not enough to remove the tightly stitched coat of flesh; one must also be delivered from his tortured thought, the foolish game of "Revolving on his spinal column." Rejection of one restraint necessarily involves rejection of the other, for analytical thought results from "seeing" with the body, and he who would see clearly (intuitively, through the spirit) must move beyond his restrictions, beyond all centripetal activity, beyond analysis as well as flesh.

This relationship between flesh and analysis is even more clearly expressed in the following short poem found among the manuscripts:

> In ecstasy at being sure
> Of what Time has reserved for it,
> The flesh will burn a meaning pure
> And make its dying exquisite.
>
> O this mortality will break
> The false, dissembling brain apart,—
> The uninstructed soul will quake
> In terror at the knowing heart! (21 #4)

In "Epidermal Macabre" the senses were described as "false"; here it is the brain to which that adjective is applied. Significantly, the brain's deception ends when the flesh dies because the brain is tied to the flesh. It is not transcendent, nor is what it knows. However, the heart possesses a knowledge that can frighten the "uninstructed soul." Of course, brain and heart, as used here, are equivalents for analysis and intuition, in the best poetic tradition. I take it that the soul is uninstructed because it has been deceived by the brain and been held back from any contact with real knowledge. Consequently, at the moment of death, when the analytical brain and its related senses stop functioning, the intuition takes over and discloses to the soul the *truth*.

"The Envenomed" (19 #28), another manuscript poem that deals with the flesh / spirit dichotomy, is worth consideration because of its similarity to "Epidermal Macabre," in form as well as content:

> All those who by design would clean
> Old refuse from the cluttered vein,
> Are doomed to rankest failure, for
> Corruption is the body's store.
> Who play at love from breast to knee
> Traffic in gross iniquity;

Our virtues carry venom and
There's danger in a proffered hand.
Like whales, we gather all that comes
Too near our mouths; we spoil our homes.
We vainly wash but never cleanse
The increment of tainted sense.
No degradation is more foul
Than what is suffered by the soul
Impounded in a carnal sty,
To root and wallow till we die.

We recognize immediately the iambic tetrameter couplets of "Epidermal," and a quick count reveals the same number of lines. As was noted previously, in his early years Roethke seems to have been fond of writing several versions of the same poem, and definitely we may regard "The Envenomed" as a variation of "Epidermal." It is basically the same poem, expressing a loathing of the flesh, though here the "savage blood's obscenity" is made somewhat more explicit, and the "carnal ghost" is replaced by the soul. Overall, "Epidermal" is probably the better poem because of the cleverness of its metaphor, but "The Envenomed," with its specific (and unpleasant) imagery, has more impact. In the earlier poem, the soul is merely restricted by a tight garment, but here it is reduced to the status of a pig by the filthy flesh.

The speaker in "Silence" (CP, 22) displays some of the "witless agony" that was promised in "Open House" in his revelation of private torment. As in "Prayer Before Study," the spirit is imprisoned, "crying in a cage," and struggling to get out. But here the struggle is much more desperate and determined. The internal din is that of a demolition crew: hammers strike; wheels grind; and the spirit cries out amid the undiminished noise that threatens to shake the speaker's skull "to disrepair." This pounding, grinding activity recalls the imagery employed in "The Adamant," where the "great sledge" and "knitted gears" steadily but vainly attempt to crack open the core of truth. Here, though, the object is to free the spirit from its cell, and so a hammer pounds steadily "on the crystal walls / Of sense." This symbolizes the attempt to break through the barrier of the senses as well as through sense, or analytical thought. At the same time, "the wheels of circumstance" grind away like the "teeth of knitted gears" in "The Adamant." In this case, however, it is not the core of truth but "Confusion's core" that rests at the center. The spirit is frightened and confused, and like a trapped bird that crashes into walls and windows in an effort to escape from a room, it recklessly tears away at the walls of its prison. Behind his calm exterior, the speaker conceals a desperate, frantic struggle between spirit and flesh.

This silent, interior battle is waged with negligible results, with the exception of the modest rising of the spirit in "The Auction" and the spirit's tentative excursion in "Against Disaster" (CP, 19):

> Now I am out of element
> And far from anything my own,
> My sources drained of all content,
> The pieces of my spirit strewn.
>
> All random, wasted, and dispersed,
> The particles of being lie;
> My special heaven is reversed,
> I move beneath an evil sky.
>
> This flat land has become a pit
> Wherein I am beset by harm,
> The heart must rally to my wit
> And rout the specter of alarm.

This is the mystic's familiar experience of the abyss, wherein the soul "looks upon itself as one that is placed in a profound and vast solitude whither no creature can come, and which seems an immense wilderness without limits."[13] The mystic arrives at this perception through contemplation of the Absolute, and his initial reaction upon finding himself in the black abyss is fear. He is out of his "element," disoriented and frightened, for the ultimate reality he seeks has suddenly become terrifying; his "special heaven is reversed." This is a necessary step for the mystic who perceives ultimate truth or reality as transcendent, something external toward which he must strive. Like Dante, he must descend into the depths if he is to ascend to the heights: the way down is the way out and up.

But he who descends into the abyss must have the courage to remain there, for ultimately the downward path will turn upward; the darkness of the depths will become bright, and what is initially frightening will become soothing and beautiful. The speaker in "Against Disaster" is unable to remain in the abyss, because his fear overwhelms him. When he discovers that the "flat land has become a pit," that his spirit has been strewn and his being dispersed, he feels threatened and vulnerable and calls upon his heart to help regain his wit and pull him out of danger. His wit, or analytical thought, must be assisted by the heart, or intuition, if the "disaster" is to be avoided. It is only by rallying his intuitive faculties under the banner of wit that he is able to recover himself, for the analytical intellect cannot sustain the perception of the abyss of the Absolute. To invoke the wit is to end the perception. This, then, is an abortive attempt to perceive ultimate reality. At this point, the speaker is unfamiliar with the terrain, and so he views the desolate crags of the abyss not as a precursor of true mystical vision, but as a potential disaster. In later poems, most notably "The Abyss," the speaker is less afraid and remains in the depths until he ascends to true vision.

Though Roethke's various attempts to free the spirit are unsuccessful, the general movement in the early poems and in *Open House* is out of self, away from flesh and analytical thought. This movement is sustained in such poems as "Feud" and "Prognosis," which view particular families, perhaps the entire race of man, as "an infected brood" (*CP*, 4). The tainted blood in these poems reflects a disdain for the flesh; the spirit is felt to be starving within a diseased body. Also, the analytical mind is rejected, as in "Prognosis," where "The ruminant, reason, chews a poisoned cud" (*CP*, 5). Essentially, these poems represent a less personal treatment of the themes that are dealt with more intimately in "Epidermal Macabre," "Silence," and the other poems discussed in this section. The view is broadened to show that the restrictions of the flesh and the inadequacies of analysis pertain to everyone. It is not only the private house of the speaker that is opened to the public view, but an ancestral house, the house of mankind as well. This generalization of theme is best exemplified by "Sale," that, though similar in many ways to "The Auction," is concerned not simply with the sale of one person's rubbish, but an entire family's horrors.

The early poems, particularly those of *Open House*, represent a preliminary excursion along the road of the mystic quest. After awakening to an apprehension of a reality that transcends that of everyday life, Roethke sets about, through the process of purgation, to journey toward it. Though his attempts are unsuccessful, insofar as they never lead to illumination, they are valuable experiences that provide a basis for future exploration. The lessons learned in *Open House* are not forgotten in the subsequent poetry, and the first tentative steps into mysticism start Roethke on his journey to the self beyond self, the ultimate reality.

I have devoted considerable space to this examination of Roethke's early poetry because, unlike many of his readers, I do not regard it as desolate country to be traversed as quickly as possible. One sometimes gets the impression that nothing before *The Lost Son* (or precious little, at any rate) really matters, and that is an unfortunate point of view because the poems Roethke published during that first decade (1930–1941) reveal much about the direction he was later to take. Of course, no one then could have guessed that he would write anything like "The Lost Son" sequence, but looking back from our vantage point we can detect the movement from those stiff little poems of *Open House* to the vegetal freedom of the greenhouse verse.

Roethke's early work truly reflects a period of purgation, in both the mystical and the artistic sense. For, while he was struggling spiritually to find some deeper meaning in the world, he was also struggling to find his proper voice and style. In many ways, the early poems collectively depict a writer's purgatory, a time of trial and effort during which the poet is made ready to "take the fire" (*CP*, 61). We might acknowledge that every artist goes through a similar stage, but for Roethke things were not typical. For him, the process of writing poetry and the poetry itself were the same thing, for he was himself both the poetic medium and the poetic subject. To stretch his own boundaries was to stretch the boundaries of his art, and so we see him straining and longing for a personal and poetic breakthrough of some kind during those early years. He attained it in the fall of 1935 when he had his first breakdown or, as he once called it, "break-up." From that moment, his poetry was destined to change, for he had changed.

Roethke's manic (or mystical) experience brought home to him the true significance of what had been, prior to his breakdown, mere poetic conventions. In particular, he was made aware of the tensions between the rational and the nonrational, between the body and the spirit. Consequently, many of the poems written after 1935 (most of those in *Open House*) reveal a struggle to break away from the restraints of the intellect and the body. They demonstrate symbolically Roethke's outward journey, which was prompted by his awakening to the existence of another level of reality, another more profound truth.

Once Roethke began pulling at the bonds that limited his perceptions, it was inevitable that he would begin to break down the restrictive form of his poetry. The beginning stages of that effort can be seen in his early work, particularly in the tension that exists between form and content in many of the poems. *Open House* is, in a very real sense, not a first book of poems so much as it is a transitional book. It is the link between Roethke's initial manic episode and his eventual utilization of that experience (and a similar one in 1945) in *The Lost Son*. The poems it contains reveal a man in a state of change, moving from awakening through the difficult stage of purgation.

In his provocative study *Escape from the Self*, Karl Malkoff offers some interesting speculations about the relationship between form and content in Roethke's work:

> When Roethke is exploring the psychology of self . . . he chooses open forms, rhythms dictated by the emotional energy of the lines. However, when he attempts to convert those same impulses into theology, or at least some religious or philosophical context . . . Roethke uses iambic meters (predominantly pentameter) and clearly defined stanzaic patterns, end-stopping his lines to emphasize the effect. In other words, when he is fitting his feelings into a rationally understandable system he uses stock

forms; when the nonrational is allowed to find its own path, he uses organic forms.[14]

Roethke never completely abandoned the formal poem but reserved it for those occasions when he was trying to be most rational, as in the 1962 villanelle "The Right Thing." However, free verse became his principal mode after *Open House* because it was more compatible with his unusual experience, his nonrational perceptions.

III. Inward Growth

6.

Preparation Through Contemplation

"To gain a contemplative mind / All these extremes
have I endured."—Roethke Notebooks (32A #11)

Open House was generally well received and earned Roethke
recognition as a skillful poet, but it was *The Lost Son and Other
Poems* and *Praise to the End!* that established his reputation, and
that, even today, are considered by many critics to be his most
significant works. Although no one familiar with *Open House*
at the time of its publication, including Roethke, knew the direction his poetry would take during the next seven years, at
least one reviewer of the first book sensed the need for
change. Stephen Baldanza observed in Roethke's poetry "a
caution which is at the core of his artistic impulse" and pre-
dicted that Roethke's artistic development would depend on
his "willingness to expose his true self more courageously in
form and content."[1] Roethke himself was aware of a certain
over-neatness in those early poems, and he must have realized
that the naked revelation of self promised in *Open House* was
restricted by narrow poetic forms; that the process of freeing
the spirit involved not only stripping away the cloak of flesh
but abandoning the formal garment of exact meter and rhyme
as well.

In the greenhouse poems and "The Lost Son" sequence, the
line expands or contracts to reflect the stretching and turning
of the spirit as it extends itself like the tendril of some young
plant, and exact rhyme gives way to the more subtle sound
effects of assonance, consonance, and alliteration.[2] These stylistic changes augment and reflect Roethke's struggle for identity, as he moved away from the "knitted gears" of *Open House*
and into the light, free-moving air of the greenhouse world of
The Lost Son. In a sense, this movement was inevitable if
Roethke was to make advances in his search for a true identity.
The greenhouse poems and the longer sequence that follows

76

are the result of Roethke's willingness to take his own advice: reject analysis and perceive reality intuitively. The security of fixed form was abandoned in favor of feeling the way, learning by going, even as the spirit must find its own direction.

Roethke's impulse in *Open House* was to get outside himself by breaking down the walls of flesh to free his spirit. But in *The Lost Son*, he stopped battering those "crystal walls / Of sense" (*CP*, 22) and turned within himself for a route to the outside. Like a man trapped within a cave, he first tried to push away the stones that obstructed his exit, and when that attempt failed he turned into the cave itself, groping down dark tunnels to find a way out. The change in direction denotes a more fundamental change in perspective. Roethke no longer viewed ultimate reality as an external emanation, but as something immanent, within himself, and his altered viewpoint necessarily brought with it a change in the dominant symbolism. According to Underhill, the journey symbol is most usually associated with those who view ultimate reality as something external, as Roethke does in *Open House*, but those who perceive it as something within themselves employ another kind of symbolism:

> Those who are conscious . . . of the Divine as a Transcendent Life immanent in the world and the self, and of a strange spiritual seed within them by whose development man, moving to higher levels of character and consciousness, attains his end, will see the mystic life as involving inward change rather than outgoing search. Regeneration is their watchword, and they will choose symbols of growth or transmutation.[3]

Roethke's greenhouse is the ultimate symbol of growth, a "womb of cypress and double glass" containing countless flowers and plants, all straining to be born.[4] Young stems and shoots struggling to push through the earth and rise toward the light provide an exact parallel for the spirit in its struggle to rise to a new level of reality. The flesh / spirit dichotomy of *Open House* is still operable, but the prisoner / cage symbol is not, even though Roethke continued his attempt to "Transmute and purify [his] 'life.' "[5] His frenzied banging on the walls is replaced by the slow, determined process of growth, and the spirit is viewed as a delicate, young plant capable of extending itself beyond the surface that holds it back.

It was not unusual that Roethke should turn to the plant world as a poetic source, because his childhood was spent in and around several large greenhouses operated by his father in Saginaw, Michigan. His choice of sources was a particularly fortunate one, because he found in returning to the lost environment of his youth a medium peculiarly suited to his poetic talents. Underhill notes, "Plant life of all kinds . . . can easily become, for selves of a certain type, a 'mode of the Infinite'" and further, "The flowery garment of the world is for some mystics a medium of ineffable perception, a source of exalted joy."[6] Certainly, this was the case with Roethke, for he found in plants and the related world of lice, snails, beetles, and other "minimals" the truest reflection of his own striving for identity, and his close observation of those small worlds led to the production of most of the poems in *The Lost Son* and his successive books.

Roethke discovered that by carefully observing the lives in his greenhouse world he could attain the clarity of vision that had eluded him in *Open House*. For him, plants and flowers truly were a "mode of the Infinite," a gateway to ultimate reality. Speaking of this technique in "On 'Identity,'" Roethke says:

> It is paradoxical that a very sharp sense of the being, the identity of some other being—and in some instances, even an inanimate thing—brings a corresponding heightening and awareness of one's own self, *and*, even more mysteriously, in some instances, a feeling of the oneness of the universe. Both feelings are not always present, I'm aware, but either can be an occasion for gratitude. And *both* can be induced. The first simply by intensity in the seeing. To look at a thing so long that you are a part of it and it is a part of you.[7]

Roethke's remarks could pass as an excerpt from a primer on mysticism; in fact, they closely resemble Underhill's comments on contemplation:

> The education which tradition has ever prescribed for the mystic, consists in the gradual development of an extraordinary faculty

of concentration, a power of spiritual attention. It is not enough that he should naturally be "aware of the Absolute," unless he be able to contemplate it. . . . The condition of all valid seeing and hearing, upon every plane of consciousness, lies not in the sharpening of the senses, but in a peculiar attitude of the whole personality: in a self-forgetting attentiveness, a profound concentration, a self-merging, which operates a real communion between the seer and the seen—in a word, in *Contemplation*.[8]

As noted earlier, Roethke was interested in contemplation at least as early as 1936, though his contemplative efforts at that time seem to have been unproductive. But he apparently continued his attempt to attain to "a degree of Quietness: an inward nakedness" (47 #8), as the following notebook entry indicates:

> *St. Theresa* Meditation, Quiet, nameless intermediate,
>   Orison of Union
> Hugh, St. Victor: Meditation, Soliloquy, Consideration,
>   Rapture
> The new silence upon me
> My first lesson too hard.
> St. Theresa: 1) meditation / / Stilled in a whirlwind:
>
> Hindus brooding on a word; Christians on an attribute
> of God
>
> In suspense, yet I remember who I am
> I scraped the mould from the noble lineaments of the soul.
> I attained to a degree of quietness: an inward nakedness
> I was empty: *I was filled*.
> Emptied the small pail of my consciousness.
> My ears saw, *my tongue felt*, my eye tasted
> I teach & *understand out* of utter ignorance
> Beginning of ingathering; folding the strands over (47 #8)

Unquestionably, meditation is the focal point of this entry, but of particular interest is the juxtaposition of what appear to be Roethke's own contemplative efforts with the mystics' technique. While it does not assert that Roethke thought himself a mystic, this entry does suggest his awareness of a relationship between his own strivings and those of the mystics. Clearly, he regarded contemplation as the way to reach the perception he wanted. After all, it is the first step listed for both St. Theresa and Hugh, St. Victor. It is a beginning.

Contemplation is the route by which the mystic moves to a new perception of reality. His objective is still to get outside the self, to free the spirit, but he does this through long and intense looking. Being merely "aware of the Absolute" is no more than seeing tail flicks at the corner of the eye; one must learn to focus upon those fleeting glimpses of a transcendent reality in order to get anywhere. He must learn to exercise a Keatsian "negative capability" to enable him to move beyond himself so that he can see things from a different angle. The movement is "from I to Otherwise, or maybe even to Thee." Contemplation, then, is closely allied with the mystical stage of awakening. It is the process by which the mystic, aware of a higher level of reality that glimmers faintly from the world around him, cleanses his "windows of perception" so that he can behold what he believes to be ultimate reality in its full radiance.

So central is contemplation to Roethke's poetry, so closely is it allied with the creative act itself, that we may say with Arnold Stein: "What contemplation was to some philosophers, composition was to Roethke."[9] His poems are not simply the result of contemplation but are themselves the contemplative act, as "Cuttings" (*CP*, 37) illustrates:

> Sticks-in-a-drowse droop over sugary loam,
> Their intricate stem-fur dries;
> But still the delicate slips keep coaxing up water;
> The small cells bulge;
>
> One nub of growth
> Nudges a sand-crumb loose,
> Pokes through a musty sheath
> Its pale tendrilous horn.

This poem has the clarity and detail of time-lapse photography. There is no analytical commentary, no blinking or looking away, just the steady, intensely perceptive eye fixed on the cuttings. It is as though we were contemplating those "sticks-in-a-drowse" ourselves, and indeed that seems to be the effect Roethke intends, for he provides objective description only, no hints as to what the poem might mean. This straightforward simplicity, a quality of most of the greenhouse poems, creates difficulties for the critic, because as Blessing notes, "Critical apparatus is not designed for a primitive, descriptive poetry, a poetry with few tropes, no allusions, a clear vocabulary and syntax, and almost no abstractions."[10] The poem means what the cuttings themselves mean. This is pure contemplation, perception without analysis, wherein the object is simply to see the cuttings as they are.

In a companion piece, "Cuttings (later)" (CP, 37), Roethke shifts the point of focus from the young plants to his own re-action to their struggle:

> This urge, wrestle, resurrection of dry sticks,
> Cut stems struggling to put down feet,
> What saint strained so much,
> Rose on such lopped limbs to a new life?
>
> I can hear, underground, that sucking and sobbing,
> In my veins, in my bones I feel it,—
> The small waters seeping upward,
> The tight grains parting at last.
> When sprouts break out,
> Slippery as fish,
> I quail, lean to beginnings, sheath-wet.

Objective description gives way to subjective response as Roethke attains the basic goal of contemplation: "to look at a thing so long that you are a part of it and it is a part of you." The experience is essentially spiritual, as revealed in the first four lines, most notably in the words "resurrection" and "saint." When the "tight grains" finally part and sprouts "break out," we cannot avoid making flesh/spirit associations. The struggle of the cuttings parallels the struggle of the spirit, and by contemplating those small sprouts as they rise above the soil Roethke participates in their ascension. This sense of communion is typical of the contemplative experience, and to some extent even the language used to describe it is not pe-culiar to Roethke. For example, echoes of fourteenth-century mystic John Ruysbroeck's description of the contemplative act can be found in "Cuttings (later)": "This driving and drawing we feel in the heart and in the unity of all our bodily powers, and especially in the desirous powers."[11] Though Ruysbroeck does not specifically employ plant imagery, there is an osmotic, plantlike quality about his description, particularly in the words "driving and drawing," that could well describe the struggle of Roethke's sprouts. This similarity indicates that the contemplative experience varies little from person to person and even from century to century, being viewed most often as a process of absorbing and being absorbed, simultaneously— "driving and drawing," "sucking and sobbing."

"Cuttings" and "Cuttings (later)" taken together comprise the contemplative act: intense, objective looking that leads to a strong sense of identification between contemplator and the object contemplated. This is the technique Roethke employs in the rest of the greenhouse poems in an attempt to bring himself closer to illumination. His goal is to break up his ordinary perception of reality so that he can see things clearly, as they really are.

Although "Root Cellar" (*CP*, 38) contains no references to the speaker or to the human world in general, the plant/human associations that were initiated in "Cuttings (later)" are central to the poem:

> Nothing would sleep in that cellar, dank as a ditch,
> Bulbs broke out of boxes hunting for chinks in the dark,
> Shoots dangled and drooped,
> Lolling obscenely from mildewed crates,
> Hung down long yellow evil necks, like tropical snakes.
> And what a congress of stinks!—
> Roots ripe as old bait,
> Pulpy stems, rank, silo-rich,
> Leaf-mold, manure, lime, piled against slippery planks.
> Nothing would give up life:
> Even the dirt kept breathing a small breath.

Once the relationship between the struggle of plants and the struggle of the human spirit has been established, it becomes an implicit part of all the greenhouse poems, and though the description may be objective, as in "Cuttings," we automatically make associations similar to those made in "Cuttings (later)." Roethke has, in effect, taught us how to contemplate. Thus, in "Root Cellar" the shoots that dangle from crates and the bulbs that break out of boxes "hunting for chinks in the dark" become a metaphor for the spirit groping toward the light of true perception, struggling to ascend from its own black cellar.

In "Weed Puller" (*CP*, 39) the re-appearance of the speaker makes the relationship between plant and human more explicit, but this time the comparison involves burrowing roots rather than climbing sprouts. The speaker's perspective is altered, and he finds that he has more in common with the underground parts of the plant than with the rising, flowering stems:

> Under the concrete benches,
> Hacking at black hairy roots,—
> Those lewd monkey-tails hanging from drainholes,—
> Digging into the soft rubble underneath,
> Webs and weeds,
> Grubs and snails and sharp sticks,
> Or yanking tough fern-shapes,
> Coiled green and thick, like dripping smilax,
> Tugging all day at perverse life:
> The indignity of it!—
> With everything blooming above me,
> Lilies, pale-pink cyclamen, roses,
> Whole fields lovely and inviolate,—
> Me down in that fetor of weeds,
> Crawling on all fours,
> Alive, in a slippery grave.

Roethke once referred to his greenhouse as "This hell and heaven at once,"[12] and that duality is nowhere better expressed than in this poem. The speaker is beneath the benches that hold the plants, crawling along on hands and knees amid the "perverse life," while above him bloom "Whole fields lovely and inviolate." For Roethke, as for Dante and most mystics, the route to heaven leads through hell, or as John Senior puts it: "To discover the highest form of Self, we must live through the lowest first—Hell is a necessary condition of heaven."[13] In order to look upon those inviolate flowers, as Dante looked upon the Celestial Rose, Roethke must first pass through a kind of plant inferno occupied by lewd roots, webs, weeds, grubs, snails, sharp sticks, and coiled "fern-shapes." In short, he must be purged and purified. This process, as we saw in *Open House*, follows the stage of awakening and must be experienced before the mystic can attain illumination.

The abjuration and hatred of flesh that marked the stage of purgation in *Open House* are replaced in *The Lost Son* by a slow, determined struggle to be born. No longer is the spirit viewed as a caged prisoner who must escape, but as a shoot or foetus that must struggle toward birth. This imagery is implicit in almost all the greenhouse poems but is most obvious in the final three lines of "Weed Puller": "Me down in that fetor of weeds, / Crawling on all fours / Alive, in a slippery grave." Karl Malkoff maintains that " 'fetor' suggests 'foetus,' "[14] but with or without that verbal similarity the "all fours" posture resembles the foetal position, and the implications of being "Alive, in a slippery grave" are obvious. Roethke himself made frequent references to the greenhouse as a womb, and in his "Open Letter" statement concerning "The Lost Son" sequence, which seems applicable to the greenhouse poems as well, he says: "Each poem . . . is a stage in a kind of struggle out of the slime; part of a slow spiritual progress; an effort to be born, and later, to become something more."[15] Roethke senses that, like a cutting or a root, he has the potential for growth, the ability to extend himself beyond the slime. The ultimate reality he seeks resides within him, just as the flower is contained within the bulb, but to realize that potential he must exercise his entelechy. The process is one of transformation, of birth or evolution, from womb to open air, from all fours to an upright posture. This is the stage of purgation, and as always it is a difficult, even painful struggle toward illumination and self-fulfillment.

In "Moss-Gathering" (*CP*, 40) the relationship between plant and human is broadened to the philosophical nature/ man level, and what was dealt with suggestively in the other greenhouse poems is here presented analytically:

To loosen with all ten fingers held wide and limber
And lift up a patch, dark-green, the kind for lining
   cemetery baskets,
Thick and cushiony, like an old-fashioned doormat,
The crumbling small hollow sticks on the underside
   mixed with roots,
And wintergreen berries and leaves still stuck to the top,—
That was moss-gathering.
But something always went out of me when I dug loose
   those carpets
Of green, or plunged to my elbows in the spongy yellowish
   moss of the marshes:
And afterwards I always felt mean, jogging back over
   the logging road,
As if I had broken the natural order of things in that
   swampland;
Disturbed some rhythm, old and of vast importance,
By pulling off flesh from the living planet;
As if I had committed, against the whole scheme of life,
   a desecration.

Obviously, what comes through is the sense of unity, the feeling that the planet is an animate entity, but also that the moss-gatherer is not a part of this whole. Consequently, he feels "mean," and he jogs "back over the logging road," a criminal running from the scene of the crime where he has "broken the natural order of things." His running away is somewhat like the flight of the protagonist of "The Lost Son" who is "hunting, like a primitive, for some animistic suggestion, some clue to existence from the sub-human."[16] And like the speaker in "Weed Puller," who looks up from his "fetor of weeds" toward the blossoming flowers, the speaker here perceives "some rhythm, old and of vast importance" from which he is separated.

The plants in the greenhouse are assisted in their struggle by the florist, "That hump of a man" (*CP*, 42), the resident god in this "heaven-on-earth" who pinches and picks, weeds and sprays, and transplants with great skill[17]:

Lifting the young plants with two fingers,
Sifting in a palm-full of fresh loam,—

One swift movement,—
Then plumping in the bunched roots
A single twist of the thumbs, a tamping and turning,
All in one . . . .

He provides the plants with the environment most conducive
to their growth: good soil and "long days under the sloped
glass" (*CP*, 42). The human, however, receives no such help in
his struggle to grow; no beneficent god lifts him to a better
plane.

Nevertheless, in "Child on Top of a Greenhouse" (*CP*, 43),
the young boy, through his own efforts, has been transplanted:

The wind billowing out the seat of my britches,
My feet cracking splinters of glass and dried putty,
The half-grown chrysanthemums staring up like accusers,
Up through the streaked glass, flashing with sunlight,
A few white clouds all rushing eastward,
A line of elms plunging and tossing like horses,
And everyone, everyone pointing up and shouting!

He has moved from the slime beneath the benches into the
wind and sunlight and, to continue the symbolism established
in "Weed Puller," is outside the womb. Unfortunately, this initial excursion out of the slime earns him—in addition to the
chrysanthemums' accusing stares and everyone's shouts—
only a brief and partial illumination. Like the moss-gatherer,
he is still separated from the true order of things. The light is
there, flashing off the glass, and there is that one splendid
vision of "elms plunging and tossing like horses," but basically
the perception is a limited one. Like the transplanted flowers,
the boy breaks "into nakedness . . . extending / Out into the
sweet air, . . . Stretching and reaching" (*CP*, 42). But unlike
that of the transplants, his position is too precarious to be sustained, and he does not have the time to grow, to fully realize
that reality toward which he strives.

A good deal of attention has been given by critics to the
child's sense of guilt, primarily as reflected in the "half-grown
chrysanthemums staring up like accusers." Obviously, the
child feels guilty because he is doing something dangerous,
something of which the adults disapprove. But I do not think,

as Malkoff does, that his feelings arise simply because "There is clearly a great deal of guilt involved in growing up."[18] Rather, the child, like the moss-gatherer, feels guilty because he senses a unity in the world of which he is not a part. The chrysanthemums convey directly the sense of guilt that is felt implicitly by the moss-gatherer as he flees from his unseen accusers. The sexual suggestiveness of these poems has been emphasized by a number of critics to the exclusion of other resonances. While we may concede the onanistic symbolism of "Moss-Gathering" or the sensuality of "Cuttings (later)," it is dangerous to insist too much on the Freudian element. William Meredith offers the best advice in this area in his commentary on "Cuttings (later)": "It is one of a great many poems that can be damaged by overt sexual interpretation. Insofar as we are sexual beings—and happily that is quite far—things lurk in our minds. But insofar as a skillful artist speaks of experience other than the sexual, we must suppose that he intends to treat other experience, and pay attention to that."[19] The sexual aspect of the greenhouse poems has been more than sufficiently explicated. It is time we discovered what else Roethke had to say in those poems.

The theme of "Flower Dump" (*CP*, 43) is essentially the same as that of "Child on Top of a Greenhouse," but it is expressed exclusively in terms of plants:

> Cannas shiny as slag,
> Slug-soft stems,
> Whole beds of bloom pitched on a pile,
> Carnations, verbenas, cosmos,
> Molds, weeds, dead leaves,
> Turned-over roots
> With bleached veins
> Twined like fine hair,
> Each clump in the shape of a pot;
> Everything limp
> But one tulip on top,
> One swaggering head
> Over the dying, the newly dead.

The single tulip, like the child, is above the heap, one "swaggering head" lifted over the crowd, and the determination and bravado it manifests in lifting itself up from mortality's dump amount to a kind of floral nose-thumbing in the face of death. The pursuit of ultimate reality involves disengaging oneself from "the dying, the newly dead," stretching toward the Absolute despite the risks, despite one's own mortality.

"The Return," which expresses a self-loathing reminiscent of the hatred of flesh in *Open House*, stands in counterpoint to the child's perception atop the greenhouse. Whoever would advance along the road of the mystic quest must be prepared to experience both pain and pleasure, for the mystic's progress is actually a vacillation between purgation and illumination. Each flash of intuition or fleeting perception of ultimate reality reveals to the mystic his own unworthiness and frequently throws him into a depressed state. His desire is to sustain the stage of illumination, but until he is completely purged he can attain that level only momentarily: The child cannot remain precariously perched on the glass roof. It should not be surprising, then, that Roethke's brief illumination atop the greenhouse leads eventually to "The Return" (*CP*, 47), where he views himself as a cowering dog creeping back to his "self-infected lair." Once again on all fours, as in "Weed Puller," Roethke finds himself, so to speak, back beneath the benches.

Despite occasional lapses into depression, Roethke was able to sustain a basically optimistic outlook, as this uncollected poem, "After Loss" (18 #9) reveals:

> A man lies down in his sweat,
> Tears dry before the wind,
> What the heart remembers half,
> Stays with us to the end.
>
> Our truths are learned piece-meal;
> By littles we must live;
> The weed crushed by the heel
> Grows to the flower we love.
>
> The heart's blood, drop by drop,
> Replenishes the vein;
> The things that we gave up
> Become our own again.

For the mystic, the way down is the way out. He expects to experience some pain, but he knows that he will ultimately attain his goal, if he perseveres. In Roethke's words, "There is a perpetual slipping-back, then a going-forward; but there is *some* 'progress.' "[20] Advances are made "piece-meal," and at a cost, but the crushed weed eventually becomes "the flower we love."

There is, of course, something here of the Christian doctrine of losing oneself to find oneself: "The things that we gave up / Become our own again." This is standard mystical doctrine as well. Only through purgation can one hope to move toward illumination; only by abandoning himself can he truly hope to find himself. The movement inevitably involves considerable struggle and effort.

In "Last Words" (*CP*, 48) the speaker's plea for illumination recalls the two prayer poems of *Open House* ("Prayer" and "Prayer Before Study"), where similar requests are made for light and deliverance:

> Solace of kisses and cookies and cabbage,
> That fine fuming stink of particular kettles,
> Muttony tears falling on figured linoleum,
> Frigidaires snoring the sleep of plenty,
> The psyche writhing and squirming in heavy woolen,—
> O worm of duty! O spiral knowledge!
>
> Kiss me, kiss me quick, mistress of lost wisdom,
> Come out of a cloud, angel with several faces,
> Bring me my hat, my umbrella and rubbers,
> Enshroud me with Light! O Whirling! O Terrible Love!

This is the mundane, uninspiring life of suburbia, where kisses mean as much as cookies or cabbage, and the spirit is stifled. Like the weed puller, who looks up from the slime beneath the benches to see fields of flowers blooming overhead, the speaker here looks up from his domestic swamp toward the stair of "spiral knowledge," the way to illumination and a different level of reality. Desiring more than cabbage kisses, he would be kissed by the "mistress of lost wisdom" and enshrouded with light.

The prayer for illumination is answered in "Night Crow" and "River Incident," not with a blinding light but with a dim glow of intuition in which the desired knowledge manifests itself as a kind of racial memory. In "Night Crow" (*CP*, 49), while watching a crow "Flap from a wasted tree," the speaker taps a collective unconscious that causes him to sense some vague kinship with that bird:

> A shape in the mind rose up:
> Over the gulfs of dream
> Flew a tremendous bird
> Further and further away
> Into a moonless black,
> Deep in the brain, far back.

And in "River Incident" (*CP*, 49) he experiences an evolutionary *déjà vu* as he wades into the water:

> And I knew I had been there before,
> In that cold, granitic slime,
> In the dark, in the rolling water.

These intuitions suggest a close relationship among apparently unrelated things, or, in mystical terminology, a *universal oneness*. The goal of the mystic is to apprehend that oneness, and by apprehending, to merge with it. Here, however, there is no mergence, just a fleeting sense of kinship similar to that expressed earlier in "The Bat" and "My Dim-Wit Cousin." The speaker feels that he has something in common with both fowl and fish, but as yet he is not sure what it is.

In "The Waking" (*CP*, 51), the final poem before "The Lost Son" sequence, the speaker moves from vague feelings of kinship to a true sense of union with the world around him. His desire to be enshrouded with light is fulfilled, for as he strolls through an open field he experiences "an abnormal sharpening of the senses—whereby an ineffable radiance, a beauty and a reality never before suspected, are perceived shining in the meanest things"[21]:

> I strolled across
> An open field;
> The sun was out;

Heat was happy.

This way! This way!
The wren's throat shimmered,
Either to other,
The blossoms sang.

The stones sang,
The little ones did,
And flowers jumped
Like small goats.

Stones and blossoms sing with the wrens, and the animate world is suffused with the presence of God. The unity that was felt indistinctly in "Night Crow" and "River Incident" is here experienced fully, and the speaker feels that "all the waters / Of all the streams / Sang in my veins / That summer day."

At this point in his mystic quest, Roethke has achieved an important goal, a brief but clear perception of the ultimate reality he seeks. No longer will he have to base his pursuit on insubstantial tail flicks, for he has seen the real thing in all its brilliance. As a result of this breakthrough, illumination will occur more frequently, though in varying degrees, and always as a result of contemplation and purgation.

The simplicity of the greenhouse poems recalls in many ways Blake's "Songs of Innocence," which have the same kind of surprising depth despite their apparent straightforwardness. Indeed, it is tempting to establish "Innocence" and "Experience" categories for Roethke's greenhouse and "The Lost Son" sequences, because such a division, though it may not hold in strict parallel to Blake's, can help to clarify the progression of the poems in *The Lost Son* volume. The movement is from external to internal, from the beautiful, perfect world of the greenhouse plants to the morass of the protagonist's subconscious. As with Blake's songs of *Innocence* and *Experience*, the two groups of poems depend upon and modify each other. "The Lost Son" sequence is rendered more comprehensible than it might be because of the presence of the greenhouse poems, and they in turn are given an added depth by "The Lost Son" sequence.

Roethke was acutely aware of this interdependence, as the following notebook entry suggests:

> The greenhouse. All of a sudden, though I have not exhausted the subject, I am tired of it as if I have the impulse to go forward before having finished what is necessary. (47 #7)

What was necessary, of course, was to prepare the way for "The Lost Son" sequence. Things had to be set up properly despite Roethke's inclination to rush ahead. In a later notebook, he wrote:

> These damned greenhouse poems bore me, in a way, but I respect them; I had to write them that way—and I'm doing a few more. (37 #97)

This comment suggests something inevitable or inexorable about the greenhouse poems. They had to be done, and they had to be done a certain way. Perhaps it was their simplicity that bored Roethke, but he apparently knew the simplicity was necessary, even essential, as preparation for the longer, more complex sequence he was about to write.

7.

Movement Into the Self

"The pit and the peak are the same."—Roethke Notebooks (43 #200)

At first glance, "The Lost Son" sequence appears to be as far removed from the greenhouse poems as a Rorschach print is from a snapshot, but a closer analysis reveals that the "psychic shorthand" of the former and the vivid description of the latter actually represent different perspectives on the same contemplative experience.[1] Because mergence involves an interpenetration of identities, a mutual absorption, whereby the contemplative moves into the thing he is focused upon and, at the same time, takes it into himself, it is possible to view the experience both with the perspective of one who is absorbed and one who absorbs. This double viewpoint accounts for the basic difference between the greenhouse poems and "The Lost Son" sequence: In the first group, Roethke moves into the plants and participates in their struggle, and in the second the plants are internalized to become a part of Roethke's psychological landscape. This out/in movement, sensed by the contemplative as a simultaneous occurrence, represents the complete experience of mergence, and the greenhouse poems and "The Lost Son" sequence are actually complementary halves of the same whole, opposite sides of one contemplative coin.

Roethke's method is to "begin from the depths and come out," to start in his own subconscious from the point at which he too was a "nub of growth" and follow his struggle to be born and later "to become something more." In this sense, each poem is "a stage in a kind of struggle out of the slime; part of a slow spiritual progress,"[2] and the sequence represents an attempt to "trace the spiritual history of a protagonist (not 'I' personally but of all haunted and harried men)."[3] Roethke believed that "the spiritual man must go back in order to go forward,"[4] clearly a variation on the familiar mystical paradox "The way down is the way out": "To mount to God is to enter one's self. For he who inwardly entereth and intimately penetrateth into himself, gets above and beyond himself and truly mounts up to God."[5] For Roethke this involves plunging into the unconscious and reenacting his life from zygote to fetus to infant to child to adolescent to adult, stages of growth that can be used to describe the progress of the entire sequence. There is considerable overlapping from poem to poem, "A perpetual slipping-back, then a going-forward; but there is *some* 'progress'" as the protagonist, like the greenhouse cuttings, moves slowly upward and outward.[6]

As in the greenhouse poems, growth is the central metaphor, but in the sequence it is rendered in terms of the subconscious and preconscious. The language, though simple and straightforward, is often difficult because it follows "the motion of the mind itself: hence some of the associational jumps, the shifts, in subject matter and rhythm, the changes in speed."[7] Roethke's aim is to "keep the rhythms 'right,' *i.e.*, consistent with what a child would say or at least to create the 'as if' of the child's world." It is the "spring and rush" that he is after, "a kind of psychic shorthand" reflective of the protagonist's mind when it is under great stress.[8] Roethke felt that "in this kind of poem, the poet should not 'comment,' or use many judgement-words; instead he should render the experience, however condensed or elliptical that experience may be."[9] The result is a line of varied length, sometimes clear, sometimes cryptic, filled with aphorisms and enigmatic questions.

Because he provides no commentary and includes few "judgement-words," Roethke's symbols are open-ended, and the language, generally, is supercharged with meaning. This wide-open quality is at once an asset and a liability, for, while it deepens and enriches the poetry, it increases the difficulties of interpretation. Some critics, such as Karl Malkoff, have virtually lost themselves in a Freudian maze, and others, most notably Richard Blessing, have backed away from any attempt at a close textual reading, electing instead to discuss the sequence in its entirety, from a distance.[10] The proper approach lies somewhere between those two extremes: one should take care not to restrict Roethke's meaning but at the same time should not shirk the responsibility of interpreting the poems.

We should take our cue from Roethke himself, who said in a draft of "Open Letter" that the "obscurity will yield more likely to the sudden insight rather than to the line-by-line exegesis" (28 #6).

The basic difficulty is with the language itself, for Roethke is, as he once parodied himself, fishing "in that dark pond, the unconscious," or diving into it "with or without pants on, to come up festooned with dead cats, weeds, tin cans, and other fascinating debris." What he dredges up is significant because it comes from the unconscious, but we are likely to be hard pressed to say what a dead cat or a tin can means—or, perhaps more accurately, which of its meanings we are to take. Roethke himself provides little assistance in this matter, saying only "The clues will be scattered richly—as life scatters them; the symbols will mean what they usually mean—and sometimes something more."[11] In other words, Roethke is merely the diver who brings interesting debris to the surface; he assumes no responsibility for explaining its significance. This, as we have already seen, is the technique of contemplation: perception without analysis. In the greenhouse, the objective was to see the plants as they were, to participate in their "is-ness," their identity; the same objective operates in "The Lost Son" sequence, except that this time the eyes are turned inward to perceive the identity of the self.

This is not to imply that Roethke has no control over his language, for he picks his words carefully. And although he declines to comment on the debris he brings to the surface, Roethke does decide what to pull up and what to leave on the bottom and is therefore unquestionably in control of his poetry. When Kenneth Burke suggested that certain passages in the sequence could be rearranged, Roethke responded:

> Your remark about the redistribution of the jingles,—which I don't think is right—may suggest to some readers that the piece is a kind of *collage*. The way I struggle for the "rightness" in feeling and phrase: they're not that, I think.[12]

As he claims in "Open Letter," he is not an instrument, nor are the poems in any sense a gift.[13] In fact, Roethke states in a notebook entry that "They came out of a special and terrifying experience: I took chances on my life to write them, and I was a fool for doing so."[14] He is referring, apparently, to his manic-depressive episodes. Thus, each poem represents not a smooth flow from the stream-of-consciousness, but a dangerous dive into the depths of the unconscious.

It is important here to make a few observations about Roethke's manipulation of the language in this sequence, specifically his use of puns and other types of word play. Roethke obviously considered the humorous element of the poems to be of considerable importance, as this comment from a draft of "Open Letter" indicates:

> I insist that much of the sequence is comic—or is nothing: particularly the nonsense songs, some of the rants, the dialogues,— what Mr. Robert Fitzgerald has called "eerie back-chat." It distressed me that a younger commentator, Mr. Peter Viereck, should find "The Shape of the Fire" "absurdly humorless." (28 #6)

Unfortunately, a number of critics since Viereck have missed the comic element in the sequence, and many of those who have found it seem unsure about what to do with it. The problem, of course, is the odd mixture of the serious and the funny. Some of the suggestive songs and shameless puns seem inappropriate in an otherwise serious context. And after all, Roethke himself claimed he took chances with his life to write the sequence. Surely, then, the poems are meant to be taken seriously.

Similar appearances of the comic in serious places in other literature, most notably in Shakespeare's plays, have been explained (albeit tenuously) as comic relief—as when Mercutio, fatally wounded, puns, "Ask for me tomorrow and you shall find me a grave man."[15] In more contemporary literature, such occurrences have been accounted for as black humor or existential irony. However, these explanations will not work for Roethke's word play. Instead, we need to account for the comic element in Roethke's own terms and in the terms of his manic experience.

When Roethke claims to have risked his life for "The Lost Son" poems he is speaking of his deliberate attempts to provoke another manic episode. Allan Seager has recorded Roethke's desire for "an illness, something I can get my teeth into."[16] Apparently he got his wish, for in the fall of 1945 an unusually creative period signaled the onset of his second attack. Seager further records that Roethke worked on "The Lost Son" sequence during the time that he was recovering from his episode.[17] The notebooks substantiate this. This is not to say that Roethke wrote the sequence while he was in a manic phase. That would not have been possible. However, it is important to note that the periods immediately before and after the episode were very productive times during which Roethke exploited his illness for poetic material.

I contend that "The Lost Son" sequence is largely the product of Roethke's manic experience. To be sure, it is not simply an effusive, uncontrolled outpouring—Roethke refined and shaped it—but the impetus, the driving force behind it is manic. Roethke knew this, and that is why he took such chances by courting his illness, virtually wishing it upon himself. Consequently, it may be profitable to consider the nature of the manic experience when attempting to make sense of the sequence, especially where the word play is concerned.

Significantly, clinical studies of mania indicate that the manic frequently describes his experiences by saying that he feels "newborn." This is a particularly revealing description because mania, rooted deeply in the infantile, is essentially a return to the childish state, a time of few inhibitions and few repressed desires. The manic, like the child, is essentially carefree and happy, and he derives pleasure from the same things that please a child. One of his characteristic sources of pleasure is word play. According to Karl Abraham, "Abolition of logical control and playing with words [are] two essential features of manic ideational processes [which] indicate an extensive 'return to infantile freedom.'"[18] This is one way to create the "as if" of the child's world.

Psychologists usually emphasize that a considerable amount of pleasure is derived by the manic from his word games; that in fact it is the pleasurable aspect of manipulating language that motivates him to play with words in the first place. Obviously, this pleasure is associated with the regressive nature of the illness because the manic, like the child, is fond of nonsense, repetitions, and the sound of language. For the child, the pleasure in such word play comes from the process of learning to master something difficult—language as a means of communication. This may also be a source of pleasure for the manic in his regressed state, but it has been proposed that his basic source of pleasure is in the saving and eventual release of energy that, in the normal person, is used up in focusing on the meaning rather than on the sound of words.[19] The manic's principal concern is not with logic.

Although it is possible to follow the psychology of mania considerably further, I prefer to end the pursuit short of making speculations about oral satisfaction and Roethke's libido. My intent is not to put Roethke on the psychoanalytic couch but simply to point out the characteristics of mania that may have influenced "The Lost Son" sequence. If we can accept the sequence as a regression to childhood and before, then it does not seem unreasonable to assume that Roethke's mania may have been the source of the regression, and further, that the characteristics of mania may help to account for many of the enigmatic passages in "The Lost Son" sequence.

It is essential to keep in mind, however, that although Roethke's mania may explain the presence of skip-rope songs, nonsense verse, puns, and other kinds of word play, it in no way explains their meanings. And that is as it should be, for the meaning is not the important thing—rather, it is the sound we should pay attention to. This, of course, calls to mind Roethke's repeated plea that the sequence be read aloud. The poems open themselves to the ear, not to the analytical eye. This brings us not only to the most crucial element of the sequence but also to a crucial question: If the words Roethke uses in the sequence are more significant in terms of sound than sense, what effect does he hope to achieve by using them? The way this question is answered determines how the sequence is interpreted, but of course, not everyone is willing to allow the question. Depending on to whom you listen, the sequence is either so simple as to be worthy of only a quick reading or so complex that it deserves a lengthy exegesis. It is either an arbitrary listing of skip-rope songs and nonsense

verse or a clever arrangement of symbols from the unconscious. Paradoxically, these divergent viewpoints proceed
from a similar experience—an inability to explain the sequence. But in one instance the reader yields to his frustration,
saying, "This is nothing but gibberish," and in the other he
submits to his analytical side, thinking, "All this *has* to mean
something." Actually, both positions are valid and not mu-
tually exclusive. "The Lost Son" sequence is "gibberish," although a very special kind, and it does mean "something,"
though it may not "mean" in the usual sense of the word.

I wish to suggest a way to read "The Lost Son" sequence
that will accommodate both points of view, because the polar-
ized critical positions are the product of something more than
a mere difference in taste or aesthetics. Rather, they are rooted
in the poetry itself, provoked by it. Roethke deliberately im-
merses the reader of the sequence in nonlogical, manic word
play in an effort to jam his logical thought processes. This is a
game critics are ill-equipped to play, since we traffic primarily
in analysis. Consequently, any attempt to explicate the poems
in a logical, line-by-line fashion must result either in frustration or a forced reading. This is not to imply that the poems
cannot be interpreted, for indeed they can be, but it is necessary first to recognize and subsequently to yield to Roethke's
manipulative tactics. Only by accepting the poems on his
terms can we move toward a satisfactory understanding of the
sequence.

The speaker in "The Lost Son" sequence is a kind of latter
day sphinx, a poser of riddles who demands to be answered:
"A whisper of what, / You round dog?— / Is the wasp ten-
der?" (*CP*, 81) "Has the dark a door?" (*CP*, 82) "Who's bishop
of breathing?" (*CP*, 83) "What's a thick?" (*CP*, 92) "Who untied
the tree?" (*CP*, 93). Confronted with these and other questions, the reader either improvises or despairs. However, contrary to tradition, those who are as clever as Oedipus lose the
game. Only those who despair and yield to the illogic of the
questions can hope to move toward a real understanding of
the poems. Unfortunately, most of us do not know how to deal
with illogic. And the more assiduous we are in the application
of our analytical powers, the more certain we are to be con-

sumed by our own interpretations. I have only to point to Karl Malkoff's Freudian maze, where kittens' feet and parents' teeth become symbols for the protagonist's libido in the simple passage "A kitten can/Bite with his feet;/Papa and Mamma/ Have more teeth" (*CP*, 71)[20]; or to Harry Williams's insistence that the line "Beware Mother Mildew" (*CP*, 55) in "The Pit" section of "The Lost Son" is a warning to the mother figure that she "will be physically weakened in the cause of the speaker's nourishment."[21] Such overinterpretations are commonplace because critics have generally failed to understand the nature of Roethke's riddles.

The determination to "crack" the code of Roethke's gnomic verse has frustrated many a reader, especially when confronted with a passage like the following one from "I Need, I Need" (*CP*, 75):

> Even steven all is less:
> I haven't time for sugar,
> Put your finger in your face,
> And there will be a booger.
>
>> A one is a two is
>> I know what you is:
>> You're not very nice,—
>> So touch my toes twice.
>
> I know you are my nemesis
> So bibble where the pebble is.
> The Trouble is with No and Yes
> As you can see I guess I guess.
>
>> I wish I was a pifflebob
>> I wish I was a funny
>> I wish I had ten thousand hats,
>> And made a lot of money.

Despite Roethke's admonition that the child's language he employs here and elsewhere is neither "cutesy prattle" nor a "suite in goo-goo,"[22] critics generally have lumped such passages under the rubric of skip-rope songs or nursery rhymes, commenting only in passing that they reflect the world and identity of the child. And those who have given more serious attention to the jingles have perhaps looked too closely, miss-

ing their real significance. The key to understanding lies in
Roethke's repeated insistence that the poems in the sequence
were "written to be heard,"[23] because the true meaning of such
nonsense verse is in the sound of the language and the effect
that sound produces rather than in semantics. For example, it
is less important to attach a specific meaning to "bibble" than
to hear the sound of the word itself as it rebounds off "pebble"
and is echoed by "Trouble" and "pifflebob" in the lines that
follow.

Similarly, the following passage depends more for its meaning on the reader's ear and an intuitive response than on his
mind and a rational analysis:

> Mips and ma the mooly moo,
> The likes of him is biting who,
> A cow's a care and who's a coo?—
> What footie does is final. (*CP*, 86)

There is magic in the varied alliteration and sustained assonance, but only if the reader hears those sounds and yields to
them. He must participate in the word game, not by digging
for symbols but by letting the sound of the language operate
subliminally. Who goes in search of a Freudian explanation for
"mooly moo" and "footie" without listening to those words
misses their fundamental significance. He finds his symbols at
the expense of a deeper meaning.

Chants and incantations have, of course, always been an integral part of occult rites and religious ceremonies, taking the
form of magic spells and charms in one case and formal liturgy
in the other. In contemplation, too, the power of words, as
reflected in the mantra, is useful in attaining the desired level
of consciousness. "It is the resonance reverberating through
the mind, rather than the actual meaning of the words which
is of importance to the user of the mantra."[24] Further, "the true
magic 'word' or spell is untranslatable; because its power resides only partially in that outward sense which is apprehended by the reason, but chiefly in the rhythm, which is addressed to the subliminal mind."[25] When Roethke's jump-rope
verse is looked at in this way, as a device intended to alter the
level of consciousness, rather than as childish gibberish or a

puzzle that must be solved, it takes on a new significance, becoming an aid to understanding rather than an obstacle, a way for Roethke and for us (if we can keep ourselves "loose and alert"[26]) to enter the subliminal world and begin advancing toward a more complete understanding of things. This, of course, brings us back to contemplation, to the process of clearing the mind of its logical clutter to make room for perceptions that transcend logic.

In addition to the jingles, the sequence also contains many aphorisms and questions similar to those mentioned earlier. Some of these are simple—"Can I have my heart back?" (*CP*, 76); "The mouth asks. The hand takes." (*CP*, 80)—but others are so cryptic and absurd that they defy understanding. One of the best examples of this kind is found in "The Long Alley" (*CP*, 60):

> If we detach
> The head of a match
> What do we do
> To the cat's wish?
> Do we rout the fish?
> Will the goat's mouth
> Have the last laugh?

It is possible to make a kind of sense out of this passage; in fact, Roethke himself suggests some symbolic equations: cat = woman; goat = animal in man.[27] But such an interpretation leaves much to be desired, and it is perhaps impossible to arrive at a completely satisfactory explanation of these lines, at least as long as we expect them to make sense. However, if we accept them as nonsense, as koans, "confusions of the intellect deliberately induced by paradoxical logic in order to evoke that dizziness which Zen Buddhists say opens the mind to a perception of higher consciousness," then their true significance becomes apparent.[28] By asking questions that cannot be answered and then focusing the logical mind on them, it is possible to jam the analytical processes, thereby permitting the intuition to take charge. Much of Roethke's language does just that and, similar to the mantra-like jingles, provides a way into another level of consciousness, both for Roethke and the reader. Again, the process is that of contemplation.

The main point is one Roethke made many times himself: "The Lost Son" sequence is meant to be heard, for there is power in the sounds of the language. The critic who sits silently at his desk, defining words and digging for symbols without listening to the composition of sounds, will miss perhaps the most significant aspect of the poems—their auditory suggestiveness. The word has power that goes beyond its connotations and denotations, and Roethke knew this, knew that the mind has an intuitive as well as a rational side to which those sounds could appeal. By manipulating the sounds in his poems and at the same time confronting the reader with insoluble verbal dilemmas, Roethke hoped to subvert the rational mind and elevate the intuitive faculties. Perhaps most of us are incapable of subordinating our rational sides to the extent Roethke subordinated his, but even so, there is something in "The Lost Son" sequence that we comprehend subliminally, perhaps instinctively, something that we simply cannot explain in the context of traditional analysis.

This position is neither anti-critical or anti-intellectual, nor am I denying the possibility of explicating the poems of "The Lost Son" sequence. However, in order to get the most out of the poems, we must take them on their own terms, for to impose our own logic upon the poems is to deny them their true meaning. How dreary it is to find one so intent upon explaining the various meanings of a word such as "near" in the line "God, give me a near" (CP, 73) that he misses the clever auditory pun; or one who is so involved in the onomatopoeic qualities of "ching" in the line "Water birds went ching. Went ching" (CP, 73) that he fails to smile at the bawdy word play. Such readers are trapped inside their own reason, "That dreary shed, that hutch for grubby schoolboys!" (CP, 92), as Roethke described it.

In the context of the entire sequence, Roethke's word play is not superfluous, and it is more than simply clever; it is essential to the meaning of the poems. Throughout the sequence, Roethke's aim is to "keep the rhythms 'right,' *i.e.*, consistent with what a child would say or at at least to create the 'as if' of the child's world."[29] And that partly explains the predominance of the jingles, aphorisms, and impossible questions. But the language, more than a witty attempt to depict the child's world, represents a serious effort to recreate the consciousness and the perception of the child, specifically as it is revealed through the regressive aspects of mania. The focus is not on the objective world, but on the child as the perceiver of that world and on *how* he perceives it; that is, on the process. This is perhaps what ultimately saves the sequence and prevents it from becoming, to borrow Roethke's phrase, merely "cutesy prattle."

The child, particularly the very young one (and the manic), is not so much a rational as an intuitive creature. For him, the world is alive and dancing with limitless possibilities. He understands not so much by thinking as by feeling. For example, when the child in "Where Knock Is Open Wide" says, "I know it's an owl. He's making it darker." (*CP*, 72), he expresses an understanding that lies outside the pale of logic. Owl and darkness are, for him, related in a way that the adult consciousness cannot accept, and yet the relationship is not an invalid one.

Roethke's goal in the sequence is to create *in* us as well as *for* us the "as if" of the child's world. By confronting us with language that appeals more to the intuition than to the intellect and by deliberately confounding our analytical minds with unanswerable questions, Roethke attempts to make us feel rather than think. We are, in a very real sense, invited to regain the child's perception, if we can. The only obstacle that stands between us and an intuitive understanding of the sequence is our insistence on logic and analysis. By yielding and entering the poetry with our ears and senses, not merely our minds, we can perhaps gain an understanding that is otherwise impossible. We can participate in, not simply explicate, the world of "The Lost Son."

The relationship of all this to mysticism should be obvious. As noted earlier in this study, the mystic, like the manic, frequently describes his experience in terms of birth, awaking into another life, another reality. Many psychologists feel that mysticism essentially involves a regression to the unified world of infancy. Establishing the validity of this claim is beyond the scope of this study. However, the important thing is not to establish that mania and mysticism are identical but that they are similar in a great many ways. In the context of our discussion of mania and "The Lost Son" sequence, the most significant parallel involves the rejection of logic in favor of some other way of knowing. The mystic, like the manic, finds analysis and the language of which analysis is made to be inadequate to describe his perceptions. But if he does try to convey some sense of his experience, he inevitably uses words that are highly symbolical or metaphorical—that is, language at its most suggestive and least analytical. This is definitely Roethke's technique in "The Lost Son" sequence. He employs language that is designed to circumvent or block the logical mind. His words, like those of the mystic, appeal not so much to our intellectual as to our intuitive understanding. They afford us a "way in" to his experience.

Perhaps the most remarkable thing about "The Lost Son" sequence is that it makes any sense at all. But there is a narrative line, and the reader can follow the general movement of the protagonist through the fourteen poems even though he may not understand specific passages along the way. The struggle "to become something more" is paramount, and if the reader can follow that movement, all the difficult passages ultimately make sense in relation to the various stages of the protagonist's struggle.[30] Consequently, rather than attempt a line-by-line explication of the poems, I will follow the general movement of the sequence in an effort to show how it relates to the mystic's push for ultimate reality.

Like the "Cuttings" poems, "Where Knock Is Open Wide" (*CP*, 71–74), which initiates the sequence, begins with the urge and wrestle to be born, to rise on "lopped limbs to a new life":

> Once upon a tree
> I came across a time,
> It wasn't even as
> A ghoulie in a dream.
>
> There was a mooly man
> Who had a rubber hat
> The funnier than that,—
> He kept it in a can.

What's the time, papa-seed?
Everything has been twice.
My father is a fish.

The language in this passage recalls the opening lines of *A Portrait of the Artist*—"Once upon a time and a very good time it was there was a moocow coming down along the road . . ."—but unlike Joyce's account, which begins at infancy, Roethke's history of self begins in the womb at the moment of conception, when one "comes across" time.[31] In the prenatal world the father is viewed as a seed ("papa-seed") and a fish, both descriptive of the sperm cell, and also a "mooly man" who wears a rubber hat (a probable reference to penis and condom). Subsequent sections carry the protagonist through memories of childhood—the death of an uncle and a fishing trip—to the death of his father:

Kisses come back,
I said to Papa;
He was all whitey bones
And skin like paper.

God's somewhere else,
I said to Mamma.
The evening came
A long long time.

I'm somebody else now.
Don't tell my hands.
Have I come to always? Not yet.
One father is enough.

Maybe God has a house.
But not here.

The poem ends on a despondent note with the expression of a tenuous faith: If there is a God, he is not here. The son has not yet "come to always," has not attained the illumination he desires.

It is essential to keep in mind that the sequence represents not just a psychological history but a spiritual struggle. The effort is not simply to be born but "to become something more," to push toward a higher plane of reality. The initial desire is for illumination; the ultimate goal is union with the One. However, in order to arrive at the second stage of the mystic quest one must first be purged. In the greenhouse poems purgation is represented by the plants' struggle to push through the soil and grow toward the light, and in "The Lost Son" sequence it is reflected in the protagonist's struggle to be born. He is, on the mystical level, knocking on the door of illumination. Malkoff notes that the title "Where Knock Is Open Wide" is from a line from Christopher Smart's *A Song to David* and that in Smart's poem it precedes "the glorious floods of light of the last stanzas."[32] For Roethke, too, the knocking is a prelude to illumination, though the floods of light are yet to come. Like the child atop the greenhouse, the sequence's protagonist longs to be outside the womb, but his initial exposure to the world beyond leaves him unfulfilled.

"I Need, I Need" (*CP*, 74–76) begins not where the initial poem left off but with a regression to early infancy:

> A deep dish. Lumps in it.
> I can't taste my mother.
> Hoo. I know the spoon.
> Sit in my mouth.

Though the inevitable slipping back has occurred, some progress has been made because the poem begins with the child outside the womb. The initial emphasis is on "the child's world of sucking and licking. Then there is a shift to a passage in which two children are jumping rope. The reader isn't *told* the children are jumping rope: he simply hears the two reciting, alternately, jingles to each other."[33] These rhymes, as we noted earlier, do not necessarily make logical sense, or at least not profound logical sense, but they are not frivolous. The sound produced by such passages helps establish the "as if" of the child's world and creates in the reader the proper state of consciousness. Eventually, the jingles resolve themselves into "a vaguely felt, but definite, feeling of love in one of the children"[34]:

> Stop the larks. Can I have my heart back?
> Today I saw a beard in a cloud.
> The ground cried my name:

> Good-bye for being wrong.
> Love helps the sun.
> But not enough.

The incomplete love sensed by the protagonist and the melancholy tone of these lines recall the incomplete faith and despondency of the final section of "Where Knock Is Open Wide," a similarity made even more obvious by the "beard in a cloud" that symbolizes the dead father, and the "sun" (son) that is not helped enough. However, this time the protagonist manages to rally from his depression:

> Her feet said yes.
> It was all hay.
> I said to the gate,
> Who else knows
> What water does?
> Dew ate the fire.
>
> I know another fire.
> Has roots.

Although one fire has been extinguished, the son is certain that there is another one with roots that cannot be put out. Fire, like light, is a symbol of illumination, and the son is here reaffirming his belief in and desire for the illuminated state.

Significantly, the skip-rope songs lead to the feeling of love in the third section of the poem and prepare the child and the reader for what at this point in the sequence is only a vague sensation of the Absolute. They perform this function by emphasizing sound rather than meaning. In an incantatory fashion, they shift the child into another state of consciousness where his intuition, his vaguely felt sense of love, is manifested.

In the next four poems, which complete Part I of *Praise to the End!*, "we hear the young adolescent, half a child, then the randy young man boasting and caterwauling": "She asked her skin / To let me in: / The far leaves were for it" (*CP*, 77); "In the high noon of thighs, / In the springtime of stones, / We'll stretch with the great stems" (*CP*, 80); "I'm the serpent of somebody else. / See! She's sleeping like a lake: / Glory to seize, I say" (*CP*, 81). In the midst of the protagonist's discovery of his own sexuality, the purgative process continues. In "Bring the Day!" he determines that "It's time to begin! / To begin!" (*CP*, 78), but in "Give Way, Ye Gates" (*CP*, 79–80) he learns that the road to illumination is not easy:

> Touch and arouse. Suck and sob. Curse and mourn.
> It's a cold scrape in a low place.
> The dead crow dries on a pole.
> Shapes in the shade
> Watch.
>
> The mouth asks. The hand takes.
> These wings are from the wrong nest.
> Who stands in a hole
> Never spills.
>
> I hear the clap of an old wind.
> The cold knows when to come.
> What beats in me
> I still bear.
>
> The deep stream remembers:
> Once I was a pond.
> What slides away
> Provides.

The "Suck and sob" of the first line recalls the "sucking and sobbing" of the cuttings as they strain to break through the soil, and like those plants, the protagonist must endure a "cold scrape in a low place" before he can rise to a new life. As always, the way down is the way up, and though the son may not like the pit he can find at least some consolation in knowing that he "Who stands in a hole / Never spills."

This wry acceptance of the purgative state is short-lived, however, for in "Sensibility! O La!" (*CP*, 81–82) the son becomes more anxious:

> It's a long way to somewhere else.
> The shade says: love the sun.
> I have.
> La, la,
> The light turns.
> The moon still abides.
> I hear you, alien of the moon.

Is the sun under my arm?
My sleep deceives me.
Has the dark a door?
I'm somewhere else,—
I insist!
I am.

The tension here is between darkness and light, obfuscation and illumination. The son looks for a door out of the darkness and, finding none, tries to imagine that he is not really in the darkness, that his sleep deceives him. Because "It's a long way to somewhere else," it is tempting for him to imagine that he is already there and that he does not have to make the trip at all. But such self-deception is unsuccessful, and the son's stubborn insistence that he is somewhere else seems desperate and hollow.

Desperation gives way in "O Lull Me, Lull Me" (CP, 83–84) to partial illumination for, in Roethke's words, "Disassociation often precedes a new state of clarity."[35] The mystic quest, as noted earlier, is actually a series of vacillations between states of pleasure and states of pain—each flash of illumination is earned at the cost of purgation—so it is not surprising that the son's depression resolves itself into mild euphoria:

The air, the air provides.
Light fattens the rock.
Let's play before we forget!

A wish! A wish!
O lovely chink, O white
Way to another grace!—
I see my heart in the seed;
I breathe into a dream,
And the ground cries.
I'm crazed and graceless,
A winter-leaping frog.
Soothe me, great groans of underneath,
I'm still waiting for a foot.
The poke of the wind's close,
But I can't go leaping alone.
For you, my pond,
Rocking with small fish,

> I'm an otter with only one nose:
> I'm all ready to whistle;
> I'm more than when I was born;
> I could say hello to things;
> I could talk to a snail;
> I see what sings!
> What sings!

The son's wish for a door out of the darkness is partially ful-filled, for he discovers a "lovely chink" through which he sees the "white / Way to another grace." But he himself is "crazed and graceless," standing, as it were, with his eye to the chink, looking at "What sings" in the light on the other side. At this point the son is merely beginning to grope toward the light like the bulbs in "Root Cellar," breaking out of his box, "hunt-ing for chinks in the dark."

Part II of *Praise to the End!* begins with "The Lost Son" (*CP*, 53–58), a poem that Roethke called "the 'easiest' of the longer ones . . . because it follows a narrative line indicated by the titles of the first four sections: 'The Flight,' 'The Pit,' 'The Gib-ber,' 'The Return.'" "The Flight" is "just what it says it is: a terrified running away" in which the son is "hunting, like a primitive, for some animistic suggestion, some clue to exis-tence from the subhuman"[36]:

> Tell me:
> Which is the way I take;
> Out of what door do I go,
> Where and to whom?
>
> > Dark hollows said, lee to the wind,
> > The moon said, back of an eel,
> > The salt said, look by the sea,
> > Your tears are not enough praise,
> > You will find no comfort here,
> > In the kingdom of bang and blab.
> >
> > Running lightly over spongy ground,
> > Past the pasture of flat stones,
> > The three elms,
> > The sheep strewn on a field,
> > Over a rickety bridge
> > Toward the quick-water, wrinkling and rippling.

> Hunting along the river,
> Down among the rubbish, the bug-riddled foliage,
> By the muddy pond-edge, by the bog-holes,
> By the shrunken lake, hunting, in the heat of summer.

As in "Sensibility! O La!," the son is searching for a door out of the darkness, but his imaginary running away ("I'm somewhere else,— / I insist! / I am!") has become actual flight. The desire to find the door to illumination is so overpowering that it leads him on a frenzied search that slows temporarily in "The Pit," "a period of physical and psychic exhaustion,"[37] but begins again in "The Gibber," ending with a partial illumination similar to that experienced in "O Lull Me, Lull Me":

> These sweeps of light undo me.
> Look, look, the ditch is running white!
> I've more veins than a tree!
> Kiss me, ashes, I'm falling through a dark swirl.

The perception is only temporary, for the "sweeps of light" once again become "a dark swirl." In the final section of the poem, after the serene recollection of the greenhouse world, the illumination comes again, although this time the son is nearly grown:

> Light traveled over the wide field;
> Stayed.
> The weeds stopped swinging.
> The mind moved, not alone,
> Through the clear air, in the silence.
>
> > Was it light?
> > Was it light within?
> > Was it light within light?
> > Stillness becoming alive,
> > Yet still?
>
> A lively understandable spirit
> Once entertained you.
> It will come again.
> Be still.
> Wait.

As at the close of "Where Knock Is Open Wide," the son reaffirms his faith in illumination, but here the reaffirmation is more explicit, the faith more solid, and a sense of unity is implied in the line "The mind moved, not alone." Though "the illumination is still only partly apprehended," the son is certain that it will return; he must simply be patient and wait.[38]

"The Long Alley" and "The Shape of the Fire" present a line of development very similar to that of "The Lost Son," closely following the pattern of flight, pit, gibber, and return. "A Field of Light," which stands between these two poems, functions as a short interlude. The three poems together represent the continuing process of purgation, and in each one the protagonist moves a little closer to illumination. "In 'The Long Alley' a serenity of 'light' was achieved, at a cost; but it was only partial and only for a time."[39]

> Light airs! Light airs! A pierce of angels!
> The leaves, the leaves become me!
> The tendrils have me! (*CP*, 61)

This illumination, as Roethke observes, is of short duration, but the protagonist remains ready to receive further illumination, as the concluding lines reveal: "Give me my hands: / I'll take the fire."

The final passage of "A Field of Light" (*CP*, 62–63) is "another 'light' passage, with much more activity" than at the end of "The Long Alley"[40]:

> I could watch! I could watch!
> I saw the separateness of all things!
> My heart lifted up with the great grasses;
> The weeds believed me, and the nesting birds.
> There were clouds making a rout of shapes crossing
>   a windbreak of cedars,
> And a bee shaking drops from a rain-soaked honeysuckle.
> The worms were delighted as wrens.
> And I walked, I walked through the light air;
> I moved with the morning.

The clarity of perception and the feeling of separateness in unity revealed here recall the euphoric stroll across the field in "The Waking," when the speaker felt that "all the waters / Of all the streams / Sang in my veins / That summer day." The illumination is more complete than any the protagonist has previously experienced.

Full illumination finally comes, however, at the end of "The Shape of the Fire" (*CP*, 64–67):

> To have the whole air!—
> The light, the full sun
> Coming down on the flowerheads,
> The tendrils turning slowly,
> A slow snail-lifting, liquescent;
> To be by the rose
> Rising slowly out of its bed,
> Still as a child in its first loneliness;
> To see cyclamen veins become clearer in early sunlight,
> And mist lifting out of the brown cat-tails;
> To stare into the after-light, the glitter left on
>   the lake's surface,
> When the sun has fallen behind a wooded island;
> To follow the drops sliding from a lifted oar,
> Held up, while the rower breathes, and the small boat
>   drifts quietly shoreward;
> To know that light falls and fills, often without
>   our knowing,
> As an opaque vase fills to the brim from a quick pouring,
> Fills and trembles at the edge yet does not flow over,
> Still holding and feeding the stem of the contained flower.

This vision is experienced by the mature man, and perhaps that accounts for the fullness, the completeness of the perception. The protagonist has been filled to the brim with light, with understanding.

The movement in each of these four poems may be described as two steps forward, one step back: there is inevitably some lost ground, but when the poems are examined together they exhibit considerable progress. Thus, the lost son moves, slowly but steadily, from fleeting flashes of light to a perception of the "full sun," from tail flicks at the corner of the eye to a full view of that elusive reality.

In the final four poems of the sequence, the protagonist is able to sustain his illumination, as in the closing lines of "Praise to the End!" (*CP*, 85–88):

I believe! I believe!—
In the sparrow, happy on gravel;
In the winter-wasp, pulsing its wings in the sunlight;
I have been somewhere else; I remember the sea-faced
    uncles.
I hear, clearly, the heart of another singing,
Lighter than bells,
Softer than water.

Wherefore, O birds and small fish, surround me.
Lave me, ultimate waters.
The dark showed me a face.
My ghosts are all gay.
The light becomes me.

He no longer has to imagine that he is somewhere else, for he
has truly been there, and he remembers, and the light that
falls and fills in "The Shape of the Fire" here illuminates him
to the point that he and the light are one.

Even when the illumination fails in "Unfold! Unfold!" (*CP*,
89–91), and the cliffs fling him back, the protagonist knows
how to regain the light:

A house for wisdom; a field for revelation.
Speak to the stones, and the stars answer.
At first the visible obscures:
Go where light is.

Revelation is obtained in the field, not in the house—that is,
through intuition, not analysis. The way to the stars is through
the stones, and the way to the visible is through the obscure.
This, as noted several times previously, is basic mystical doctrine: to attain the light (illumination) it is necessary to pass
through the darkness (purgation).

In "I Cry, Love! Love!" (*CP*, 92–93) the protagonist proclaims
"once more a condition of joy," but there is something ominous
about the owls in the hemlocks and the bats among the willows, almost a death wish, a desire to perish in the euphoria
of illumination:

I hear the owls, the soft callers, coming down from
    the hemlocks.
The bats weave in and out of the willows,

> Wing-crooked and sure,
> Downward and upward,
> Dipping and veering close to the motionless water.

The protagonist is "So alive I could die!," as he exclaims in "O, Thou Opening, O" (*CP*, 97–99), but he ultimately rejects that temptation, deciding instead to continue seeing and seeking, asking his skin to be true:

> Going is knowing.
> I see; I seek;
> I'm near.
> Be true,
> Skin.

Although illumination holds great joy and beauty for those who attain it, it also poses a danger, for, like the diver who experiences rapture of the deep, the mystic often feels an over-powering urge to surrender himself to the perception. If he is to continue upon the mystic quest, he must resist that attraction and, as Roethke does, make a conscious effort to continue seeking ultimate reality, to continue learning by going where he has to go.

The best summary that can be made of Roethke's use of growth symbolism in the greenhouse poems and "The Lost Son" sequence is made by Roethke himself in "A Light Breather" (*CP*, 101), which he regarded as "a kind of epilogue, or little comment poem"[41]:

> The spirit moves,
> Yet stays:
> Stirs as a blossom stirs,
> Still wet from its bud-sheath,
> Slowly unfolding,
> Turning in the light with its tendrils;
> Plays as a minnow plays,
> Tethered to a limp weed, swinging,
> Tail around, nosing in and out of the current,
> Its shadows loose, a watery finger;
> Moves, like the snail,
> Still inward,
> Taking and embracing its surroundings,
> Never wishing itself away,

Unafraid of what it is,
A music in a hood,
A small thing,
Singing.

The spirit moves like a plant, pushing steadily toward the light; yet, at the same time it moves like the snail "Still inward, / Taking and embracing its surroundings." Such is the motion of contemplation, a simultaneous unfolding and embracing, a going forth and a taking in, the upward struggle of the cuttings and the downward flight of the lost son. Also reiterated here is the important lesson learned by the protagonist in "O, Thou Opening, O": the spirit never wishes itself away, no matter how enticing annihilation in illumination may be; the road to union stretches beyond, so the mystic quest must continue.

Paradoxically, the movement of "The Lost Son" sequence is in and out simultaneously. The poems are derived from Roethke's exploration of his sub- and preconscious mind, his movement into himself, but they describe an outward movement, a push to be born and "to become something more." This paradox, as I have pointed out several times, is central to mysticism. For the mystic, the way down (or in) is the way out, and this is also true for Roethke in "The Lost Son" sequence. By exploring the most remote parts of himself, his darkest and deepest interiors, he begins to move beyond himself, into the light of illumination. The sequence describes, in Roethke's own words, "an effort to be born," a struggle to attain the mystic's (or the manic's) sense of being "newborn" and at one with the universe.[42]

In a 1946 notebook, Roethke remarked, "I seem to want to write of nothing but light" (36 #86). Definitely, the overwhelming preoccupation in *The Lost Son* is with light. The emphasis is established in the greenhouse pieces by the plants that move irresistibly toward the sun. That movement is sustained in "The Lost Son" poems and paralleled by the protagonist's struggle for birth and illumination. Significantly, it is the "sun" that is lost (clearly, Roethke means both words—"son" and "sun"—to be operable) and so the sequence is essentially, almost exclusively, a movement toward recovery of the lost source of light. Underhill makes some remarks that are particularly applicable here:

> A new sun rises above the horizon, and transfigures their [the mystics'] twilit world. Over and over again they return to light-imagery in this connection. Frequently, as in their first conversion, they report an actual and overpowering consciousness of radiant life, ineffable in its splendor, as an accompaniment of their inward adjustment.[43]

Because light implies its opposite, darkness, the condition out of which the protagonist moves, the extremes between which the lost son oscillates—darkness and light, pain and pleasure, death and life—are clearly established and account for the back-and-forth movement in the sequence. Roethke has been awakened, made aware of a higher level of reality, and so his movement is toward illumination and ultimate union, even though the road he must travel passes through the darkness of purgation and despair.

IV. The Lovers

8.

The Lovers

"The 'I' or the ego—always the soft idiot softly me-ing—
that 'I' must be broken beyond."—Roethke Notebooks (28 #26)

Words for the Wind, published in 1958 under the subtitle *The Collected Verse of Theodore Roethke*, includes—in addition to an exact reprint of the Pulitzer-Prize-winning volume *The Waking*, itself a rather complete compendium of Roethke's previous books—a considerable number of new poems. Most notable among the latter are "The Dying Man" and "Meditations of an Old Woman," and a section titled "Love Poems," significant because it marks a new direction in Roethke's symbolization of the mystic quest.

In the total context of Roethke's poetic development the love poems of *Words for the Wind* and subsequently those of *The Far Field* represent a shift from the naive, self-involved sexuality of "The Lost Son" sequence to a more mature consideration of love and its importance in the quest for identity. Typically, the mystic views the flesh as something that must be abjured. Roethke, too, begins with this perspective, but in the love poems he discovers the possibility of going through the flesh to attain the spirit.

In recognizing the relationship between sexual and spiritual love, Roethke is operating not only in the tradition of the medieval Mariolatry poets and such Elizabethans as Donne and Herbert, but in accordance with a considerable number of mystics as well. Perceiving that sexual union, like mystical ecstasy, effects a transcendence of reason and self, a reconciliation of opposites, and a sense of mergence, many mystics have relied on the correspondence to help convey some sense of their ineffable spiritual experiences:

> It was natural and inevitable that the imagery of human love and marriage should have seemed to the mystic the best of all images of his own "fulfilment of life"; his soul's surrender, first to the

call, finally to the embrace of Perfect Love. It lay ready to his hand: it was understood of all men: and moreover, it certainly does offer, upon lower levels, a strangely exact parallel to the sequence of states in which man's spiritual consciousness unfolds itself, and which form the consummation of the mystic life.[1]

The "strangely exact parallel" that Underhill mentions may be stated thus: the mystic is, in a sense, smitten by a fleeting perception of ultimate reality and feels that he must possess it. His initial awakening is a kind of falling in love, and his subsequent travails during the period of purgation resemble the desolate yearnings of the forlorn lover. If he is a constant suitor, his perseverance will result eventually in acceptance, the period of illumination when he is permitted to look upon the full beauty of his loved one, and marriage, the union of his soul with the Absolute. So exact is the parallel that it is possible for the mystic to describe his spiritual ventures exclusively in terms of physical love, and many have done so.

Roethke, too, makes use of this correspondence in his love poetry, which functions simultaneously on the sensual and spiritual levels. This duality is reflected primarily in Roethke's lady, who, despite her sensuality, seems to be something of an ethereal being, appearing (in "The Visitant" and elsewhere) as in a vision or a dream. Certainly, she is more than an ordinary woman, and in the context of Roethke's quest for identity she becomes the embodiment of that Absolute toward which he strives.

The love poems represent a new development in Roethke's poetry and reflect how closely his art was tied to events in his own life. It was not until after his marriage to Beatrice Heath O'Connell in January 1953 that Roethke began writing what must stand as some of the finest love poems of our time. His bent was to see everything in his life in terms of poetry and so, just as he had exploited his own manic-depressiveness for new perceptions, he explored his relationship with Beatrice for poetic material. If that sounds coldly utilitarian, it should not. Poetry was for Roethke a total obsession; it was life itself, and he could no more readily have stopped mining his experiences for poetry than he could have stopped living.

It is important to note that the love poems were not a digres-

sion for Roethke. They simply afforded him another set of
symbols for his familiar themes: the search for self—this time
through another person—and his struggle to perceive and
unite with the Absolute, the Godhead above God. Significantly, the love poems are characterized by a mystical symbolism that makes them wholly compatible with Roethke's earlier
work, and this compatibility also links the love poems, at least
indirectly, with Roethke's manic perceptions. Just as the manic
episodes allowed him to escape the limitations of self and participate in the larger unity of creation, love with another person gave him the opportunity to see himself "In another being,
at last" (*CP*, 126). The movement is from "I to Otherwise, or
maybe even to Thee."[2] Certainly, marriage did not signal the
end of the manic episodes; another one occurred in the fall of
1953, and they were to recur throughout the remainder of his
life.

Roethke's familiarity with the mystical symbolism of the lovers is revealed throughout the notebooks in references to St.
Theresa and to other mystics. For example, the following passage is found in a 1942 notebook:

> St. Theresa
> unitive mysticism
> epithalamic mysticism (33 #31)

The term *epithalamic mysticism* is apparently taken from *Love in
the Western World*, which Roethke read and made copious notes
on. Similarly, terms such as *agape* and *eros*, which appear ran-
domly throughout the notebooks of the early 1940s, also are
derived from that source. These terms refer specifically to the
love that passes between the mystic and the divine Absolute.
As Roethke succinctly expresses it in another 1942 notebook
entry, "Orthodox mysticism: marriage of God & ind. soul" (33
#31).

"The Visitant" (*CP*, 100–101), though not one of the love
poems proper, is nevertheless the best point of departure for
this analysis because it exhibits characteristics of "The Lost
Son" sequence as well as the love poems and thereby functions as an effective transition between the two. The poem begins with the protagonist waiting (like his "Lost Son" counter-

part) by the "slip-ooze" (inevitable starting point for the struggling spirit). As he waits, the visitation begins:

> Slow, slow as a fish she came,
> Slow as a fish coming forward,
> Swaying in a long wave;
> Her skirts not touching a leaf,
> Her white arms reaching towards me.
>
> She came without sound,
> Without brushing the wet stones,
> In the soft dark of early evening,
> She came,
> The wind in her hair,
> The moon beginning.

The imagery here echoes a passage in "The Long Alley" in which the protagonist invokes the flowers, concluding: "What fish-ways you have, littlest flowers, / Swaying over the walks in the watery air, / Drowsing in soft light, petals pulsing" (CP, 61). The spectral woman, too, has "fish-ways," swaying forward through the watery air, but unlike the flowers in "The Long Alley" she brings no illumination. For some reason the spell is broken and the protagonist wakes the next morning to find himself wondering "Where's she now, the mountain's downy girl?" This initial experience, like tail flicks at the corner of the eye or the child's momentary perception atop the greenhouse, is fleeting and only partially assimilated, but it awakens the protagonist to an awareness of another level of reality.

The vision recurs in "The Dream" (CP, 119–20), with the visitant once again approaching through the flowing air, but this time the perception is more intense, and the protagonist is able to sustain it for a longer period:

> She came toward me in the flowing air,
> A shape of change, encircled by its fire.
> I watched her there, between me and the moon;
> The bushes and the stones danced on and on;
> I touched her shadow when the light delayed;
> I turned my face away, and yet she stayed.
> A bird sang from the center of a tree;
> She loved the wind because the wind loved me.

Even though he turns his face away, the protagonist still sees the spectral woman, as one perceives the afterimage of a brilliant light, and when he subsequently yields himself to her, he becomes immersed in fire:

> She held her body steady in the wind;
> Our shadows met, and slowly swung around;
> She turned the field into a glittering sea;
> I played in flame and water like a boy
> And I swayed out beyond the white seafoam;
> Like a wet log, I sang within a flame.
> In that last while, eternity's confine,
> I came to love, I came into my own.

The meeting of the shadows signifies a uniting of souls, as the protagonist links himself with the incorporeal woman, symbol of the Absolute, and becomes engulfed in flame. There can be no question that the experience presented in these lines is that of illumination, for many mystics have described their perceptions of ultimate reality in the same way, as an immersion in fire. The result of such an engulfment in what Underhill calls the Fire of Love is perfect love and understanding.[3] Thus, the protagonist's claim in the last line of the poem, "I came to love, I came into my own," transcends the purely sensual meaning.

I do not wish to downplay the erotic nature of the love poems because the sensual experience leads directly to mystical perception. In Roethke's words, "The flesh can make the spirit visible." However, I do want to emphasize that the poems function on the spiritual as well as the physical plane. No doubt, Roethke reveled in the ambiguity of a line like "I came to love, I came into my own." Yet it is equally certain that he intended the sexual experience to represent a greater sense of union. The erotic imagery is not incidental, but essential to the poem's larger meaning.

"All the Earth, All the Air" (*CP*, 121–22) begins with the speaker standing "with standing stones" and ends with him lurking in "A lurking place," "One with the sullen dark." The euphoric activity of illumination has been replaced by the static depression of purgation, leaving the speaker to dispel his gloom by rationalizing: "This joy's my fall" and "The ground needs the abyss." Both aphorisms may be taken as variations on the familiar paradox "The way down is the way up," for both imply the necessity of opposites: The joy of illumination is defined by the fall of purgation just as the ground is best understood in the context of the abyss; each is a necessary and inherent condition of the other. The consideration of such paradoxes coupled with the recollection of illumination helps to rally the speaker, and he realizes that despite his present position, "The field is mine! Is mine!," a line which recalls the glittering field of illumination in "The Dream." And, as though the afterimage of the spectral woman still remains upon his mind's retina, he concludes, "who faced with her face, / Would not rejoice?"

The concern with opposites continues in "Words for the Wind" (CP, 123–26) as the speaker declares:

> Love, love, a lily's my care,
> She's sweeter than a tree.
> Loving, I use the air
> Most lovingly: I breathe;
> Mad in the wind I wear
> Myself as I should be,
> All's even with the odd,
> My brother the vine is glad.

The assertion "I wear / Myself as I should be" is virtually a duplication of a passage in "Open House," "Myself is what I wear / I keep the spirit spare" (CP, 3), and as in that early poem, the speaker here has stripped himself of all but the essential. The implication, of course, especially in light of the "Open House" allusion, is that the flesh has been subdued and the spirit extended, producing a clearer perception of things. The result of such a heightened state of awareness (illumination) is the conviction that "All's even with the odd," the mystic's characteristic sense of unity. Because all things are related it is possible to speak to the stones and have the stars answer—as the lost son does in "Unfold! Unfold!"—or to stare until a garden stone slowly becomes the moon. Similarly, the speaker can maintain that "All things bring me to love" because his love is all things:

The breath of a long root,
The shy perimeter
Of the unfolding rose,
The green, the altered leaf,
The oyster's weeping foot,
And the incipient star—
Are part of what she is.

The sense of unity is complete when the speaker himself, having kissed "her moving mouth, / Her swart hilarious skin," becomes a part of the everything that is a part of his love and can
"see and suffer myself / In another being, at last."

The sexuality of this poem is unavoidable, particularly when
Roethke seems to be grinning through the transparency of a
double entendre, as in the last line cited above, where he obviously intends the phrase "in another being" to be construed
in all its senses. Such ambiguity has the effect of contributing
yet another pair of opposites to the general fund, and in the
context of "Words for the Wind" these antithetical elements
work together, thereby providing another manifestation of
unity. Roethke's ability to see himself in another being allows
him to transcend the narrow restrictions of his own identity
and participate in a larger self.

The movement in "Words for the Wind," and in the love
poems generally, is out of self. As we have seen, this is the
basic movement of most of Roethke's poetry, though the
method changes. In *Open House*, Roethke tries to push beyond
himself to attain the Absolute; in *The Lost Son* he struggles to
rise above himself by moving inward; and in the love poems
he attempts to move outside himself by focusing his attention
on another person. Writing of "Words for the Wind" Roethke
says, "I was able to move outside myself—for me sometimes
a violent dislocation—and express a joy in another, in others"
(28 #25). Physical love, then, can become an avenue of escape
for the spirit.

The movement from the physical to the spiritual is an element of most of the love poems, but it is perhaps nowhere
better expressed than in "Toward, Toward" (24 #28), apparently an early draft of "The Tranced":

Is it the nature of all love to rise?
Our small souls hid from their small agonies;
Love-longing of a kind
Rose up within the mind,
Rose up and fell like an erratic wind.

Eyes brooded on a point of light so fine
Subject and object sang and danced as one;
Slowly we moved between
The unseen and the seen,
Our bodies light, and lighted by the moon.

We struggled out of sensuality
As best we could. Being, we had to be;
We paced the barren ground;
The stones rang with light sound;
The birds, the leaves waved the slow wind around.

And then we faced, alone, the pure profound,

The silent air, the widening abyss
That shifted toward us when we bent to kiss;
Remembering less and less
Of mere appearances,
Groping that way, and this,
We faltered toward our everlastingness.

The initial question, "Is it the nature of all love to rise?", is
eventually answered affirmatively. (In "The Tranced," the
question is changed to a declarative statement.) But the poem
makes it clear that the final rising is preceded by a necessary
falling. The "love-longing" rises in the mind only to fall "like
an erratic wind." However, the lovers are able to struggle out
of sensuality and make a clumsy movement toward "everlastingness." The flesh, then, is seen as a way to elevate the spirit,
but only if a kind of spiritual union is achieved. This union
involves the obliteration of the distinction between subject and
object, between lover and loved one. The self must be transcended if a merging with the lover (and consequently with
the Absolute) is to be effected.
 The method employed here is not so different from that
found in the greenhouse poems where a mergence was at-

tained by long-looking. In fact, the title of this poem, "Toward, Toward," suggests not simply a persistent struggle to move in the direction of the Absolute but also the mutual interpenetration that occurs during contemplation. Observer and the thing observed move toward one another and merge, if the contemplative is successful. The movement is observer toward object and object toward observer, as he becomes a part of the thing he contemplates and it becomes part of him. Significantly, this fusion is often referred to as the mystic marriage. In similar fashion, the lovers merge with one another and transcend the physical.

The sensuality of Roethke's lady is an element of all the love poems, but so is her transcendent, beatific nature. Even in "I Knew a Woman" (*CP*, 127) the provocative woman can "move more ways than one." To be sure, she is shapely and sexy, well-learned in the art of love and lovemaking, but she also casts "a shadow white as stone" and puts the speaker in touch with the eternal. Caught up in her motion, the speaker loses his sense of time and apparently transcends the temporal. His focus is on "how a body sways" because her movement, which is obviously erotic, is also cosmic, as seen in the line "She moved in circles, and those circles moved." She is, in effect, the *primum mobile*, responsible for all movement, and by concentrating on her the speaker is able to commune with the Absolute.

Elsewhere, the sensual qualities of the lover become secondary. In "The Voice" (*CP*, 128), for example, the woman is not visible at all, but she still has the power to attract the speaker and lift him to another plane of perception:

> One feather is a bird,
> I claim; one tree, a wood;
> In her low voice I heard
> More than a mortal should;
> And so I stood apart,
> Hidden in my own heart.

Something of Blake's notion of seeing the world in a grain of sand comes through here, as the speaker asserts that the part contains the whole. This is the mystic's perception of unity.

The feather is the bird; the tree the wood; and the voice the woman—and something more. The voice enables the speaker to hear "More than a mortal should"; it calls him out of himself "out where / Those notes went, like the bird," and leads him to a perception of unity:

> Desire exults the ear:
> Bird, girl, and ghostly tree,
> The earth, the solid air—
> Their slow song sang in me;
> The long noon pulsed away,
> Like any summer day.

The bird, girl, and tree have all merged, and the mergence has expanded to include "The earth, the solid air" and the speaker, who feels their combined song singing within him. Significantly, the experience takes place at noon, when the sun is brightest, symbolizing the speaker's sense of illumination.

The relationship between flesh and spirit is dealt with more explicitly than in any other of the love poems in the aphoristic passages of "The Sententious Man" (CP, 131–32):

> Spirit and nature beat in one breast-bone—
> I saw a virgin writhing in the dirt—
> The serpent's heart sustains the loveless stone:
> My indirection found direction out.
>
> Pride in fine lineaments precedes a fall;
> True lechers love the flesh, and that is all.

Because spiritual yearnings and sexual desires reside within the same breast, they are at the least related through proximity, which makes it possible to arrive in the vicinity of one by traveling to the other. Thus, the sententious man's claim, "My indirection found direction out." By loving only the flesh one can never become more than a "true lecher," but by recognizing the relationship between flesh and spirit and loving the spirit as well he can begin to get somewhere. The flesh may be a means to an end, but it is never an end in itself: "The spirit knows the flesh it must consume."

Later in the poem, the speaker provides a more vivid description of his indirect route to illumination:

> Though all's in motion, who is passing by?
> The after-image never stays the same.
> There was a thicket where I went to die,
> And there I thrashed, my thighs and face aflame.
> But my least motion changed into a song,
> And all dimensions quivered to one thing.

The subtle sexual imagery of this passage reveals itself fully only when the infinitive "to die" is read in its archaic sense, to achieve sexual climax. In that context, the thrashing motion, the flaming thighs, and the thicket where the dying occurs take on a particularly erotic significance as the entire passage becomes a description of the sex act. The result of this physical encounter is spiritual illumination and a sense of unity, as indicated in the last line of the passage and in the subsequent claims, "I taste my sister when I kiss my wife," and "Each one's himself, yet each one's everyone."

The sentimental man, "having found out all I could of all desire," understands the relationship between flesh and spirit. He knows that those who love only the flesh are like "small waters" that "run toward a miry hole." But he also knows it is possible to move beyond the purely sensual, as "water moves until it's purified" or as "the weak bridegroom strengthens in his bride." The latter image is a familiar one in mystical literature, where the individual spirit and the Absolute are often referred to as bride and groom, and its appearance here reinforces the symbolic quality of the poem.

Because marriage affords the mystic a surprisingly accurate analogy for his mystical experience, it is not unusual (especially among Catholic mystics) to encounter descriptions of the ineffable couched in terms of human love and marriage. Thus, St. Bernard writes:

> "'Let Him kiss me with the kisses of His mouth.' Who is it speaks these words? It is the Bride. Who is the Bride? It is the Soul thirsting for God. . . . She who asks this is held by the bond of love to him from whom she asks it. Of all the sentiments of nature, this of love is the most excellent, especially when it is rendered back to Him who is the principle and fountain of it—that is, God. Nor are there found any expressions equally sweet to signify the mu-

tual affection between the Word of God and the soul, as those of
Bridegroom and of Bride."[4]

As noted earlier, the notebooks reveal that Roethke knew of
this convention as epithalamic mysticism from his reading of
Love in the Western World, and much of his love poetry is
charged with the symbolism of the spiritual marriage. This is
undeniably true of "Her Dream" (20 #25), a poem found
among the manuscripts. Though it is a little long, I will repro-
duce it in its entirety because it was never collected in any of
Roethke's volumes:

> I went down to the river
>   In the mild light of the moon;
> The willows wrapped around me
>   All the smells of middle June;
> But when I sighed and raised my eyes,
>   The scene had fled and gone.
>
> I had a dream—would you believe?—
>   I dreamt about a horse;
> A lion bit an adder;
>   I cried out in remorse;
> I was driving up a mountain
>   When the car went in reverse.
>
> My backwheels hung far over
>   A gully dark and wide;
> It seemed an entrance made for me:
>   I took myself inside,
> And there I saw, straight up an aisle,
>   A bridegroom and a bride.
>
> The guests rose up to stretch their knees
>   And see what they could see:
> The burly bridegroom had a look
>   Of dour perplexity;
> The bride, poor naked shivering shape—
>   I swear she looked like me.
>
> The parson frowned; he hemmed and hawed;
>   He fumbled with his book;
> And every face, it looked at me
>   With the same sneery look;

When I tried to cover up myself,
   I stood there, and shook.

But suddenly the chancel cracked
   With a jagged lightning stroke;
The pillars streaked with balls of fire;
   There was a smell of smoke;
The bells began to ring themselves
   Before the heavens broke.

The rain came down, the rain came down,
   The bride and bridegroom kneeled;
Then all the guests ran naked out
   Upon a shimmery field
To dance and sing. And the bridegroom sighed
   As my lips began to yield.

This poem with its Yeatsean title, spoken by a female persona, was written in 1960 about the same time as "Her Words," "Her Reticence," "Her Longing," and "Her Time." The woman, of course, is Roethke's alter ego or, in St. Bernard's terms, the soul. Because the poem describes a dream, we are invited to derive as much symbolic value from the images as we can. However, the symbols are not terribly enigmatic if we begin, as Roethke apparently did, with the idea of the mystic marriage.

The first stanza actually frames the entire poem by telling what happened immediately before and after the dream. The speaker, apparently affected by the moonlight and the smells of summer, is transported to the visionary or dream state, which lasts until she lifts her eyes to find the vision dispelled. The description of the dream begins in the second stanza, and it captures the kaleidoscopic effect of the early phases of the dream cycle when inexplicable images float up from the subconscious mind—a horse, a lion, an adder. But very quickly, the imagery becomes consistent and a story begins to develop.

Significantly, the speaker is traveling up a mountain when her progress is reversed, and she enters a dark gully. This movement symbolizes the by now familiar mystical paradox, the way down is the way up and out. Her climb toward the summit of the mountain, toward perception and illumination, is turned into a descent, a journey through the dark abyss, but that is the way she must go. It is an entrance made for her. Within the abyss, the speaker sees a marriage ceremony taking place, and the bride, who looks like her, eventually becomes her, naked and shivering before the guests. The notion of being stripped bare, of wearing only the essential self, goes back as far as "Open House" and conveys the same sense of being made worthy by casting off the trappings of the ego. Illumination comes in the form of lightning bolts and fireballs, pealing bells and the rain that cleanses and purifies. The guests, formerly "sneery," now run out to cavort naked on the "shimmery field," always a symbol of illumination in Roethke's poetry, and the wedding ceremony is completed with a kiss, not unlike that described by St. Bernard in the passage quoted previously.

There is little room to doubt that Roethke was consciously employing symbols of the mystic or spiritual marriage in "Her Dream." In fact, the imagery is so consistent with that used by such mystics as St. Theresa, with whom Roethke was familiar, that it is difficult to read the poem in another context. Certainly, no other reading opens the poem so completely. I would place "Her Dream" alongside "In a Dark Time" as a poem influenced by Roethke's readings in mysticism and philosophy, which were quite extensive during the 1950s. The poem seems almost to have been written "by the book," and it makes explicit what is only implicit in most of the other love poems.

In "The Pure Fury" (*CP*, 133–34) the contemplation of the Absolute as the ideal love is replaced by what Underhill calls "dark contemplation," "the self's immersion in that paradoxical splendor of the Abyss"[5]:

> Stupor of knowledge lacking inwardness—
> What book, O learned man, will set me right?
> Once I read nothing through a fearful night,
> For every meaning had grown meaningless.

This is the dark night of the soul, the entry into "a plane of experience to which none of the categories of the intellect apply." Reason finds itself, in a most actual sense, "in the dark."[6] Nothingness predominates, flying loose when the "woman with an empty face," herself a kind of nonentity, tries to think.

Despite its negative aspects, the dark night is a necessary stage of the mystic quest, acting as a further purgation of the spiritual traveler, and if the mystic has the strength to remain in its overwhelming darkness the light will eventually become visible, disclosing to him the brilliance of the Absolute; thus the wish expressed in the closing lines of the poem:

> I live near the abyss. I hope to stay
> Until my eyes look at a brighter sun
> As the thick shade of the long night comes on.

The movement is cyclical, similar, as the image suggests, to the movement of night and day.

Though "The Renewal" (*CP*, 135) begins on a whimsical note with a centaur and sibyl romping and singing, it soon becomes apparent that "the thick shade of the long night" has not yet been dispelled: "Dark hangs upon the waters of the soul." Knowing that "Love alters all" (a variation on the "Love conquers all" adage), the speaker seeks renewal by demanding, "Unblood my instinct, love," and it is by loving that he is eventually delivered from the darkness:

> Sudden renewal of the self—from where?
> A raw ghost drinks the fluid in my spine;
> I know I love, yet know not where I am;
> I paw the dark, the shifting midnight air.
> Will the self, lost, be found again? In form?
> I walk the night to keep my five wits warm.
>
> Dry bones! Dry Bones! I find my loving heart,
> Illumination brought to such a pitch
> I see the rubblestones begin to stretch
> As if reality had split apart
> And the whole motion of the soul lay bare:
> I find that love, and I am everywhere.

The dark night is a time of disorientation and terror, a time of desperation when the speaker paws the darkness like a frightened animal and seems in danger of losing himself completely. But at the crucial moment illumination comes, a "sudden renewal of the self." And as though he has reached the end of an arduous search, he exclaims, "I find that love." The reference here is to spiritual love, the love of an individual spirit for the Absolute, which enables the speaker to experience the feeling of unity, the sense that "I am everywhere" and, as the ambiguity of the line suggests, that love itself is all pervasive.

"The Pure Fury" and "The Renewal" are remarkable among the love poems because they deal exclusively with the spiritual. There is none of the sensuality that is characteristic of the sequence as a whole, for Roethke's lady is abstracted out of existence, becoming a faceless woman in one poem and disappearing altogether in the other. She no longer stands as a symbolic representation of the Absolute but becomes that Absolute herself, the true object of Roethke's love.

"The Sensualists" (CP, 136) is an abrupt turnabout from the two preceding poems, concerned, as the title implies, with sexual rather than spiritual love:

> "My shoulder's bitten from your teeth;
>   What's that peculiar smell?
> No matter which one is beneath,
>   Each is an animal,"—
> The ghostly figure sucked its breath,
>   And shuddered toward the wall;
> Wrapped in the tattered robe of death,
>   It tiptoed down the hall.

These "true lechers" wake a ghost, a woman "pure as a bride," reminiscent of the spectral woman in "The Visitant" and "The Dream," who comes this time not as a manifestation of the Absolute but as a symbol of death. She signifies that those who love only the flesh must be prepared to accept flesh's mortality; without the involvement of the spirit it is impossible to approach the Absolute. Unlike the bride in "Her Dream," she attains no illumination, nor do the two lovers. Instead of being "naked to the bone," she is "Wrapped in the tattered robe of death," and her departure indicates that the sensualists have lost their opportunity for a spiritual experience. This poem stands as a clear statement that the obvious sensuality, here and in the rest of the love poems, cannot be an end in itself.

"Love's Progress" (CP, 137–38) takes the next step and describes what can be accomplished by lovers if the physical is transcended. They can experience a "rare propinquity," which is considerably different than the closeness of the sensualists, who are locked in a restrictive embrace that affords "no place to turn." The lovers in "Love's Progress" attain not only a nearness but a kinship, a mergence that allows them a freedom of movement similar to that of the vine, the light, a woman naked in water. The movement is toward illumination. Here, as elsewhere in the love poems, the woman is closely associated with light—"Light of my spirit, light / Beyond the look of love"—and the speaker, feeling himself far from home and vulnerable, awaits her arrival:

> The close dark hugs me hard,
> And all the birds are stone.
> I fear for my own joy;
> I fear myself in the field,
> For I would drown in fire.

The speaker is waiting for the darkness to turn to light, as it inevitably does for those who can endure the blackness of the abyss, and his anticipation of the coming illumination is so keen that it frightens him. It is worthwhile to note here that a number of mystics have expressed a similar apprehension about the joyous state of illumination, fearing that the sense of pleasure derived from perceiving the Absolute might prevent them from ultimately uniting with it. Whether this is Roethke's concern is not clear, but certainly he regards the coming experience as so exquisite that his own joy may consume him.

What happens when illumination is slow in coming is vividly described in "Plaint" (*CP*, 139), an oddity among the love poems because it does not focus on the love between a man and a woman. Instead, it deals with a broader love of mankind, perhaps even of God:

> Day after somber day,
> I think my neighbors strange;
> In hell there is no change.
> Where's my eternity
> Of inward blessedness?
> I lack plain tenderness.

> Where is the knowledge that
> Could bring me to my God?
> Not on this dusty road
> Or afternoon of light
> Diminished by the haze
> Of late November days.
>
> I lived with deep roots once:
> Have I forgotten their ways—
> The gradual embrace
> Of lichen around stones?
> Death is a deeper sleep,
> And I delight in sleep.

Lacking "plain tenderness," the speaker is incapable of loving his neighbors and perceiving God. Unlike Paul on the road to Damascus, he sees no blinding light of illumination because the already weak light of afternoon is further weakened by a late November haze. He tries to remember the ways of roots, their struggle to rise toward the sunlight, to blossom, and he invokes the image of lichen embracing stone, a kind of primordial love. But he is unable to pull himself out of despondency, and so the poem ends with a death wish. Obviously, "Plaint" describes a dark night of the soul experience, and it is significant among the love poems because of what it says about love. Without love, no apprehension of a higher reality is possible. One must be capable of loving not only his neighbors but everything if he is to perceive that unity which is itself a manifestation of love.

"The Swan" (*CP*, 140) presents another sensualist, one who finds himself "tangled in that lively hair" asking:

> Is there no way out of that coursing blood?
> A dry soul's wisest. O, I am not dry!

The sexual imagery is obvious, as is the implicit rejection of sexuality. Still the speaker cannot escape his own sensual nature but lives "alive and certain as a bull," traditional symbol for male potency. He seems unable, and perhaps a little unwilling, to overcome his physical desire, so he accepts himself as he is:

A man alive, from all light I must fall.
I am my father's son, I am John Donne
Whenever I see her with nothing on.

As a "man alive"—that is, sexually potent—he realizes that he
can never attain spiritual illumination, for the attraction of the
flesh is too strong. Nevertheless, there is a tone of happiness
in his submission to the thought of his lady with nothing on
(though this may call to mind the nothingness of the abyss).

The second section of "The Swan," printed entirely in italics
as though it is an aside or an editorial comment, differs considerably from the first:

The moon draws back its waters from the shore.
By the lake's edge, I see a silver swan,
And she is what I would. In this light air,
Lost opposites bend down—
Sing of that nothing of which all is made,
Or listen into silence, like a god.

The woman with nothing on has been transformed into a silver swan, symbol of the Absolute, and the speaker's desire for
a spiritual mergence with her leads to the familiar sense of
unity as "Lost opposites bend down." The spiritual experience
that was beyond the reach of the speaker in the first part of
the poem is here attained, and the dual structure reflects the
dual nature of love throughout the sequence. In addition, the
poem unmistakably alludes to Zeus and Leda, thereby deep-
ening the relationship between the physical and the spiritual,
the temporal and the Absolute. The allusion to Yeats's "Leda
and the Swan" is also unavoidable as the poem's "lost opposites" put on the knowledge of the gods and find their proper
place in a unified universe.

The final poem, "Memory" (*CP*, 141), ends the sequence as
it was begun with a dream:

In the slow world of dream,
We breathe in unison.
The outside dies within,
And she knows all I am.

> She turns, as if to go,
> Half-bird, half-animal.
> The wind dies on the hill.
> Love's all. Love's all I know.
>
> A doe drinks by a stream,
> A doe and its fawn.
> When I follow after them,
> The grass changes to stone.

Though the woman is not quite as elusive this time, she still departs, leaving the speaker to follow a doe and its fawn over grass that changes to stone. This final surrealistic image evokes a sense of death, perhaps even an attraction to it, for the petrification of the perennial grass symbolizes the stoppage of time and the creation of an eternal now. When the speaker tries to pursue his lady he becomes the only moving thing in a static world, a temporal being in the midst of the eternal. To pursue further is futile, and to remain is to die. In a sense, "Memory" leaves Roethke with two alternatives: he can abandon the pursuit of his lady or he can enter the world of stone grass. Thus, the way is prepared for the final poems of *Words for the Wind*, for Roethke's ultimate consideration of the possibilities of death and death's relation to the Absolute.

Before ending this discussion, I would like to examine some of the love poems published in *The Far Field*, several of which were composed about the same time as those in *Words for the Wind*. These poems are frequently neglected by critics, perhaps because they are overshadowed by the rest of *The Far Field*, but they are, nonetheless, significant in Roethke's symbolization of the lovers. "Light Listened" (*CP*, 212), composed around 1957, is metrically like "Words for the Wind" and thematically like "I Knew a Woman." The lady described in the poem is sensual and provocative, with "more sides than a seal," but like the woman who taught Roethke "Turn, and Counter-turn, and Stand," she is more than merely sexy. She leads the speaker to conclude, "All's known, all, all around," and when she sings a final song, light listens. By identifying her with light, Roethke indicates that she has certain transcendent qualities, that she is, in fact, the way to illumination. She opens up the speaker to an awareness of everything around him, provides him with a knowledge he did not previously have.

"His Foreboding" (*CP*, 215) calls to mind "Love's Progress" both because of its metrical similarities and its content. The speaker here is separated from his loved one and must endure the purgatory of his own company:

> I sing the wind around
> And hear myself return
> To nothingness, alone.
> The loneliest thing I know
> Is my own mind at play.

Living within himself affords him no opportunity for perception. "Thought upon thought can be / A burden to the soul," but he finds himself alone, engaged in "Activity centripetal." What he needs, to enable him to get beyond himself, is his lover, but she is not there. He senses an even more difficult time approaching:

> Is she the all of light?
> I sniff the darkening air
> And listen to my own feet.
> A storm's increasing where
> The winds and waters meet.

Because he cannot attain the light on his own, he speculates that his love may be "the all of light." The darkening air signifies the approach of the dark night of the soul. As the speaker's preoccupation with self intensifies, he listens, to the sound of his own feet, waiting for the storm to strike.

Among the love poems in *The Far Field*, one titled "Her Wrath" (*CP*, 216) has been consistently overlooked, probably because it appears to be a light poem, and on one level it is:

> Dante himself endured,
> And purgatorial ire;
> I, who renew the fire,
> Shiver, and more than twice,
> From another Beatrice.

Undeniably, Roethke is referring to his wife Beatrice in these lines, jokingly comparing her to Dante's Beatrice, but he also had something else in mind. Like Dante, Roethke strove for a perception of the ultimate, and in a very real sense his Beatrice helped him move toward that perception. Like the woman described in all the love poems, Beatrice is both physical and spiritual. It seems that Roethke found in love another avenue to the Absolute, an opportunity to see and suffer himself in another being, thereby transcending himself. Clearly, this is the message of all the love poems: Love provides a way for him to "put off myself and flee / My inaccessibility."

By way of concluding this chapter, I would like to consider "Four for Sir John Davies" (*CP*, 104–7), which, although it precedes most of the love poems chronologically, nonetheless functions as a fitting summary for a discussion of the lovers. In fact, the four sections of the poem, which generally follow the steps of awakening, purgation, and illumination, collectively embody all the elements I have been concerned with in the love poems.

Roethke's claim that "The Dance" essentially wrote itself is well known, and his insistence that the poem was inspired by Yeats and other dead poets who were present in the room has raised more than a few disbelieving brows. Yet Roethke's assertion seems peculiarly appropriate for a poem that initiates the struggle for illumination carried out in "The Partner," "The Wraith," and "The Vigil." The sequence, then, properly begins with an unwilled visitation, with awakening.

Unquestionably, "The Dance" shows the influence of John Davies's "Orchestra," which describes the harmonious movement of the universe, and the sixteenth-century notion of the cosmic dance is implicit in the poem from the beginning: "Is that dance slowing in the mind of man / That made him think the universe could hum?" Yet, there is another influence, one older than Davies. Plotinus, writing of the relationship between the individual and the Absolute, uses the metaphor of the choral dance:

> We are like a choir who stand round the conductor but do not always sing in tune, because their attention is diverted by looking

> at external things. So we always move round the One—if we did not, we should dissolve and cease to exist—but we do not always look towards the One. . . . But when we *do* behold Him, we attain the end of our existence and our rest. Then we no longer sing out of tune, but form a truly divine chorus about Him; in the which chorus dance the soul beholds the Fountain of life, the Fountain of intellect, the Principle of Being, the cause of good, the root of soul.[7]

While Roethke probably was not thinking of this passage from Plotinus when he wrote "The Dance," certainly there is some relation, via Davies, between Roethke's poem and Plotinus's comments. Plotinus maintains that in order for a man to place himself in proper relation to the Absolute, he must learn to dance by concentrating on the One. Unless he concentrates on the conductor, he will be out of step and not a part of the whole. Roethke attempts to teach himself to dance so that he may be brought to a perception of the unity he seeks.

Another interesting gloss for Roethke's poem may be found in the Apocryphal "Hymn of Jesus," in which Christ says:

> "I am the Word who did play and dance all things." "Now answer to My dancing." "Understand by dancing what I do." "Who danceth not knoweth not what is being done." "I would pipe, dance ye all!" "All whose Nature is to dance, doth dance!"[8]

Dancing, then, is a way of knowing, a way of creating a harmonious relationship between the individual and the One and bringing oneself into proper alignment with that which he seeks. As in Yeats, the dancer and the dance become indistinguishable, if we identify the dance as the larger movement of the whole universe. Roethke is like the caged bear, moving his lumbering body, "remembering to be gay," learning more than "the joyless motion of a stone."

Unable to dance alone very long, Roethke takes a partner in the second poem, and their dance becomes explicitly sexual. The woman, like her counterparts in the love poems, is highly sensual, able to "set sodden straw on fire." Yet she has other attributes, too, and she enables her partner to transcend himself and proclaim, "we live beyond / Our outer skin." As in the majority of the love poems, the sensual provides a way to the spiritual. By doing "what the clumsy partner wants to do," the speaker discovers that "The body and the soul know how to play / In that dark world where gods have lost their way." The dark world, of course, is the world of the senses, void of true illumination. But the body and the soul know how to function together to get beyond that darkness. As we have seen so many times in Roethke's poetry, the way down into the pit is the way out into the sunlight. However, the journey is not without risks, as indicated by the ghost the dancers awaken. If the dance is purely sensual, the ghost is a manifestation of death, as in "The Sensualists," but if the sensual is transcended, the ghost becomes a symbol of the dancers' mergence and movement beyond the body.

The sense of danger involved in what the dancers are doing is apparent from the first lines of "The Wraith": "Incomprehensible gaiety and dread / Attended what we did." Although they find pleasure in their dance, by now an explicit metaphor for sexual intercourse, they fear the ghost of death, for around them lie "all the lonely pastures of the dead." Sexual love without spiritual involvement serves only to underscore the lovers' mortality. They must move beyond the purely physical that is mutable and temporal. Consequently, they find that on "a darkening day" it is necessary to take "arms against our own obscurity." The result of their efforts is a mergence:

> Did each become the other in that play?
> She laughed me out, and then she laughed me in;
> In the deep middle of ourselves we lay;
> When glory failed, we danced upon a pin.
> The valley rocked beneath the granite hill;
> Our souls looked forth, and the great day stood still.

The sexual imagery here, of being laughed out and in, is obvious, but so is the spiritual. While the lovers' bodies unite, another union takes place, in the deep middle of themselves. This image performs double duty, being at once a sexual and a spiritual reference. The deep middle refers anatomically to the sex organs, located roughly in the middle of the body, but also to the souls of the lovers, their deep middle. And indeed, their souls are involved in the dance they perform: "Our souls looked forth, and the great day stood still." What the lovers learn is something we have seen demonstrated numerous times in the love poems: "The flesh can make the spirit visible." Significantly, the ghost aroused by the sensual play becomes a strange shape, a "Sea-beast or bird," perhaps an angel, and no longer threatens to be an image of death. Ultimately, it becomes a reflection of the lovers' union: "It was and was not she, a shape alone, / Impaled on light, and whirling slowly down." The light, of course, symbolizes illumination, and the fact that the shape both is and is not the partner suggests that each has become the other and a mergence has been effected. Through a union of the flesh, the lovers' combined spirits have been made visible as a single shape.

The final poem in the sequence, "The Vigil," ends the way many of *The Lost Son* poems end, with a vision of light. The movement throughout the sequence, like Dante's, has been indirect, and as Dante found paradise by going through hell, Roethke finds spiritual illumination by indulging in the sensual. As in many of the love poems, Roethke's lady is closely associated with light: "The waves broke easy, cried to me in white; / Her look was morning in the dying light." Dancing together, the lovers are able to endure the dark night of the soul, the sense of mortality that accompanies sexual love, and rise to a new perception: "We danced to shining; mocked before the black / And shapeless night that made no answer back." Together, they shine with the brilliance of illumination before the amorphous darkness of the abyss, having "dared the dark to reach the white and warm." Echoed here is the familiar mystical attitude: Whoever can endure the terrible darkness of the abyss will find therein a brilliant light, which is divine illumination and a sense of unity. This paradox is clearly expressed in the final two lines of the poem: "Who rise from flesh to spirit know the fall: / The word outleaps the world, and light is all." In order to rise from flesh to spirit, one must use the flesh to make the spirit visible; in other words he must fall. This, of course, is an established paradox in Roethke's poetry: To go forward, it is necessary first to go back. This concept is expressed earlier in "The Vigil" this way: "Who leaps to heaven at a single bound?" The dancers, through their sexual union, have achieved a mergence: "Alive at noon I perished in her form." And that mergence enables them to attain illumination, the sense that "light is all."

"Four for Sir John Davies" presents an apt summary of the basic elements of the love poems. But on a larger scale, the sequence also embodies the essential movement in Roethke's poetry from *Open House* to *The Waking*. He begins in *Open House*, as in "The Dance," by learning to dance alone. Endeavoring without any help to fling his shadow at the moon, he tries to transcend himself. This same solitary dancing can be seen in *The Lost Son* poems, where Roethke dances to his own nonsense rhymes in an effort to escape logic and perceive ultimate reality with his heightened intuition. But in the love poems, he turns to someone else, to a lover, in his tireless attempts to get beyond himself. He finds that love of another person has much in common with love of the Absolute and that he can attain illumination by merging with his lover. That this movement is tied to Roethke's personal development should not be surprising. He inevitably translated his life into poetry, used all his experiences for poetic material. After forty-four years of learning to dance alone, he found a partner, Beatrice, and he discovered in his love for her another way to move toward the illumination and the ultimate union he desired.

V. The Final Confrontation

9.

At the Edge of the Abyss

"The Void's always before us,
Before and *behind*."—Roethke Notebooks (33 #12)

Though Roethke's death in 1963 came unexpectedly, *The Far Field*, published the following year, conveys so strong a sense of finality that one suspects Roethke knew it would be his last volume. The tone of the poetry is one of resolution, a final coming to terms with self in the context of the frightening landscape of eternity. As Allan Seager notes:

> The last years of Ted's life, as we look back on them knowing they were the last, seem to have a strange air of unconscious preparation. As the fabric of his body begins to give way, the best part of his mind, his poetry—seeming to have forgiven everyone everything, demolished its hatreds, and solved all its discords—strives toward a mystical union with his Father.[1]

Roethke's final confrontation with his own mortality is a natural development of his struggle for identity, and in a sense the "unconscious preparation" Seager speaks of is implicit in the poetry from the beginning. Death hovers nearby during all of Roethke's struggles, and the attraction it holds as an alternate way to attain "a reality of the spirit"[2] grows progressively stronger, leading him from his initial ambivalent wish to be a "carnal ghost" (*CP*, 19) to an eventual acceptance of "the windy cliffs of forever" (*CP*, 200). As late as six months before his death, while commenting that he had frequently experienced illumination and the accompanying feeling of "oneness," Roethke remarked: "I can't claim that the soul, my soul, was absorbed in God. No, God for me still remains someone to be confronted, to be dueled with: that is perhaps my error, my sin of pride."[3] In the end, this failure to attain the ultimate mystical state of union led Roethke to embrace his own mortality, fearfully at first, but with the growing conviction that death was the way to the union he had been denied.

The Far Field, then, represents the last stage of Roethke's mystic quest, the culmination of all his previous struggles. It is the final vantage point at the edge of the eternal abyss, from which he looks back over the terrain he has traveled and forward into the unknown darkness he must enter. Such a vista is ordinarily available only to the aged or those who are near death, and so it is significant that Roethke's final step toward the Absolute is initiated in the last two sections of *Words for the Wind* by poems titled "The Dying Man" and "Meditations of an Old Woman."

"The Dying Man" (*CP*, 153–56) has been identified variously as Roethke's father, W. B. Yeats (because the poem is dedicated to his memory), or a combination of the two men. But such interpretations tend to overlook the obvious conclusion that Roethke himself is the dying man and that his father and Yeats are masks he puts on in order to approach the prospect of his own death, through a kind of vicarious mortality. Thus, Rosemary Sullivan's claim that the poem "begins with Yeats' last words as Roethke imagines them to have been,"[4] though an interesting speculation is somewhat beside the point, for it is Roethke who speaks, though he may mimic the sound of Yeats's voice as well as his trimeter rhythm. The trick is to experience the final illumination of the dying man without dying, to attain that penetrating vision that will carry him beyond his fears of the possibility of death to an understanding of "Death's possibilities":

> "A man sees, as he dies,
> Death's possibilities;
> My heart sways with the world.
> I am that final thing,
> A man learning to sing."

But such illumination is attained at the cost of coming face to face with one's own finitude. The dying man sees because he has "dared to question all," "dared to fix his vision anywhere." Confronted with his death he is "A madman staring at perpetual night," but he has the courage to stare into that vertiginous blackness until he can exclaim:

> I breathe alone until my dark is bright.
> Dawn's where the white is. Who would know the dawn
> When there's a dazzling dark behind the sun?

The principal image in this passage is taken from Vaughan's poem "The Night": "There is in God (some say) / A deep, but dazling darkness."[5] Consequently, this may be one of those instances in which the dead help, as Roethke turns to one of his literary ancestors. By contemplating his death the dying man perceives the "Divine Dark, that Abyss of the Godhead, of which the mystic sometimes speaks as the goal of his quest . . . the Uncreated Light in which the Universe is bathed, and which—transcending, as it does, all human powers of expression—he can only describe to us as *dark*."[6] The dying man shares the mystic's vision because he, too, stands at the edge of eternity looking toward the Absolute, and though he has arrived at this point as a natural course of events rather than through a conscious struggle, he, too, is nearing union. It is this aspect of death that interests Roethke—the point at which the dying man and the mystic converge—for he realizes that he can truly begin to live, to perceive the brilliance of the Absolute, by confronting the darkness of his own mortality. As Roethke expresses it in the concluding lines of "The Dying Man":

> In this last place of light: he dares to live
> Who stops being a bird, yet beats his wings
> Against the immense immeasurable emptiness of things.

I do not wish to place too much emphasis on the Yeatsean influence on "The Dying Man." As I noted earlier, Roethke himself felt that he had overacknowledged his debt to Yeats.[7] But it is necessary to point out the similarities between Roethke's poem and "Sailing to Byzantium." Most obvious are the metrical parallels, especially in parts 3, 4, and 5 of "The Dying Man." Though Roethke's stanzas are two lines shorter than Yeats's, the iambic pentameter lines still rhyme ABAB, and each stanza concludes with a couplet, as in Yeats's poem. However, these correspondences are not the most striking ones. More significant are the poems' thematic similarities. Yeats's dying man, wishing to be taken into "the artifice of eternity," to become a golden bird upon a golden bough in Byzantium, is very much like Roethke's dying man who is learning to sing.[8] A passage from the Yeats poem, which

Roethke admired enough to copy out in an early notebook (32 #8), describes a deteriorating old man much like Roethke's, whose "soul's hung out to dry, / Like a fresh-salted skin":

> An aged man is but a paltry thing,
> A tattered coat upon a stick, unless
> Soul clap its hands and sing, and louder sing
> For every tatter in its mortal dress.[9]

It is likely that the idea of singing and the bird imagery in Roethke's poem were taken from "Sailing to Byzantium," as was, perhaps, the notion that "Eternity is Now" (*CP*, 153). But all of the borrowing is quickly absorbed into Roethke's own poetic strategies in the second and successive parts of "The Dying Man." For the most part, Yeats affords Roethke a point of departure and an opportunity to show that he has assimilated his influences.

I agree with Karl Malkoff, who sees in the soul "hung out to dry, / Like a fresh-salted skin" a description of "life as a 'curing' process," but I prefer to take the image a little further than Malkoff does.[10] From the perspective of the dying man, life is a purgative process, the protracted business of getting rid of the body. As Roethke says later in "Infirmity" (*CP*, 244), the dying man learns "How body from spirit slowly does unwind / Until we are pure spirit at the end." As a man approaches death, he prepares to step out of his body, a feat Roethke has tried to accomplish from "Open House" onward. Essentially, then, "The Dying Man" presents us with three of the five mystical stages: purgation, which is synonymous with life, and the approaching illumination and union, which are synonymous with death. Significantly, neither of these last two stages is attained, though they are as near as death, which looms ahead immense and immeasurably empty. Viewed from the side of the living, death appears to be a void, the abyss, but the dying man is certain (as is the mystic) that the darkness will be transformed into light if he but has the courage to endure.

In a certain sense, "The Dying Man" offers some commentary on the love poems, for the speaker in the poem is concerned with love. In the second section, he recollects:

> I burned the flesh away,
> In love, in lively May.
> I turn my look upon
> Another shape than hers
> Now, as the casement blurs.

This passage recalls a line from "The Sententious Man" (*CP*, 131–32), "The spirit knows the flesh it must consume," and indeed it would seem that the spirit had burned away the flesh when the old man was younger. But he recalls another aspect of love, the implicit danger of the sensual, "All sensual love's but dancing on a grave." And the shape he sees groping the sill is like the ghost of death raised by the two lovers in "The Sensualists." The similarity is made even more apparent in the line, "The wall has entered: I must love the wall," which calls to mind the movement toward the wall of the ghostly figure in "The Sensualists."[11] The wall, then, is a symbol of death, an obstruction with no exit that the dying man must love. In other words, he must embrace his own death if he is to turn the darkness into light. His love of another person must be transformed into a love of the thing he fears the most, his own mortality. Unquestionably, this is the ultimate way down that leads to the ultimate way out. Paradoxically, the old man realizes, "By dying daily, I have come to be."

"The Dying Man" is an appropriate transition between the love poems and the final poems of *Words for the Wind* and *The Far Field* because it reflects Roethke's shifting emphasis. Having learned to love another person and thereby transcend his own mortality, he is now prepared to confront and love mortality itself. Certainly, this is what the final poems are about, a fascination with death, an eventual embracing of the wall. Indeed, death is the final step in Roethke's search for illumination and union, and, as with all the other aspects of his life, Roethke was prepared to exploit his own death for vision and for poetry.

Roethke's consideration of death's possibilities is continued in "Meditations of an Old Woman," a sequence of five long poems presenting the reflections of another character who is near death, an old woman who, like the dying man, is a mask for Roethke, another conduit through which he approaches his own mortality. It is immediately obvious that these poems, like those of "The Lost Son" sequence, represent a "succession of experiences, similar yet dissimilar . . . a perpetual slipping-back, then a going-forward," slowly progressing.[12] The old woman discovers, as did the lost son, that it is necessary to go back before she can go forward. Her experiences are of the type that are "so powerful and so profound . . . that they repeat themselves . . . again and again, with variation and change," moving her closer and closer to an acceptance of death and a vision of union.[13]

The opening poem, "First Meditation" (*CP*, 157–60), begins with a scene of dissolution—"stones loosen on the obscure hillside / And a tree tilts from its roots"—images that parallel the old woman's moribundity. She is "nervous and cold, bird-furtive, whiskery, / With a cheek soft as a hound's ear," and her physical decay causes her to become concerned about the condition of her spirit. She knows that "the rind, often hates the life within," and so she fears that her spirit may not survive the death of her body. She imagines herself taking a lonely bus ride through the night to nowhere or missing her chance to depart altogether, "The ticket mislaid or lost, the gate / Inaccessible, the boat always pulling out." These frightening abortive journeys eventually resolve themselves into a calm, clear vision of a crab "slipping and sliding slowly backward," and a salmon, tired from swimming upstream, momentarily pausing in "a back-eddy, a sandy inlet" before continuing the journey. This is the true motion of the spirit, and indeed of the entire sequence, for the old woman is both crab and salmon, moving backward in an effort to find "Another way and place in which to continue," and forward against the current, inevitably obeying her instinct, inevitably progressing. Her destination, like the salmon's, is a place of birth as well as death, a place where beginning and end are the same. She moves toward both as the mystic moves toward union, through "a series of purifications, whereby the Finite slowly approaches the nature of its Infinite source: climbing up the cleansing mountain pool by pool, like the industrious fish . . . until it reaches its Origin."[14]

The solitude of the journey and the fearful destination toward which she moves cause the old woman to desire some sign from beyond, a "riven tree, or lamb dropped by an eagle," but the only signals she receives are those that reinforce her fears, "motes of dust in the immaculate hallways, / The darkness of falling hair, the warnings from lint and spiders." Failing to receive some external revelation, she discovers within herself, through a kind of Proustian involuntary memory, a degree of reassurance:

> A fume reminds me, drifting across wet gravel;
> A cold wind comes over stones;
> A flame, intense, visible,
> Plays over the dry pods,
> Runs fitfully along the stubble,
> Moves over the field,
> Without burning.
>> In such times, lacking a god,
>> I am still happy.

This experience of illumination is strikingly similar to the one described in the last section of "The Lost Son": "The light moved slowly over the frozen field, / Over the dry seed-crowns" (*CP*, 58). In both instances, the protagonist finds comfort in remembering a past illumination and recalling the presence of "A lively understandable spirit" (*CP*, 58). Although the old woman has received no sign from God, she finds within herself the knowledge of another reality, and that is enough to allay her fears.

In the second poem of the sequence, "I'm Here" (*CP*, 161–64), the fire of illumination is replaced by "The sun loosening the frost on December windows, / The glitter of wet in the first of morning," and the plaintive bird calls that initiated the memory of the burning field in the preceding poem turn to a bickering and cheeping that tire the old woman. In an effort to regain the happiness she had won at the close of "First Meditation," she travels backward, like the crab, to a memory of her youth, to the time when she was "queen of the vale":

> I remember walking down a path,
> Down wooden steps toward a weedy garden;
> And my dress caught on rose-brier.
> When I bent to untangle myself,

The scent of the half-opened buds came up over me.
I thought I was going to smother.

> In the slow coming-out of sleep,
> On the sill of the eyes, something flutters,
> A thing we feel at evening, and by doors,
> Or when we stand at the edge of a thicket,
> And the ground-chill comes closer to us,
> From under the dry leaves,
> A beachy wetness.
> The body, delighting in thresholds,
> Rocks in and out of itself.
> A bird, small as a leaf,
> Sings in the first
> Sunlight.

As in the preceding poem, the old woman is delivered from
her despondency into a state of spiritual equilibrium. Her
memory of the sweet, suffocating aroma of roses prompts a
vague awareness of something that flutters at the edge of the
eye (Roethke's familiar tail flicks), and she senses the exhilaration of standing at the threshold of another reality. Though
she and her geranium are dying, the old woman finds in her
memory of roses something that reassures her, something that
imparts a "still joy." Like Wordsworth in *The Prelude*, she discovers in her past life "spots of time, / That with distinct pre-
eminence retain / A renovating virtue."[15] Strengthened by her
recollection, she confronts death bravely, almost eagerly:

> It's not my first dying.
> I can hold this valley,
> Loose in my lap,
> In my arms.
>
> > If the wind means me,
> > I'm here!
> > Here.

In "Her Becoming" (*CP*, 165–67) the old woman is able to
sustain her "still joy," for she has "learned to sit quietly, /
Watching the wind riffle the backs of small birds." Hers is the
life of the contemplative, and she discovers, as did Roethke in
the greenhouse poems, that contemplation is the way to new

perceptions of reality. Through intense looking she succeeds in moving outside herself, freeing her spirit:

How sweetly I abide. Am I a bird?
Soft, soft, the snow's not falling. What's a seed?
A face floats in the ferns. Do maimed gods walk?
A voice keeps rising in my early sleep,
A muffled voice, a low sweet watery noise.
Dare I embrace a ghost from my own breast?
A spirit plays before me like a child,
A child at play, a wind-excited bird.

Contemplation leads to a sense of mergence, as the old woman sees her childlike spirit playing before her like one of the small birds she watches. These are the "times when reality comes closer," when the "cold fleshless kiss of contraries" is resolved into a sense of unity, and the old woman can declare, "I live in air; the long light is my home; / I dare caress the stones, the field my friend; / A light wind rises: I become the wind."

Although the old woman continues her contemplation in "Fourth Meditation" (*CP*, 168–70), "At the edge of the field waiting for the pure moment," she has lost the sense of oneness:

The dead make more impossible demands from their
    silence;
The soul stands, lonely in its choice,
Waiting, itself a slow thing,
In the changing body.

A light wind rises as at the end of "Her Becoming," but this time it stirs only the pine needles, for the old woman is lost in thoughts of "the self-involved: / The ritualists of the mirror, the lonely drinkers, / The minions of benzedrine and paralde-hyde, / And those who submerge themselves in trivia." Her nearness to death prompts her to consider not only her own life, but the lives of others, those who have never known "the soul's authentic hunger" or heard "the sound of another foot-step," which recalls the isolated speaker in "His Foreboding" listening "to my own feet." She is concerned for them as for the "younglings," "the small fish," who like herself "keep heading into the current." As she nears the end of the stream,

"The first and last of all things," the old woman pauses to look back at those who have never truly lived, and pronounces over them a benediction.

The final poem in the sequence, "What Can I Tell My Bones?" (*CP*, 171–73), begins in doubt and confusion:

> The soul knows not what to believe,
> In its small folds, stirring sluggishly,
> In the least place of its life,
> A pulse beyond nothingness,
> A fearful ignorance.

The old woman has become afraid in "a world always late afternoon," and she finds herself "Longing for absolutes that never come," desiring a revelation from beyond as she did in "First Meditation." The prospect of nonbeing horrifies her: "The self says, I am; / The heart says, I am less; / The spirit says, you are nothing." Whatever reassurance the old woman may have gained in her previous meditations is lost or forgotten in the presence of renewed misgivings. She is a woman divided against herself, wanting to believe that she will somehow survive her own death, but not able to believe. Failing to resolve that inner conflict, she wishes "to be delivered from the rational into the realm of pure song" in an effort "to become like God." It is this final abandonment of analysis in favor of intuition that marks the turning point in the old woman's search. Almost as if by accident, she discovers that she has been "drearily bewitched" by her deliberations and recollections and that she must become "sweetly daft" if she is to recover the lost illumination of her youth. Thus in the final section of the poem the old woman becomes once more the "learned nimble girl":

> The sun! The sun! And all we can become!
> And the time ripe for running to the moon!
> In the long fields, I leave my father's eye;
> And shake the secrets from my deepest bones;
> My spirit rises with the rising wind;
> I'm thick with leaves and tender as a dove,
> I take the liberties a short life permits—
> I seek my own meekness;

> I recover my tenderness by long looking.
> By midnight I love everything alive.
> Who took the darkness from the air?
> I'm wet with another life.
> Yea, I have gone and stayed.

This is the revelation she sought from the beginning, the assurance that "Existence dares perpetuate a soul." Like the tired salmon, whose struggle against the current ends at the headwaters, at the point where the stream springs anew, the old woman feels herself "wet with another life." What she senses vaguely in her meditations is now made clear, "As if released by a spirit, / Or agency outside me. / Unprayed-for, / And final."

Karl Malkoff's assertion that the differences between "Meditations of an Old Woman" and "The Lost Son" sequence are "more crucial than the similarities" is typical of a tendency among Roethke critics to understate the similarities that exist between the two groups of poems.[16] Actually, the reverse of Malkoff's statement comes nearer to the truth, for the sequences stand not on opposite sides of the world but at opposite ends of a continuum, opposite ends of life. Consequently, it is possible to view the meditations as a kind of latter-day lost-son sequence in which the struggle to be born has been transformed into a struggle to come to terms with death and the fragmented thoughts of the child have been raised to the level of discourse. Together these two sequences reflect the full range of Roethke's search for the Absolute—through all periods of life as well as on all levels of consciousness.

"Meditations of an Old Woman" prepares the way for the six poems of the "North American Sequence," which, to extend the lost-son parallel, resemble the greenhouse poems. They are essentially poems of nature, of the North American countryside, and, as such, they counterbalance the old woman's introspection in the same way that the greenhouse poems counterbalance the inward journey of the lost son. The theme, as always, is Roethke's struggle to attain ultimate reality, and the descriptions of the landscape, like those of the greenhouse plants, reflect the internal condition of the protagonist.

The first poem of the sequence, "The Longing" (*CP*, 187–

89), begins with a passage reminiscent of the old woman's "Fourth Meditation" catalogue of "the self-involved":

> On things asleep, no balm:
> A kingdom of stinks and sighs,
> Fetor of cockroaches, dead fish, petroleum,
> Worse than castoreum of mink or weasels,
> Saliva dripping from warm microphones,
> Agony of crucifixion on barstools.
> > Less and less the illuminated lips,
> > Hands active, eyes cherished;
> > Happiness left to dogs and children—
> > (Matters only a saint mentions!)
> Lust fatigues the soul.
> How to transcend this sensual emptiness?

The question concluding this malediction states the problem that is at the center of the entire sequence: how to transcend the sensual. Finding himself trapped in an environment where "the spirit fails to move forward, / But shrinks into a half-life, less than itself," the speaker longs to be "beyond the moon / Bare as a bud, and naked as a worm." This, of course, is the mystic's longing, the desire for a "reality of spirit," and it recalls Roethke's wish in *Open House* to rid himself of his body, thereby dispensing with the "false accouterments of sense" (*CP*, 19). The movement is outward, away from the flesh and the world of humans and into the North American landscape, into "the Dakotas, where the eagles eat well," where the stench of dead buffalo purifies the spirit.

There is also in this poem something of a death wish, or at least a fascination with death, perhaps with death's possibilities. The speaker longs for a reality of the spirit, but he is caught in a "kingdom of stinks and sighs," which recalls "the kingdom of bang and blab" in "The Lost Son" (*CP*, 53–58). Like the frightened protagonist of that earlier poem, the speaker here can find no comfort, and his question, "How to transcend this sensual emptiness?" is essentially the same as the lost son's, "Which is the way I take; / Out of what door do I go, / Where and to whom?" Like the lost son, whose desperate searching leads him to subhuman forms of life, the speaker in "The Longing" turns to "the fish, the blackening salmon,

and the mad lemmings." However, there is a fundamental difference between the lost son's regression and the longed for
regression of the speaker in this poem. The lost son's drive is
back to the point of his origin, to the beginning of life, and
though the cows and briars may say to him, "Die," he overcomes the death wish. The speaker in "The Longing," who
desires "the imperishable quiet at the heart of a form," embraces his own mortality. He pushes toward death, not toward
the beginnings of life, though paradoxically death may be a
new beginning. Having left the body of the whale, symbol for
the dark voyage of his life, he is confronted by the greater
darkness of death, symbolized by the wide mouth of the night.
But this strange country, which is permeated with the smell of
death, attracts him, calls to him as to an explorer eager to chart
new territories.

The language of "Meditation at Oyster River" (*CP*, 190–92)
creates a soporific, almost hypnotic mood as the lines wash
gently in and out like waves.

> Over the low, barnacled, elephant-colored rocks,
> Come the first tide-ripples, moving, almost without
>   sound, toward me,
> Running along the narrow furrows of the shore, the
>   rows of dead clam shells;
> Then a runnel behind me, creeping closer,
> Alive with tiny striped fish, and young crabs
>   climbing in and out of the water.

For Roethke, as for the mystic, this slowed state of consciousness (contemplation) is one way to attain a different perception
of reality. Thus the speaker in this poem, as a result of concentrating his attention on the water, exclaims:

> Water's my will, and my way,
> And the spirit runs, intermittently,
> In and out of the small waves,
> Runs with the intrepid shorebirds—

The experience is identical to that described in "Cuttings
(later)" in which the speaker, through contemplation, participates in the cut stems' struggle to rise to a new life, feeling in
his own veins their "sucking and sobbing" (*CP*, 37). This sense

of communion or mergence is invariably the result of successful contemplation, and in the mystical context it is closely associated with illumination, as at the close of "Meditation at
Oyster River" where the speaker's spiritual jaunt with the
shorebirds ends with the perception that "All's a scattering, /
A shining."

As in all the poems of the "North American Sequence," the
setting here is crucial to an understanding of the poem, because the landscape, as Malkoff astutely notes, is a reflection
of the protagonist's inner mind.[17] Significantly, the speaker's
meditations take place at sundown and at a place where a river
empties into the sea. The symbolic value of these images is
obvious, evoking thoughts of death, of the finite and the infinite. Without ever saying so, the speaker communicates to us,
through descriptions of his surroundings, that he is meditating upon his own death. As in "The Longing," he is fascinated
by the prospect of exploring death's landscape:

> At last one long undulant ripple,
> Blue-black from where I am sitting,
> Makes almost a wave over a barrier of small stones,
> Slapping lightly against a sunken log.
> I dabble my toes in the brackish foam sliding forward,
> Then retire to a rock higher up on the cliff-side.
> The wind slackens, light as a moth fanning a stone:
> A twilight wind, light as a child's breath
> Turning not a leaf, not a ripple.
> The dew revives on the beach-grass;
> The salt-soaked wood of a fire crackles;
> A fish raven turns on its perch (a dead tree in the rivermouth),
> Its wings catching a last glint of the reflected sunlight.

Dabbling his toes in the "brackish foam" that moves toward
him, the protagonist is, in effect, sampling the waters of death.
Certainly, the other images support this reading: the slowing
of the wind, the setting sun, the silence. But he is interested
only in meditating upon his death, not in accomplishing it, so
he moves farther back, away from the tidal ripples that
threaten to surround him.

What he sees in the small life before him and in the "shy
beasts" he contemplates is a kind of insouciance in the face of

death, an acceptance of life on its own terms, which leads him to exclaim, "How graceful the small before danger!" It is this observation that stirs in him a sense of joy as he recalls "the first trembling of a Michigan brook in April" and a rainbow in the spray of cascading water. He recalls also the thawing of the Tittebawasee "in the time between winter and spring" when the ice melts and everything begins to flow, "tin cans, pails, old bird nests." This memory is undeniably a symbol of re-birth, emphasizing the spring that follows winter, the life and motion that follow death and stasis. The assurance implied in the memory is not unlike the "surety" that characterizes the hummingbird and the quiet poise that shines from all crea-tures within the speaker's view. It is this vision that leads into the illumination of the final stanza. The speaker's sense of unity, "I rock with the motion of morning," recalls a similar sensation in "A Field of Light" (CP, 62–63), "I moved with the morning." Both statements capture the same feeling of one-ness, the same illumination. The sun sets, but the moon rises, and there is light: "All's a scattering, / A shining."

Contemplation, as defined implicitly in "Journey to the In-terior" (CP, 193–95), is that movement into self that ultimately leads out of self: "The way down and out." This paradox is at the very heart of mystical experience, for it is by turning his thoughts inward in pure concentration on the Absolute that the mystic transcends self and moves outward toward that Ab-solute he desires. "He must call in his scattered faculties by a deliberate exercise of the will, empty his mind of its swarm of images, its riot of thought. In mystical language he must 'sink into his nothingness': into that blank abiding place where busy, clever Reason cannot come."[18] In "Journey to the Inte-rior" this movement is expressed as an automobile trip, Roethke's metaphor for the contemplative process, for the pro-gressive elimination of everything but the desired object of contemplation. The speaker's consciousness is cluttered with a multitude of thoughts—represented by dogs, snakes, musk-rats, turtles, and jackrabbits, to list just a few—and as they pass through his mind they appear as objects viewed from the window of a moving car, though the speaker notes, "I'm not moving but they are." When all such distractions have been dismissed, the speaker arrives at the still center of his consciousness, the point at which "time folds / Into a long moment" and the soul is "at a still-stand, / At ease after rocking the flesh to sleep." It is in this moment of intense concentration that he perceives "the flower of all water, above and below me." This is "the moment of time when the small drop forms, but does not fall," "The stand at the stretch in the face of death." At this instant of pure contemplation the Absolute is perceived and understood, though only partially, "as a blind man, lifting a curtain, knows it is morning." The full view, union, is yet to come.

There is an interesting connection between the imagery in the first section of "Journey to the Interior" and that found in "Her Dream" (20 #25). Compare, for example, the following passages, the first taken from "Journey to the Interior":

> In the long journey out of the self,
> There are many detours, washed-out interrupted raw places
> Where the shale slides dangerously
> And the back wheels hang almost over the edge
> At the sudden veering, the moment of turning.

The second passage is from "Her Dream," the uncollected poem that was quoted in its entirety in the preceding section:

> I was driving up a mountain
>   When the car went in reverse.
>
> My backwheels hung far over
>   A gully dark and wide.

In each passage, the drive uphill involves the danger of the precipice and the gulf below. To attain illumination, one must risk the pit. In "Her Dream," of course, the driver enters the pit voluntarily, but in "Journey to the Interior," the upward push is more determined and is stopped only by "a fallen fir-tree, / The thickets darkening, / The ravines ugly." What ultimately stands between this driver and the peak of illumination is the pit of his own death, the black thickets and ugly ravines, and he sits before the fallen fir tree as before his own completed life, contemplating the stillness, the darkness. What he needs is the recklessness of youth, the foolish courage to drive beyond eighty on dangerous roads, "to throw the car sideways and charge over the hill, full of the throttle." Again, there is something of a death wish here, the urge to charge full in the face of mortality.

In the final section of the poem, the stalled driver of the first part and the unstoppable driver of the second merge. Stasis and motion become the same thing. This is evident in the latter part of section two when time seems to stop and the car is no longer moving, though the scene outside the window passes by. This is death, where opposites are reconciled, "the never receding, / Moving, unmoving in a parched land," where there is "Neither forward nor backward," where "The spirit of wrath becomes the spirit of blessing." It is "a place leading nowhere." This reconciliation of opposites is, as we have seen, one of the characteristics of mystical union and an integral part of the sense of unity described by those who have experienced illumination. Another characteristic of the mystical experience is a loss of the sense of time and the sensation that time is meaningless. Many mystics have described this as the awareness of the eternal now, and Roethke's statement, "time folds / Into a long moment," echoes this description and even more closely resembles it in an early draft of the poem where it appears as "time folds / Into an eternal instant" (42 #187). Significantly, Roethke's perception of death is becoming more like the mystic's vision of union.

Having glimpsed the Absolute, the speaker gravitates toward it irresistably, unable to overcome his desire for union. Thus, in the opening section of "The Long Waters" (*CP*, 196–98) he states:

> And I acknowledge my foolishness with God,
> My desire for the peaks, the black ravines, the
>   rolling mists
> Changing with every twist of wind,
> The unsinging fields where no lungs breathe,
> Where light is stone.

The confessional tone of this passage suggests that there is an implicit death wish in those "black ravines" and "fields where no lungs breathe." Though the speaker asks in the following section to be protected from "the worm's advance and retreat" he cannot help yielding to death's attraction, to the delight of "The cricket-voice deep in the midnight field" and "The dry bloom splitting in the wrinkled vale," for death leads to the Absolute.

By returning to the ocean and contemplating the water as he did in "Meditation at Oyster River," the speaker once more moves toward illumination. Looking into the bay, he observes, "These waves, in the sun, remind me of flowers," and this memory of his previous perception of the Absolute as "the flower of all water" signals the approach of illumination:

> As a fire, seemingly long dead, flares up from
> a downdraft of air in a chimney,
> Or a breeze moves over the knees from a low hill,
> So the sea wind wakes desire.
> My body shimmers with a light flame.
>
> I see in the advancing and retreating waters
> The shape that came from my sleep, weeping:
> The eternal one, the child, the swaying vine branch,
> The numinous ring around the opening flower,
> The friend that runs before me on the windy headlands,
> Neither voice nor vision.

The illumination here is much more intense than the small "shining" perceived at the close of "Meditation at Oyster River," for the speaker sees "The eternal one," the all of which everything is a part—child, vine branch, opening flower, but above all himself—and he senses the mystical oneness, exclaiming, "I lose and find myself in the long water; / I am gathered together once more; / I embrace the world."

I would like to emphasize the meditative nature of all the poems in the "North American Sequence." The speaker, longing to explore death's terrain, finds in the world about him many manifestations of death. As the protagonist of the greenhouse sequence contemplates the small plants in their struggle for life, the speaker here considers how things in nature stand in relation to death. By contemplating the urge and wrestle of the cuttings, the speaker in the greenhouse poems begins to feel a similar "sucking and sobbing" in his veins and bones, a parallel urge to push outward and break through into light. Conversely, the speaker in the "North American Sequence" begins to come to terms with his own mortality by contemplating the examples of death he finds in nature. As the cuttings may instruct one how to strive for new life, the pine, "whole with its roots," sunk in the estuary may teach him how to die. Paradoxically, both impulses lead to the same place, to illumination and union.

The attractiveness of death is the explicit concern of "The Far Field" (*CP*, 199–201). Encounters with "the shrunken face of a dead rat," the tom cat shot by the night watchman, "young rabbits caught in the mower," and speculations concerning evolution and the possibility of reincarnation have taught the speaker "not to fear infinity, / The far field, the windy cliffs of forever." Like "The Dying Man" he overcomes his fear of death by accepting death, by daring "to fix his vision anywhere" (*CP*, 155), even on the abyss of his own mortality:

> I am renewed by death, thought of my death,
> The dry scent of a dying garden in September,
> The wind fanning the ash of a low fire.
> What I love is near at hand,
> Always, in earth and air.

The pivotal word here is "Always," for it can be construed either as an adverb or a noun: "What I love is always near at hand" or "The always that I love is near at hand." The validity of the second reading is reinforced by a line in the succeeding section, "All finite things reveal infinitude," which indicates that infinity (or always) is ever near because it is reflected in all things. This recalls a line from "The Waking" (*CP*, 108): "What falls away is always. And is near." As yes is implied by no, so infinity is implied by finitude, and the speaker finds that his own mortality is substantiation for a belief in the eternal Absolute.

"The Far Field" is in many respects a final poem, though it does not conclude the sequence. I say it is a final poem not only because it shows the speaker coming to terms with death but because it seems to summarize so much of the poetry that has come before. The first section, for example, is very much like the opening of "Journey to the Interior," and it ends the same way, with the car stopped before some final obstruction. The second section recalls the greenhouse world of Roethke's childhood—the flower dump, the pheasant run, the half-grown flowers. The vision of birds prefigures the poem "All Morning," which appears later in the volume. Also in the second section is the image of the speaker "In the silted shallows of a slow river, / Fingering a shell, / Thinking: / Once I was something like this." The similarity to "River Incident" (*CP*, 49) is unmistakable:

> And I knew I had been there before,
> In that cold, granitic slime,
> In the dark, in the rolling water.

The fourth section, of course, with its old man "in garments of adieu" calls to mind "The Dying Man" (*CP*, 153–56), "that final thing, / A man learning to sing," who here becomes "the end of things, the final man." It does not seem an exaggeration to say that in the "North American Sequence," and in "The Far Field" in particular, Roethke pulls together many of the threads of his life and consequently of his poetry. He puts aside all his masks, revealing that he is the "old man with his feet before the fire," looking not only into the face of death but back on his life for understanding and courage to help him in his final confrontation.

The final poem of the sequence, "The Rose" (*CP*, 202–5), opens with the speaker in his familiar location by the sea. But this time he calls attention to the spot by insisting, "this place, where sea and fresh water meet, / Is important" and thereby underscores the symbolic quality of the setting: the place where small streams empty into the ocean, where individual spirits return to be immersed in the depths of the One. It is in this place of flux that the speaker finds his symbol for the eternal, the rose:

> A single wild rose, struggling out of the white
>   embrace of the morning-glory,
> Out of the briary hedge, the tangle of matted
>   underbrush,
> Beyond the clover, the ragged hay,

Beyond the sea pine, the oak, the wind-tipped
    madrona,
Moving with the waves, the undulating driftwood,
Where the slow creek winds down to the black sand
    of the shore.

Like "The Dying Man," who dares to live by beating his wings
"Against the immense immeasurable emptiness of things"
(CP, 156), the rose overcomes everything that would deny its
existence and thereby earns its rightful place. In the face of
death it dares to be, living in the eternal now, and evokes in
the speaker an awareness of his own pure being:

Near this rose, in this grove of sun-parched,
    wind-warped madronas,
Among the half-dead trees, I came upon the true
    ease of myself,
As if another man appeared out of the depths of
    my being,
And I stood outside myself,
Beyond becoming and perishing,
A something wholly other,
As if I swayed out on the wildest wave alive,
And yet was still.

This is not an experience of mergence because there is no
sense of oneness; rather, it is a moment in which the speaker
senses his own infinitude, his own "is-ness." What moves outside him is his own pure being, that "something wholly other"
that is beyond change, and in the landscape of death he attains
the old woman's reassurance: "Existence dares perpetuate a
soul" (CP, 173). This final illumination represents not only the
resolution of the poem but of the entire "North American Sequence," for the struggle to transcend the sensual and come to
terms with death is finally won.

In one of the notebooks, Roethke entered the following definition: "The rose: emblem of human love becoming divine"
(33 #12). For Roethke, as it was for Dante, the rose is the ultimate symbol of vision and unity as he approaches the Absolute. Unquestionably, Roethke's use of the symbol is intended
to call to mind the *Paradiso*, and that association deepens the
poem, but the symbol is nonetheless distinctly Roethke's. It

symbolizes his youth insofar as it recalls the greenhouse roses of his childhood, and his approaching death. In a certain sense the rose is the composite of the urge for life found in the greenhouse poems and the calm acceptance of death that is at the heart of the "North American Sequence." It is at once living and dying, transient and permanent. I find it peculiarly appropriate that Roethke's contemplation of death should ultimately bring him back to the struggling natural life with which he began and that he should find in that life an implicit acceptance of death. The rose brings the courage he had hoped for, to live at the edge of death and flower against the blackness of eternity, moving yet staying, embracing all.

The "North American Sequence" is characterized by the same backward and forward movement that operates in "The Lost Son" sequence, but there is, as always, some progress. The protagonist begins by longing to explore the uncharted country of death, and his successive meditations allow him to do that, to a certain extent, though he must frequently travel over territory he has already covered. As in "The Lost Son" sequence, where the movement was into the self and each successive effort began a little before the end of the preceding one, the efforts here to move out of the self overlap. But in each poem, some advance is made, and the speaker's longing is ultimately translated into a calm understanding and acceptance of death.

Despite his successes, however, Roethke has failed to attain his ultimate goal: mystical union, the state in which "Absolute Life is not merely perceived and enjoyed by the Self, as an illumination: but is *one* with it."[19] This final mergence requires total surrender, abandonment of will and desire, a transformation that can be effected only by passing through the dark night of the soul, and so Roethke, in one last push toward union, enters that place of dissociation and terror in the concluding poems of *The Far Field*. Underhill describes the dark night of the soul as a time of disorientation and fear. It is:

> the last painful break with the life of illusion, the tearing away of the Self from that World of Becoming in which all its natural affections and desires are rooted, to which its intellect and senses

correspond; and the thrusting of it into that World of Being where
at first, weak and blinded, it can but find a wilderness, a "dark."[20]

The mystic perceives this place as a pit or an abyss filled with
an overwhelming darkness in which he is utterly alone. But if
he has the strength of spirit to remain, the darkness will eventually become bright and he will see that he is not alone but in
the presence of the Absolute.

10.

Dueling with God

"Consciousness, Life & Existence are finite states &
the Infinite Godhead *is* beyond them. Can't even give
it unity for unity is distinguishable from plurality.
Super-unity which is neither one nor many."
—Roethke Notebooks (39 #125)

The illuminations Roethke attained in "North American Sequence" lead him inevitably to the dark night experiences described in "Mixed Sequence" which, as Karl Malkoff observes,
may seem too mixed, owing at least in part to the unfinished
state of the section at the time of Roethke's death.[1] Yet, the
sequence ultimately coheres, albeit rather loosely, about
Roethke's exclusive concern in this volume, death, and it represents a logical step in his drive toward the Absolute.

The initial poem, "The Abyss," deals specifically with the
dark night of the soul, the final obstacle between Roethke and
union. As we have seen in the "North American Sequence,"
this obstruction is nothing less than death, not only the figurative death of the mystic but, in Roethke's terms, the literal
death of the self. The abyss, then, is the pit of mortality
through which Roethke must pass in a final act of purgation.
Most of the other poems in the sequence are essentially visions
of death and terror that arise from the pit, and they emphasize
the vulnerability of all things: relatives ("Elegy" and "Otto"),
acquaintances ("Chums"), small creatures ("The Meadow
Mouse" and "The Thing"), and even plants ("The Geranium").
These visions are byproducts of the speaker's preoccupation
with his own mortality, and they are part of the purgative process, the getting used to the terrifying darkness. The paradox
of the abyss is that the darkness eventually turns to light, and
the penetrating sense of isolation becomes an awareness of
union. The abyss is both a place of terror and joy in which the
brilliant light of the Absolute at first blinds and terrifies but
subsequently grows beautiful as the eyes adjust to the blind-

ing vision. As Roethke expressed it in a late notebook entry, "Now's when the insight comes. Now, now in the cold dark" (42 #190).

William Heyen argues at length and quite convincingly that the five sections of "The Abyss" correspond to Underhill's five stages of the mystic way,[2] but the parallel is not exact, and Heyen occasionally stretches both Roethke's and Underhill's meanings in an attempt to get the two together. Undeniably, Roethke borrowed heavily from Underhill and from her sources, but his focus is exclusively on the dark night or mystic death. That focus is consistent with Roethke's preoccupation with death throughout his final book. The poem is essentially an account of a man who takes the step down the stair into the abyss, is purged by the overwhelming darkness of the pit, and progresses finally to illumination and a sense of union.

The opening section of "The Abyss" (*CP*, 219–22), with its questions and elliptical statements, resembles "The Lost Son" poems, and there is, in the speaker's puzzled queries, something of the lost son's frantic questioning:

> Is the stair here?
> Where's the stair?
> "The stair's right there,
> But it goes nowhere."
>
> And the abyss? the abyss?
> "The abyss you can't miss:
> It's right where you are—
> A step down the stair."

Certainly, this calls to mind the lost son's search for a way out as he, like the protagonist in "The Abyss," tries to flee his thoughts of mortality and conjures the silence, asking:

> Which is the way I take;
> Out of what door do I go,
> Where and to whom? (*CP*, 54)

In each poem, the protagonist is disoriented, wishing to move but not knowing which direction to take, and for each, the question he asks both himself and the thin air is answered the same way: There is but one way to go—down into the pit. In

"The Lost Son" the pit is presented broadly as a place of psychic exhaustion, but in "The Abyss" it is clearly meant to stand for death. The stair on which the protagonist finds himself leads one way only—down—just as life moves inexorably toward death. He cannot ascend the stair because it goes nowhere, and a descent will drop him into the nothingness of the abyss. In this respect, up and down are the same thing, and the way down is truly the way up and out.

In the second section, as the speaker looks back over his life, he realizes that he has "been spoken to variously / But heard little." The pledge in "Open House" (*CP*, 3) had been to "stop the lying mouth," but here the speaker confesses, "My inward witness is dismayed / By my unguarded mouth." He has not always extended the spirit and spoken his "witless agony" but has "taken, too often, the dangerous path, / The vague, the arid." He rationalizes his behavior by asking, "Among us, who is holy?" As he does so he hears "the noise of the wall," by now an immediately identifiable symbol of death.

Like the lost son, the speaker here realizes that he can find no comfort "In the kingdom of bang and blab" (*CP*, 54). Consequently, he invokes Walt Whitman, "maker of catalogues," to help him manage and to escape the babbling tongues, "the terrible hunger for objects." He must enter the abyss to purge himself of the things of the world, and so he becomes "a mole winding through earth, / A night-fishing otter." These images again recall "The Lost Son," specifically the otterlike creature sought by the protagonist in "The Flight" section and the mole in "The Pit" that knows who "stunned the dirt into noise." Both creatures move through the darkness, as the speaker himself must learn to do once he has entered the black abyss.

The third section seems almost to paraphrase any number of accounts mystics have given of their dark night experiences:

> Too much reality can be a dazzle, a surfeit;
> Too close immediacy an exhaustion:
> As when the door swings open in a florist's storeroom—
> The rush of smells strikes like a cold fire, the throat freezes,
> And we turn back to the heat of August,
> Chastened.
> So the abyss—

> The slippery cold heights,
> After the blinding misery,
> The climbing, the endless turning,
> Strike like a fire,
> A terrible violence of creation,
> A flash into the burning heart of the abominable;
> Yet if we wait, unafraid, beyond the fearful instant,
> The burning lake turns into a forest pool,
> The fire subsides into rings of water,
> A sunlit silence.

The traditional mystical paradox is here: the blinding light that at first appears to be darkness, the misery and fear that eventually become the pleasure of a joyous perception. As in "Unfold! Unfold!" (*CP*, 90), the protagonist knows that "At first the visible obscures." Unquestionably, this is the same experience described by St. John of the Cross in *Noche Escura del Alma*:

> The self is in the dark because it is blinded by a Light greater than it can bear—that "Divine Wisdom which is not only night and darkness to the soul, but pain and torment too." "The more clear the light, the more does it blind the eyes of the owl, and the more we try to look at the sun the feebler grows our sight and the more our weak eyes are darkened. So the divine light of contemplation, when it beats on the soul not yet perfectly purified, fills it with spiritual darkness, not only because of its brilliance, but because it paralyses the natural perception of the soul. The pain suffered by the soul is like that endured by weak or diseased eyes when suddenly struck by a strong light."[3]

If the self can endure the "blinding misery" but for a while, until it is purified, the perception that is at first a "surfeit," "an exhaustion," will become a vision of the desired Absolute.

The question that opens section four reminds us that there is no way to go but down the stair: "How can I dream except beyond this life?" Standing at the edge of death, the speaker has no alternative but to dream forward into the abyss, for he cannot "outleap the sea— / The edge of all the land, the final sea." He must take that one step down the stair. Wishing to be like the eyeless tendrils that seek the light despite their blindness and the child who, unafraid, reaches into the coiled smilax, thrusts into the unknown, the speaker begins to yield to his fate, obeys the wind at his back bringing him "home from the twilight fishing." And his resignation brings him to an understanding:

In this, my half-rest,
Knowing slows for a moment,
And not-knowing enters, silent,
Bearing being itself,
And the fire dances
To the stream's
Flowing.

Again, we are confronted with a standard element of mystical doctrine, the notion that the Absolute can never be understood by reason or logic but must be apprehended through some other channel. Obviously, this is another example of the analysis/intuition dichotomy that we have noted throughout Roethke's poetry, but this time there is a more specific mystical reference. In a 1962 notebook, Roethke remarks:

We think by feeling. What is there to know! The answer is *unknowing*—the unknowing of the cloud of un-knowing. (43 #208)

This comment alludes not only to "The Waking," the concluding poem of the volume by the same name, but also to an anonymous fourteenth-century mystical treatise titled *The Cloud of Unknowing*, found among Roethke's personal library books. The title of the work is another metaphor for the dark night of the soul, described in the following way:

At the first time when thou dost it [enter the abyss] . . . thou findest but a darkness, and as it were a cloud of unknowing thou knowest not what, saving that thou feelest in thy will a naked intent unto God. This darkness and this cloud is, howsoever thou dost, betwixt thee and thy God, and letteth thee, that thou mayest neither see Him clearly by light of understanding in thy reason, nor feel Him in sweetness of love in thine affection. And therefore shape thee to bide in this darkness as long as thou mayest, evermore crying after Him that thou lovest. For if ever thou shalt feel Him or see Him as it may be here, it behoveth always to be in this cloud and this darkness.[4]

This perception of the abyss is the result of contemplating the Absolute. Roethke's term "half-rest" may refer either to the contemplative state itself, which appears to be inactive but is not, or to the fact that one-half of his mind, the analytical half, is temporarily turned off. At any rate, when he enters the realm of not-knowing, wherein dwells the Absolute, he leaves the world of becoming and communicates directly with the world of being—that is, the infinite or God. Consequently, not-knowing is described as "Bearing being itself," that can never be known of the intellect, only not-known.

The moment of not-knowing passes, however, and the speaker asks, in the best intellectual fashion, "Do we move toward God, or merely another condition?" This reveals that he has not yet managed to surrender his intellect and his individual will completely, which he must do if the terrible darkness is to be perceived as light. For the time being, he rocks "between dark and dark / My soul nearly my own, / My dead selves singing." Like the "cold God-furious man" in "The Exorcism" (CP, 147), the speaker here has succeeded in disposing of some of his "Lewd, tiny, careless lives," and his soul is almost completely his own, almost freed from the restrictions of flesh. But he must undergo the final purgation of death before his soul is fully released. The shade that speaks at the end of this passage, "Adore and draw near. / Who knows this— / Knows all," is the shade of death as well as the shadow of the cloud of unknowing, for the two things are identical.

The final line of the section that concludes the poem, "Being, not doing, is my first joy," appears to have been taken almost verbatim from Underhill, who says in her chapter on the dark night of the soul, "Being, not doing, is the first aim of the mystic."[5] Clearly, the mystic's objective is to move from the world of becoming, which is in constant flux, into the world of being, which is absolute, where God is. Certainly, Roethke's final section reveals that he has remained in the abyss long enough to obtain a vision of that other world and a sense of union:

> I thirst by day. I watch by night.
> I receive! I have been received!

I hear the flowers drinking in their light,
I have taken counsel of the crab and the sea-urchin,
I recall the falling of small waters,
The stream slipping beneath the mossy logs,
Winding down to the stretch of irregular sand,
The great logs piled like matchsticks.

I am most immoderately married:
The Lord God has taken my heaviness away;
I have merged, like the bird, with the bright air,
And my thought flies to the place by the bo-tree.

Being, not doing, is my first joy.

The line "I receive! I have been received!" expresses the contemplative's sense of mergence, in which he seems to enter the
thing he contemplates as it enters him. The result is a feeling
of unity that permits the speaker to communicate with the
flowers, the crab, and the sea urchin. He also exclaims, "I am
most immoderately married," obviously an allusion to the
mystical notion of the spiritual marriage in which the soul becomes immersed in God. And finally, we see that he has
merged even with the air, as his thought, which is no longer
of himself or anything but the Absolute, "flies to the place by
the bo-tree," the place of illumination and vision, as if to receive instruction and enlightenment.

The final section of the poem has caused problems for many
critics who have refused to believe that Roethke ever attained
the state of union. Their skepticism is aroused principally by
Roethke's own insistence that he experienced illumination,
"the sense that all is one and one is all," but never union, the
feeling that "the soul, my soul, was absorbed by God."[6] This
remark leads Rosemary Sullivan to claim that the tone at the
end of "The Abyss" is "one of longing" and not fulfillment,
that it could not be fulfillment because Roethke himself
claimed never to have experienced union.[7] Perhaps the problem for Sullivan, and others, is fundamentally an inability to
separate Roethke the man from Roethke the poet. Admittedly,
such a division is not easy, but it seems essential if one is to
reconcile the contradictions between observations made by
Roethke about his personal struggle toward the Absolute and

his poetic account of that struggle in these last poems. I accept Roethke's claim that God remained for him "someone to be confronted, to be dueled with," but I also accept as true the sensation of union that concludes "The Abyss."[8] While Roethke could not experience union personally, poetically he could attain that state. "The Abyss," like most of the poems in *The Far Field*, is concerned with death, specifically with the prospect of Roethke's death. And several of the poems actually carry the speaker beyond the bounds of life. Clearly, this is true of "The Abyss," for the pit into which the speaker descends symbolizes more than a figurative, mystic death; it represents the literal death of the self. Consequently, what Roethke describes in this poem, and elsewhere in the volume, is his impression of what his own death will be like. Obviously, then, we do not have to take the vision of union that concludes the poem as a statement of fact, simply as a speculation of what might be. Through his poetry, Roethke is able vicariously to descend into the final abyss and describe for us what he sees there. That is his way of coming to terms with death.

Roethke approaches death obliquely in the poems that follow "The Abyss" by focusing upon the mortality of others rather than himself. This is a method of growing accustomed to the "burning heart of the abominable." He draws nearer to an acceptance of his own death by considering death in its various manifestations among people, animals, and plants. Standing with one foot poised above the terrible abyss, he prepares himself for the step he must take. His first vision of death, in "Elegy" (*CP*, 223), comes in the form of Aunt Tilly, a strong-minded but generous woman who "died in agony, / Her tongue, at the last, thick, black as an ox's." But the vision of pain and horror quickly dissipates and is replaced by a less frightening image:

> Terror of cops, bill collectors, betrayers of the poor,—
> I see you in some celestial supermarket,
> Moving serenely among the leeks and cabbages,
> Probing the squash,
> Bearing down, with two steady eyes,
> On the quaking butcher.

This abrupt transition to the concept of death as an extension of life in which Aunt Tilly continues as always signifies the speaker's inability to fix his gaze on death and hold it there. He has, in effect, averted his eyes from the terrible reality that strikes "like a fire." At this point, the blinding darkness of the abyss is too much for him, so he turns away.

In "Otto" (CP, 224–25), the speaker continues to substitute pleasant images of death for the terrifying reality, eulogizing his father but never once coming to terms with the fact of his death. Here, there is no recognition of pain or terror, only the beautiful recollection of his father's greenhouses:

> In my mind's eye I see those fields of glass,
> As I looked out at them from the high house,
> Riding beneath the moon, hid from the moon,
> Then slowly breaking whiter in the dawn;
> When George the watchman's lantern dropped from sight
> The long pipes knocked: it was the end of night.
> I'd stand upon my bed, a sleepless child
> Watching the waking of my father's world.—
> O world so far away! O my lost world!

Significantly, the father's world is not dead but lost, as if it still existed somewhere, intact and undecayed. There is in this image a desperate yearning for permanence, a desire to believe that the father's world, like Aunt Tilly's, goes on. Clearly, the speaker is still unable to confront fully "the blinding misery" of the abyss. Loss of self is the lesson of the abyss. All vestiges of personality and will must be surrendered in order to experience the unity of the larger self, the Absolute. At this point, Roethke is unable to imagine his father's annihilation in the pit and he clings to the notion of self as a last hope in the face of the selfless void.

"The Meadow Mouse" (CP, 227) and "The Geranium" (CP, 228) reveal that the speaker is drawing nearer to a confrontation with death, for he begins to identify with the vulnerable creatures of the world. As always for Roethke, the route to understanding lies not through the human but through other forms of life, small animals and plants. The meadow mouse

taken under the speaker's protection escapes, choosing instead to live, "courtesy of the shrike, the snake, the tom-cat."
This vision of life at the edge of the abyss prompts the speaker
to consider other creatures that must come to terms with
death:

> I think of the nestling fallen into the deep grass,
> The turtle gasping in the dusty rubble of the highway,
> The paralytic stunned in the tub, and the water rising,—
> All things innocent, hapless, forsaken.

Confronting death is a lonely affair, with no protector to watch
over the dying one. The nestling, the turtle, and the paralytic
must face the deep grass, the dusty rubble, the rising water
alone. This realization makes the speaker aware of all things
that stand at the "edge of all the land, the final sea," including
himself. Through the meadow mouse, he returns to the human, but the soothing images of death in "Elegy" and "Otto"
have been replaced by a sense of the real horror of dying. He
is beginning, at this point, to adjust his sight to the penetrating blackness of the abyss.

"The Geranium" is perhaps more understated than "The
Meadow Mouse," but the implicit meaning is fundamentally
the same. Instead of relinquishing a mouse to the stalking
death of the meadow, he this time gives up a dying plant to
the trash can. But his sense of identification with the plant is
so strong that he fires the "snuffling cretin of a maid" who
threw it out. The loneliness he feels after the geranium has
been disposed of is the loneliness of "All things innocent, hap-
less, forsaken," which must deal with death alone. And he
sees in the dying geranium something of his own condition,
for he, too, is seedy, not merely unkempt in appearance (as
the plant is, too), but going to seed, like the flower, having
nearly completed his life cycle.

"The Thing" (CP, 232) may appear on the surface to be only
a vehicle for irony as the speaker watches with horror while a
flock of birds attack and kill some smaller flying thing, "small
as a lark," and then turns to his picnic meal of "little larks arranged on a long platter." No doubt we are supposed to detect
a vague feeling of guilt in the speaker who implicitly identifies

with the savage birds, but we should also sense a kind of sympathy for the smaller creature that is destroyed. Not by accident does Roethke fail to name the thing. In "All Morning" (*CP*, 234–35), he can identify "towhees, finches, chickadees, California quail, wood doves, . . . wrens, sparrows, juncos, cedar waxwings, flickers," and more, but he labels the flying object only as a thing, not even a bird. By leaving its identity vague and open-ended, Roethke allows the small thing to stand for any creature hunted down by the "long terrible eyes" of death, including himself. And what he feels as he muses at the end of the poem is, perhaps more than anything else, a silent communion with the thing that was destroyed.

The sense of identification with the thing is made even more apparent by "The Pike" (*CP*, 233), in which the speaker becomes the object under attack:

> A scene for the self to abjure!—
> And I lean, almost into the water,
> My eye always beyond the surface reflection;
> I lean, and love these manifold shapes,
> Until, out from a dark cove,
> From beyond the end of a mossy log,
> With one sinuous ripple, then a rush,
> A thrashing-up of the whole pool,
> The pike strikes.

Although it is never made explicit that the speaker is attacked by the pike, the poem certainly suggests it. And even if we say the pike strikes one of the small fish in the water, the speaker's sense of identification with these creatures is so strong that he feels the pike's violence himself. He, in effect, becomes the thing that is destroyed in this "scene for the self to abjure."

Throughout this sequence, Roethke's contact with death is once removed. He approaches the terrors of the abyss through other people and through the vulnerable creatures of the world, but his vicarious experiences bring him ultimately to the point where he can confront death directly. By the end of the sequence, he has moved from a romanticized notion of death and the afterlife, to a partial acceptance of death in its most terrible shape and its relation to him. Like "The Dying

Man," he has begun to dare "to fix his vision anywhere," even on the terrible darkness of the abyss.

The poems of "Sequence, Sometimes Metaphysical" bring Roethke into closer contact with the abyss and the Absolute that lies within it. In relation to the preceding sequence, these poems are more intensely personal, bringing the speaker face to face with what he has learned not to fear. According to Roethke, the sequence was intended to represent "a hunt, a drive toward God: an effort to break through the barrier of rational experience" (28 #24). The opening poem, "In a Dark Time," offers a very close description of a mystical experience, and those poems that follow, according to Roethke, in a draft of "On 'In a Dark Time,'" "represent a gradual descent from the heights to a more human, a more understandable, a more 'rational' condition" (28 #24). "In a Dark Time" itself has received much critical attention, primarily through the Anthony Ostroff–edited symposium, to which John Crowe Ransom, Babette Deutsch, Stanley Kunitz, and Roethke himself contributed essays. I offer another interpretation that does not differ radically from those earlier ones, but that will, I hope, shed some new light on the poem.[9]

Although "In a Dark Time" (*CP*, 239) is usually placed alongside "The Abyss" as another example of the dark night, it actually deals with more than that one phase of the mystical experience. Roethke himself described the poem as an attempt "to break from the bondage of self, from the barriers of the 'real' world, to come as close to God as possible," and as such it functions as a much better paradigm of the mystical experience than does "The Abyss."[10] In fact, all five of Underhill's stages of the Mystic Way are contained within this one dark night. In the first stanza, the speaker experiences the stage of awakening: "In a dark time, the eye begins to see," but as Roethke himself cautions, "the eye only *begins* to see: this is only a stage in a long process."[11] Although another reality is intuited, it is not yet fully perceived.

Roethke's contention that the dark time in which the eye (the I) begins to see can be willed recalls his insistence that he willed his own states of perception, his periods of mania:

> But the conscious will can be a factor, I have found, in either a
> rise or a fall of a cyclic phase. The danger to the human condition
> lies in excessive acceleration, either way. The way up and the
> way down may be the same, but the pace often varies, sometimes
> disastrously. (28 #24)

Roethke's notebook observations of his first breakdown indicate essentially the same thing, that a "'descent' can be
willed," though there is real danger in "the preceding euphoria, in the exhilaration getting out of hand" (42 #194).
Clearly, that danger is averted here, and the speaker experiences the first glimmer of the Absolute, seeing in the "deep-
ening shade" his own shadow, the "reminder that I am going
to die" (28 #24), and sensing his place in the unity of things,
"between the heron and the wren, / Beasts of the hill and ser-
pents of the den."

   Mysticism and mania have come together in this poem and
Roethke implicitly acknowledges them as being very nearly
the same thing. The dark time, then, is not only the mystic's
dark night of the soul but also Roethke's own frightening periods of manic-depression. His description of how the poem
was written emphasizes the manic nature of what he himself
termed a mystical experience:

> This was a dictated poem, something given, scarcely mine at all.
> For about three days before its writing I felt disembodied, out of
> time (in the language of the day, I was very "high"). Then the
> poem virtually wrote itself, on a day in summer, 1958. (28 #24)

Interestingly, Parini finds this poem less spontaneous than
Roethke's comment suggests it was, maintaining that it "reads
like a versification of Underhill's paradigm; abstractions ob-
trude everywhere."[12] Unquestionably, the poem does follow
Underhill's five-stage mystic way rather closely, and since
Roethke had long been familiar with Underhill's work there is
reason to suspect an influence. But what do we then do with
Roethke's claim that the poem virtually wrote itself? His remark that he was "high" during the time leading up to the
poem's composition is intriguing and suggests that the piece
was produced during a manic phase. If this is true, and if the

correspondence between the manic and the mystic experience
has any validity, then the poem does not have to be seen as
something modeled after Underhill's work. Instead, it may be
said simply to correspond to Underhill's scheme because of the
shared vision of manics and mystics. The feeling of being
"very 'high'" is the principal characteristic of mania, just as
feeling "disembodied and out of time" are chief characteristics
of the mystical experience. Of course, it is possible that
Roethke was not being truthful in saying the poem came to
him spontaneously. Or perhaps it did come quickly, but
framed in the outline Roethke had absorbed from Underhill
and copied down in his notebook years earlier. We can never
know for sure. But I prefer to take Roethke at his word and to
assume that Underhill's influence on the poem was, at most,
a subconscious one. Certainly, we have seen enough similarities between the manic and the mystic experience throughout
Roethke's poetry to accept that similarity here.

A further indication that mania and mysticism parallel one
another is seen in the line "A lord of nature weeping to a tree."
This is a direct reference to Roethke's first breakdown and his
contention that during the manic phase he had a mystical experience with a tree and learned the secret of Nijinsky. If the
line is indeed a reference to that experience, Roethke's remark
that the "lord of nature" phrase is a bit of "self-mockery, a partial irony" makes a different kind of sense as a self-parody (28
#24). He is looking back on himself as on a novice, in the same
way he characteristically looked back on his early poems, with
the critical eye of age and experience.

The second stage of the mystical process, presented in
stanza two, is purgation, the time when the mystical seeker,
in his effort to perceive that ultimate reality he senses, comes
to "know the purity of pure despair." Realizing that the self
must be purged of its imperfections before it can look on the
Absolute, he undergoes a process of mortification, a symbolic
crucifixion, as reflected in the image of his "shadow pinned
against a sweating wall." Still, the self has not been purged
completely for it is the shadow that is pinned to the wall. "The
true self still maintains its choice, its mobility" (28 #24). It has
not yet entered the abyss, remaining for the present on the

edge, the winding path. Again, I see in the first lines of this stanza—"What's madness but nobility of soul / At odds with circumstance?"—a reference to Roethke's own "mad" experiences as well as to mystical perception.

In the third stanza, the speaker arrives at the third stage of the Mystic Way, illumination:

> A steady storm of correspondences!
> A night flowing with birds, a ragged moon,
> And in broad day the midnight come again!
> A man goes far to find out what he is—
> Death of the self in a long, tearless night,
> All natural shapes blazing unnatural light.

The "steady storm of correspondences" is a reference to the mystical sense of oneness and the "steady stream, a veritable storm of signs, reminders of the invisible, the divine world," that keep breaking in upon the speaker (28 #24). Of course, the "unnatural light" is an almost invariable characteristic of illumination, as is the reversal of day and night: "The time-sense is lost" (28 #24). The speaker, having prepared himself through purgation, now looks on the radiant Absolute and loses himself in the vision; "the natural self dies in the blaze of the supernatural" (28 #24).

The final stanza is the one that has received the most critical attention, partly because of its ambiguities, but I think also because of its compression. Unlike the three preceding stanzas that present one stage of the Mystic Way each, the fourth presents two, the dark night of the soul and union. Indeed, the first three lines disclose a vision of the dark night:

> Dark, dark my light, and darker my desire.
> My soul, like some heat-maddened summer fly,
> Keeps buzzing at the sill. Which I is *I*?

The concept of a dark light is by now a familiar mystical paradox. Immersed in the abyss, the speaker realizes that any light he perceives will have to come from the consuming darkness that surrounds him. But before he has that ultimate perception of the Absolute, the last vestiges of selfhood must be purged away. According to Roethke, "this is where the turn comes," and he emphasizes "the intensity of the identification with the fly: Am I this many-eyed, mad, filthy thing, or am I human? 'Which I is I?'" (28 #24). Such questioning is typical of the dark night experience in which "the purifying process is extended into the very centre of I-hood, the will."[13] Accompanying this process is the sense of defilement, the feeling of being unworthy. The soul is "overwhelmed by the purity of God, and this purity makes her see the least atoms of her imperfections as if they were enormous sins."[14] Roethke captures this sensation in the image of the fly: "My soul itself is 'like' a disease-laden, heat-maddened fly—to me a thing more intolerable than a rat" (28 #24).

If a breakthrough to union is to be effected, the soul must relinquish itself to the abyss by abandoning its will, its desires, its individual identity. Whether or not Roethke succeeds in this endeavor is uncertain, for the self possesses, even at this stage, only a "modicum of humility" (28 #24). At the moment of union, as we shall see, the self seems almost to resist annihilation in the One. Still, the dark night leads to another condition, described by Roethke in the following way:

> The moment before Nothingness, before near annihilation, the moment of supreme disgust is the worst: when change comes it is either total loss of consciousness—symbolical or literal death— *or* a quick break into another state, not necessarily serene, but frequently a bright blaze of consciousness that translates itself into action. (28 #24).

The "quick break into another state" is described in the final three lines of the poem, which unquestionably represent the mystical stage of union:

> A fallen man, I climb out of my fear.
> The mind enters itself, and God the mind,
> And one is One, free in the tearing wind.

It is the "fallen man" who has entered the pit, but significantly, he is now climbing out of his fear. For him, the way down has become the way out; the horrors of the abyss have led to the experience of unity in which God and the individual soul become one and the same thing. In fact, they become *the* One, "the Godhead theologically placed above God . . . not only the veritable creator of the universe but the creator of the revealed God" (28 #24). This movement from self to selfless absorption in the Absolute is in some ways a terrifying experience, "no jump for the timid, no flick from the occult, no moment in the rose-garden" (28 #24). The sense of terror is embodied in the ambiguous word "tearing,"[15] which suggests that the protagonist and "God Himself, in his most supreme manifestation, risks being maimed, if not destroyed" (28 #24). But the word also implies pity and the hope that "some other form or aspect of God will endure with man again, will save him from himself" (28 #24).

The standard discussion of these last lines tends to focus on whether or not Roethke actually attains union. Undoubtedly, his sense of mergence is different than that described by Underhill as "a state of equilibrium, of purely spiritual life, characterized by peaceful joy, by enhanced powers, by intense certitude."[16] And the mind seems almost to flee God (in the fashion of "The Hound of Heaven"), crawling into itself as if terrified. But the union is ultimately effected, despite the soul's resistance, and "in the poem, the self dies, for a time at least" (28 #24). If we take the poem on its own terms, we must acknowledge that union is accomplished here, in an even more definite way than in "The Abyss." To reinforce such a reading we have Roethke's claim that he "was granted an insight beyond the usual," that he was, in effect, permitted to experience death without dying (28 #24). Little wonder, then, that he found the vision of the ultimate annihilation of his individual identity to be somewhat frightening. Even so, the sense of union is no less real or valid: Though the wind may be tearing, one still becomes One.

The eleven poems that follow "In a Dark Time" do, as Roethke claimed, represent a descent from the metaphysical heights of that initial poem to the more human and the more "rational." This is not to say that "In a Dark Time" is irrational, rather that it is nonrational, beyond logic, and so the poems that follow endeavor to comprehend, in more analytical terms, the nature of the mystical experience. The first of the poems, "In Evening Air" (*CP*, 240), reveals that the speaker is still very close to the mystical experience. The "dark theme" that occupies his attention is the dark time in which the eye begins to see and the ultimate dark light of the Absolute. "Half-possessed / By his own nakedness," the speaker would be "naked to the bone," completely possessed and immersed once more in the One.[17] His state of half-possession reveals that the mystical experience has passed, though he retains a memory of its insights. His assertion, "I'll make a broken music, or I'll die," indicates a desire to sustain the vision and recalls "The Dying Man," "that final thing, / A man learning to sing." Music, of course, as we have seen elsewhere, is a manifestation of the Absolute, of the harmonious universe, and he who would bring himself into the proper relationship with that unity must add to it his own voice; he must sing. Here, however, the best the speaker can manage is "a broken music," for the sense of union has passed.

In the second stanza, the speaker invokes Roethke's familiar "minimals"—"Ye littles, lie more close!"—in the hope that they can bring him close to God again, that through those "lovely diminutives" he can perceive the infinite and escape time. Indeed, he recalls the loss of his sense of time in the brilliance of mystical vision:

> Once I transcended time:
> A bud broke to a rose,
> And I rose from a last diminishing.

The desire, of course, is to transcend his own mortality, to rise from his diminishing into the permanence of the Absolute. This image clearly refers to the greenhouse poems and to the speaker's identification with those struggling plants. It also echoes "The Rose" and the speaker's sense in that poem that he stood outside himself, "Beyond becoming and perishing" (*CP*, 205). Here, as throughout these final poems, Roethke seems to be reviewing his lifelong spiritual odyssey, looking back from the edge of the abyss.

The final two stanzas deal with the darkness of death, a crucial part of the "dark theme" that concerns the speaker. The tree in stanza three is the tree of life, which becomes "lost upon the night." Significantly, it is not obliterated by the darkness but absorbed by it, as if the tree and the night merge. Obviously, this recalls the sense of mergence in "In a Dark Time," and the similarity leads the speaker to embrace the night, "a dear proximity." That last phrase can be read several ways, as a statement of the nearness of the night or as an indication that the night and the abyss are proximate or similar. In the latter sense, the speaker embraces the night as a surrogate for the mystic (perhaps literal) death he desires. In the final stanza, the speaker stands "by a low fire," symbol of his waning life, and contemplates the darkness of death. There is in his recognition of "How slowly dark comes down on what we do" a sense of calm, as if he finds the darkness attractive. Because death descends slowly, as the night envelops the tree, the speaker finds that it is not so terrible, and perhaps he sees in it a way to regain the lost sense of mystical union.

"The Sequel" (CP, 241) is a title that should be taken in all its senses, for the poem is not only a continuation of what has gone before but a statement of the consequences of that previous activity, an evaluation of results. The principal point of focus is the mystical experience of "In a Dark Time," but the poem ranges over the breadth of Roethke's work to include all such encounters with the Absolute. The opening question, then—"Was I too glib about eternal things?"—refers not only to the initial poem of the sequence but to Roethke's entire opus. He has been, or at least has tried to be, "an intimate of air and all its songs," pursuing "all wild longings of the insatiate blood," desiring to be "Both moth and flame." The latter image refers to the drive for union, the mothlike push for the flame of the Absolute in which the seeker is consumed by the One but, as in the last stanza of "In a Dark Time," struggles until the end to keep his own identity. This is the frightening aspect of the experience, the need to relinquish the self, and the speaker's recognition of the terror of self-annihilation in the Godhead is what causes him to wonder if he has been "too glib about eternal things." He realizes that the ultimate union he has sought is "no jump for the timid" or "moment in the rose-garden" (28 #24).

The second and third stanzas recall periods of illumination in other poems. The sense of unity implied by the dance of

speaker, nestling, partridge, minnow, stone, and moon in the
second stanza seems to point back to similar experiences in
"The Waking" (CP, 51), where the speaker feels at one with
the wrens, stones, flowers, goats, and all of creation, and "A
Field of Light" (CP, 62–63), in which he exclaims, "I moved
with the morning." Certainly, the line "A nestling sighed—I
called that nestling mine" seems almost an allusion to these
lines in "The Waking": "Far in the wood / A nestling sighed,"
and the correspondence is made even stronger by the similarity of the experience each poem describes. The third stanza,
with its dreamlike imagery, recalls a number of the love
poems, but "The Visitant" comes first to mind as a parallel for
this passage:

> Morning's a motion in a happy mind:
> She stayed in light, as leaves live in the wind,
> Swaying in air, like some long water weed.
> She left my body, lighter than a seed;
> I gave her body full and grave farewell.
> A wind came close, like a shy animal.
> A light leaf on a tree, she swayed away
> To the dark beginnings of another day.

Clearly, the imagery and tone of that stanza echo the second
section of "The Visitant" (CP, 100–101):

> Slow, slow as a fish she came,
> Slow as a fish coming forward,
> Swaying in a long wave;
> Her skirts not touching a leaf,
> Her white arms reaching towards me.
>
> She came without sound,
> Without brushing the wet stones,
> In the soft dark of early evening,
> She came,
> The wind in her hair,
> The moon beginning.

"The Dream" affords another close parallel, but whichever
poem we choose to illustrate the chords being struck here in
"The Sequel," our conclusion must be the same: The stanza is

intended to evoke memories of the speaker's experiences of illumination through love.

In the final section, the questioning that began the poem is resumed: "Was nature kind? The heart's core tractable?" In other words, what was the source of previous experiences of illumination? Were those visions the product of nature's kindness or the heart's tractability (perhaps its gullibility)? Whatever their source, those experiences have failed him now, as "All waters waver, and all fires fail," and the speaker is left without illumination, "Pacing a room, a room with dead-white walls." His final sense is that he has been denied further experiences because he has "denied desire," resisted the dark desire of "In a Dark Time" that implies death of the self. And he is left speculating that he was perhaps too glib, unprepared to pay the final price for what he sought.

"The Motion" (CP, 243) marks a slight transition from the sense of loss and despondency of the two preceding poems to the conviction that "our chance is still to be." This new hope seems prompted by the recollections of love in "The Sequel" that cause the protagonist to realize that "love's a faring-forth." Such was the premise at the heart of the love poems, the notion that "The flesh can make the spirit visible" (CP, 106). This idea is expressed here in several different ways: "The soul has many motions, body one"; "By lust alone we keep the mind alive, / And grieve into the certainty of love"; and "Love begets love." What the speaker rediscovers is a fundamental truth concerning the uniformity of love: To love anything is to love the Absolute, for all things are a part of the encompassing One. Further, love is the principal element of the mystic's drive toward union. His desire is to attain another reality, to be joined by love with the eternal object of love. This explains the lines that conclude the third stanza by describing "This reach beyond this death, this act of love / In which all creatures share, and thereby love." Beyond death is union, the "final certitude," which is itself an act of love, in which every creature participates.

In the final stanza, the speaker resembles "The Dying Man" (CP, 153–56) who has stopped "being a bird, yet beats his wings / Against the immense immeasurable emptiness of things." He continues moving toward the abyss, his "Wings without feathers creaking in the sun," because he knows God has smiled a loving smile "down this space," and recognition of his love brings the hope that the darkness of death will be transformed into the brightness of "broad day."

The vision of transcendent love that concludes "The Motion" is replaced in the opening stanza of "Infirmity" (*CP*, 244) by a cynical view of self-love:

> In purest song one plays the constant fool
> As changes shimmer in the inner eye.
> I stare and stare into a deepening pool
> And tell myself my image cannot die.
> I love myself: that's my one constancy.
> Oh, to be something else, yet still to be!

As these lines reveal, the speaker's "infirmity" goes beyond the physical. Though he may have a bad knee and shoulder, he is more handicapped by his selfish desire to retain his life, his identity, than by any of his physical disabilities. His is a spiritual weakness that must be overcome if he is ever to attain union. Dying is a natural process, like the decaying of a tree, and as the "meager flesh breaks down," the soul becomes aware of and delights in "a pure extreme of light." But the ego intrudes upon the vision, cynically asserting, "Blessed the meek; they shall inherit wrath," and proclaiming, "I'm son and father of my only death." Implicit here is a refusal to acquiesce to the gradual decay, a determination to be anything but meek, to be in control.

Recognizing that stubborn resistance is the wrong stance, the speaker declares, "a mind too active is no mind at all," thereby proclaiming the primacy of intuition over analysis, the God-loving soul over the self-loving ego. Instead of fighting approaching death, he decides to yield to it, but that requires a reorientation of the analytical mind and the senses on which the mind relies. "When opposites come suddenly in place," he must teach his eyes to hear and his ears to see. Such nonrational perceptions are, as we have seen, common elements of the mystical experience. The principal opposites operable here are those of life and death, body and spirit, self and selfless-

ness, and the speaker must teach himself to confront the ultimate reconciliation of these opposites in death and union, to
strive to become not some extension of his aging self but "pure
spirit at the end."

The next three poems in the sequence represent the inevitable "slipping-back" that characterizes all of Roethke's drives
toward ultimate reality. The reassurances gained in "The Motion" and "Infirmity" are swallowed up in a frightening vision
of the abyss of death. First among these poems is "The Decision" (CP, 245), which declares, "Running from God's the
longest race of all" and then describes the culmination of that
futile flight in this familiar way:

> Rising or falling's all one discipline!
> The line of my horizon's growing thin!
> Which is the way? I cry to the dread black,
> The shifting shade, the cinders at my back.
> Which is the way? I ask, and turn to go,
> As a man turns to face on-coming snow.

Echoed here are Roethke's early flight in "The Lost Son,"
where he cries, "Which is the way I take; / Out of what door
do I go, / Where and to whom?," and his later queries in "The
Abyss," "Is the stair here? / Where's the stair?" In those poems
as in this one, the speaker seeks a way out, and his plaintive
cries for directions invariably lead to the same conclusion: The
way down is the way out. "Rising or falling's all one discipline!" To arrive at the ultimate stage of union, it is necessary
to pass through the abyss. The decision, then, is inevitable;
the speaker must confront his own death, "As a man turns to
face on-coming snow." The dark night of the soul or death, as
depicted in this poem, is an unavoidable part of the process of
becoming pure being.

"The Marrow" (CP, 246) is a poem of penance in which the
self, confronted with the inescapable reality of death, burns
with the pure desire for knowledge of the Absolute. The poem
begins with the singing of "small flies" in the mist, an apparent reference to the fly imagery of "In a Dark Time": "My soul,
like some heat-maddened summer fly, / Keeps buzzing at the
sill." Clearly, the soul of the speaker, who is nearing death, is

pushing for release, but is, as yet, still trapped within the body. The image of the crow in a burnt pine underscores the moribundity of the speaker who, surveying his life, sarcastically determines that the worst that could befall him is "A pensive mistress, and a yelping wife." By contrast, the worst that could happen beyond his mortal life is not so funny. The stakes there, between being and nonbeing, are much higher.

The second stanza shows the speaker "Brooding on God" in an attempt to gain understanding. His contemplation brings him so near the blinding reality of the Absolute that it dazzles him, and he realizes that "One look too close can take my soul away." Still, he longs to look on that "white face" "brighter than the sun," for the desire he denied in "The Sequel" has flared up again and impels him to let his soul be taken away. This, of course, implies union, absorption of the individual soul in the One. But even though he desires to look upon the face of God, on the Godhead itself, he is still possessed by fear, crying, "Lord, hear me out, and hear me out this day: / From me to Thee's a long and terrible way." This exclamation expresses not only the fear of a terrible journey, but the fear of union as well. The distance "From me to Thee" may be long and terrible, but the change "From me to Thee" in union, when the soul merges with and becomes God, is even more horrifying (as shown in the final stanza of "In a Dark Time"). At this point, the protagonist reveals that he is still afraid of the ultimate annihilation of the self. Yet what he is unable to do is what must be done if union is to be attained, for before union "The Self . . . surrenders itself, its individuality, and its will, completely."[18]

The final stanza is almost a complaint, a protest in which the speaker claims that he has been "flung back from suffering and love" of God despite his strenuous efforts to effect union. He even claims that he has slain his will in the endeavor, though ironically the last lines reveal a will that is strong and healthy: "I bleed my bones, their marrow to bestow / Upon that God who knows what I would know." Obviously, the speaker still clings to his identity and is not yet prepared to relinquish himself. His impulse here, as revealed by the last lines of the poem, is not the mystic's drive to be but the self's desire to know.

"I Waited" (*CP*, 247) is the last of the poems that mark a backswing into terror and fear. Recounted here is a period of illumination, but it is illumination with a different twist than elsewhere in Roethke's poetry. Accompanying the vision is no feeling of happiness or joy. Instead, the sense of unity is almost sinister and seems to grow out of the plodding, somnambulant walk that precedes it:

> It was as if I tried to walk in hay,
> Deep in the mow, and each step deeper down,
> Or floated on the surface of a pond,
> The slow long ripples winking in my eyes.
> I saw all things through water, magnified,
> And shimmering. The sun burned through a haze,
> And I became all that I looked upon.
> I dazzled in the dazzle of a stone.

When the sensation has passed, the speaker once again finds himself struggling along as if walking in sand, moving "like some heat-weary animal." Curiously, he claims, "I went, not looking back. I was afraid." Normally, the impulse in Roethke's poetry is to sustain the period of illumination, but here the speaker wants to escape it, is frightened by it. And when he finally arrives at a small plateau where the wind he waited for at the beginning of the poem comes toward him, he is glad.

This poem epitomizes Roethke's fear of losing his identity. After the terrible sense of union experienced in "In a Dark Time," he is even afraid of illumination and its accompanying sense of oneness. Consequently, the feeling, "I became all that I looked upon," does not provoke the usual euphoria. The appearance of the shimmering vision between two sections in which the protagonist's movement becomes slow motion emphasizes its relationship to the motionless world of death, a place of no wind. Rather than immerse himself in the perception, the speaker struggles to resist death and affirm his own identity. This effort is in no way better depicted than in the multiple repetitions of the first-person pronoun *I*—fourteen in all. No matter what illumination death may hold, the speaker fights for life, for the fresh sea winds.

Unlike the meadow that seems almost to swallow up the speaker in "I Waited," the fields in "The Tree, The Bird" (*CP*, 248) rise up to meet him. No longer weighted down and frightened, the protagonist is "At ease with joy, a self-enchanted man." He has learned again to perceive the happiness of illumination and not to fear it, though his sense of transcendence, the feeling that "I stood outside my life," and his subsequent identification with the willow and its singing bird stir some of his old anxieties:

> The willow with its bird grew loud, grew louder still.
> I could not bear its song, that altering
> With every shift of air, those beating wings,
> The lonely buzz behind my midnight eyes;—
> How deep the mother-root of that still cry!

The bird within the tree represents the soul within the speaker's body, and he hears in the bird's song the flylike buzzing of his soul to escape the flesh. But this vision that previously brought a sense of terror is now endured, and the speaker overcomes his fear:

> The present falls, the present falls away;
> How pure the motion of the rising day,
> The white sea widening on a farther shore.
> The bird, the beating bird, extending wings—.
> Thus I endure this last pure stretch of joy,
> The dire dimension of a final thing.

He accepts the reality of the passing of the present and, thereby, he implicitly accepts his own mortality. The farther shore of the white sea no longer frightens him, nor does the realization that he is the dying man, "A final thing." Though the "dimension" of his situation may be "dire," he still finds reason for joy and, like "The Dying Man" (*CP*, 153–56), "beats his wings / Against the immense immeasurable emptiness of things."

The final three poems of the sequence mark a return to joy and a sense of unity. The equilibrium won in "The Tree, The Bird" is capitalized upon and extended into a pervasive sense of happiness in these last pieces. The first of them, "The Restored" (*CP*, 249), represents a return to one of Roethke's oldest dichotomies and one of the basic principles of mysticism: the need to subvert the logical mind and elevate the intuitive faculties:

> In a hand like a bowl
> Danced my own soul,
> Small as an elf,
> All by itself.
>
> When she thought I thought
> She dropped as if shot.
> "I've only one wing," she said,
> "The other's gone dead,"
>
> "I'm maimed; I can't fly;
> I'm like to die,"
> Cried my soul
> From my hand like a bowl.
>
> When I raged, when I wailed,
> And my reason failed,
> That delicate thing
> Grew back a new wing,
>
> And danced, at high noon,
> On a hot, dusty stone,
> In the still point of light
> Of my last midnight.

The way to extend the soul, as we have seen throughout Roethke's poetry, is to dispense with analytical thinking, for the logical mind and its senses are unreliable. Thought cripples the soul. Only by permitting the intuition to take charge can one allow for the possibility of illumination. In a certain sense, this poem is a commentary on the entire sequence. Having been unsuccessful in rationally understanding the mystical experience described in "In a Dark Time" (that effort represented by the preceding eight poems), Roethke decides to stop analyzing it. He realizes that the way to happiness and a sense of union lies through the nonrational, through raging and wailing and the failure of reason, not through metaphysical deliberations.

It is the retreat from analysis and the return to intuition that mark the opening passage of Roethke's villanelle "The Right Thing" (*CP*, 250):

> Let others probe the mystery if they can.
> Time-harried prisoners of *Shall* and *Will*—
> The right thing happens to the happy man.

Taken out of context, this poem may appear to express a facile philosophy, but within the scope of "Sequence, Sometimes Metaphysical" it represents the culmination of Roethke's attempts to explain the mystical experience. Confronted with a multitude of enigmas, the speaker abandons his efforts to understand them rationally and turns instead to the nonrational, to the assertion that "The right thing happens to the happy man." There is little of logic in this claim, as in all such articles of faith, but there can be no other resolution, for the things that defy logical analysis are manifold: "The bird flies out, the bird flies back again; / The hill becomes the valley, and is still"; "Body and soul are one! / The small become the great, the great the small." The happy man leaves the how and why of such mysteries to others, finding his own answers by ceasing to seek them, "surrendering his will / Till mystery is no more." He is the "Child of the dark" in that he has no answers, but "he can outleap the sun" because by surrendering his will in the face of the ultimate mysteries he has placed himself in perfect communion with the All, the Absolute.

"Once More, the Round" (*CP*, 251), the final poem in the sequence, continues along the lines of "The Right Thing" by asking questions that look very much like riddles or koans:

> What's greater, Pebble or Pond?
> What can be known? The Unknown.
> My true self runs toward a Hill
> More! O More! visible.

To the first question there is no answer, and the answer to the second is vintage Roethke and standard mystical doctrine. To illustrate my meaning, a passage from the notebooks that was quoted earlier in this study is especially pertinent here:

> We think by feeling. What is there to know! The answer is *un-knowing*—the unknowing of the cloud of un-knowing. (43 #208)

Elsewhere, Roethke instructs himself, "In the very real and final sense, don't *know* anything."[19] The trick, of course, is to stop the analytical mind so that "knowing slows for a moment, / And not-knowing enters, silent, / Bearing being itself" (*CP*, 221). As the anonymous author of *The Cloud of Unknowing* says of God, "By love he may be gotten and holden, but by thought of understanding, never."[20] By abandoning his attempts to know, the speaker learns by going, and as he progresses, the Absolute he seeks becomes more visible. Again now, he senses his place in the ultimate unity of things, with the bird, the leaf, and the snail, realizing that love is the key that binds all together in a kind of cosmic dance that forms the ultimate One.

"Sequence, Sometimes Metaphysical" begins in despair and ends in joy. At the outset, the protagonist is determined to make sense of his mystical experience, even to recapture it if he can overcome his fear. But all his questions and deliberations prove pointless, so he is ultimately forced to abandon his attempts. Ironically, when he stops trying to understand, understanding becomes implicit, as does the resolution of all his fears. Curiously enough, Roethke seems at the end of his career finally to have gained the deliverance from "all / Activity centripetal" (*CP*, 24) he had sought from the beginning, in the pages of *Open House*. This final sequence in his final volume shows him coming to terms with death, readying himself for the ultimate immersion in the Absolute, for the union with the Godhead above God, the union he feared so long, yet so fervently desired.

11.

Poets and Mystics

"Manic-depressives hand in hand, / Romping through
the promised land."—Roethke Notebooks (33 #29)

Most critics feel uneasy with the term *mysticism*, even
though they do, with varying degrees of reluctance, acknowledge the mystical element in Roethke's poetry. Their concern,
as I suggested earlier, arises from a very significant question:
If we label Roethke's poetry mystical, do we by implication
identify him as a mystic? The problem, which exists from the
very beginning, grows acute when we approach Roethke's final volume, for it is in the poems of *The Far Field* that Roethke's
poetic persona most resembles the mystic. His overwhelming
concern is with union, and as we have seen, in at least one
instance, "In a Dark Time," he effects a merging with the Absolute, with God himself. Accepting Roethke's periods of illumination and his dark night travails is less problematic than
accepting his claim of union because these experiences are
well within the range of the artistic sensibility. Union, however, is another matter, exclusively in the domain of the mystic. Jay Parini deals with the problem this way:

> One simply cannot equate Roethke with St. Theresa, Richard of
> St. Victor, or any other classical mystic. Like most other mystical
> poets, he attained illuminations, *intimations* of immortality; noth-
> ing more. With the possible exceptions of St. John of the Cross
> and Dante, poets rarely even try to portray the final union in
> their verse. Attempts to express this union in the language of
> poetry, as in Blake's Prophetic Books, often end in failure.[1]

Parini neatly resolves the problem by making the distinction
between calling Roethke a mystical poet and calling him a
mystic. However, this distinction deserves elaboration, particularly if we are to put Roethke's poetic accounts of union
into perspective, and if we are to understand the degree of his
success or failure in describing that most elusive and ineffable

aspect of the mystical experience. It is not enough to declare flatly, as Rosemary Sullivan does, that Roethke "was a poet and not a mystic."[2] Although we may agree with her, the implied difference must be explained.

According to Underhill, "all real artists, as well as pure mystics, are sharers to some degree in the Illuminated Life."[3] The very nature of artistic inspiration implies seeing beyond the surface of things to a deeper truth or significance. The poet does not see different things than other people; rather, he sees things differently, with a kind of vision that resembles the mystic's insight. This faculty of seeing the radiance within things is obviously better developed in some poets than in others; in fact, it is totally lacking in many. However, the sense of illumination is highly refined in Roethke, as it is in many of his literary ancestors—Vaughan, Traherne, and Blake, in particular. Obviously, the same dilemma exists for the reader of these poets: Are they poets or mystics or mystical poets?

Northrop Frye, in his formidable study of Blake, *Fearful Symmetry*, devises a linguistic escape from the problem by calling Blake a visionary and avoiding the troublesome term *mystic* altogether.[4] However, Frye is engaging in more than a mere verbal shuffle. He is establishing, as Blake did himself, a separate designation for poets who have a heightened sense of the Absolute but whose ultimate loyalty is to the artistic creation rather than to the perception which inspires it. According to Frye, the poet's apprehension "is not an end in itself but a means to another end, the end of producing his poem. The mystical experience for him is poetic material, not poetic form, and must be subordinated to the demands of that form."[5] Such an attitude is clearly incompatible with the goal of the genuine mystic, to immerse himself in God. Beyond that ineffable experience there is nothing. For the poet, there is the poem. This calls to mind Auden's remarks on the incompatibility of Christianity and art:

> A poet must intend his poem to be a good one, that is to say, an enduring object for other people to admire. Is there not something a little odd, to say the least, about making an admirable public object out of one's feelings of guilt and penitence before God?[6]

It does not seem unusual at all that Roethke turned his personal drive toward God into poetry. For Roethke, the struggle toward a final union with the Absolute and his poetic account of that struggle were the same thing. In a certain sense, the poetry was not so much a summing up of his mystical experiences as it was the medium through which he explained them to himself and made use of them. Consequently, the question of where to place final allegiance, with the mystical perception itself or with its poetic description, seems never to have troubled Roethke the way it did Yeats, for example, in "Vacillation." There is no comparable dialogue in Roethke's poetry between the soul and the heart, revealing the tension between the desire to find God and the urge to create poetry; no pledge of loyalty to the poetic craft instead of the spiritual pursuit, as symbolized by Yeats's acceptance of the poet Homer as his model and his dismissal of the mystical scholar Von Hügel.[7] Blessing records one instance in a 1948 notebook when the conflict between mystic and poet was apparently on Roethke's mind: "Creativeness requires that a man forget about his own moral progress and sacrifice his personality—If a man feels nothing but humility and a perpetual sense of sin, he can do no creative work."[8] However, this was apparently not an overriding concern; at least it never found its way into the poetry. Definitely, Roethke did not consider himself a mystic, but he did acknowledge, on numerous occasions, a familiarity with the mystic vision, and his notebooks reveal that he thought "the poet's path is closer to the mystic than we think" (42 #194). Blessing observed, "Roethke seems to have come to hope that creativeness might serve as a way of forgetting the self, that it might, if a man could detach himself sufficiently from its fruits, take the place of the more conventional mystic's asceticism."[9] That was how Roethke resolved the problem that concerns us here and that must concern anyone interested in his mysticism.

The relationship between Roethke's poetry and his pursuit of ultimate reality helps to explain one of the most problematic aspects of several of his final poems, the description of union. "The Abyss" and "In a Dark Time," in particular, have been criticized for their pat and, in some critics' opinions, contrived final lines that describe a mergence with God, an ultimate bonding with the One. If such an experience is reserved for the genuine mystic, and if Roethke was not a mystic, how can we accept his accounts as anything other than fabrications? The answer is, we cannot. However, accepting them as fabrications should not in any way diminish their significance or their authenticity, for they are accurate and true to the mystical experience. The problem central to Roethke's last poems is the final abandonment of self, a step Roethke desired to take, though he found himself incapable of following through. Ultimately, this is what distinguishes Roethke from the genuine mystic: his inability to escape the bonds of "I-hood" and experience the resulting union. However, what he could not bring himself to do spiritually he could accomplish poetically, and because of the connection between his spiritual pursuit and the poetic process he was able to effect, at the very least, a vicarious union. Perhaps Roethke believed he could induce the sense of union by experiencing it poetically, by drawing poem and experience so close together that they would become indistinguishable, making what he wished for not only figuratively but literally true. Roethke's explanation of this process is much more to the point: "I believe the poem should create its own reality" (42 #196).

Every reader must recognize that Roethke's final poems, those composing *The Far Field*, are not so much a reflection of experiences as a foreshadowing of things to come. They prefigure Roethke's death, but even more significantly they extend beyond dying to the final confrontation with God. Those last poems represent a stage of preparation, of becoming accustomed to the idea of death and the resultant immersion of self in the union beyond, enabling Roethke to deal with the loss of individual identity, for him the ultimate horror. In a poem like "In a Dark Time," the distinction between artistic creation and personal experience disappears, and the imagined becomes the actual. There is a precedent for this technique, of course, in "The Lost Son" sequence where the movement of the poetry and the movement of the mind are the same thing. I do not agree with those critics who find Roethke's accounts of union forced and awkward. Rather, I find in them a remarkable example of a man coming to terms with his gravest fears. Moreover, I feel the descriptions of union are as real and truthful as a person can possibly make them on this side of dying.

God, for Roethke, was the ultimate one to come to terms with, and even though he longed for a final union, he resisted it. Nevertheless, even in his resistance we may see, paradoxically, a final acquiescence. Roethke suggests this possibility himself in a comment found among the notes he made while writing his essay "On 'Identity' ":

> Plotinus says . . . "Running from God is the longest race of all." But the running from *may* be a running *toward*. How do we know? This is related to Yeats' "Hatred of God can bring the soul to God." (28 #26)

Certainly, this process of yielding while resisting describes the whole movement of Roethke's final poems. Although the self fights to sustain its individual identity, it gradually gives up its separateness.

By his own definition, Roethke was religious: "Take a crude definition of a religious man: that he believes in an Other, a power greater than himself" (28 #26). However, he never felt comfortable with orthodox religion, and even the traditional concept of God caused him some difficulty as the following remarks indicate:

> I believe that man should find out God in his own terms. This is nothing more or less than Protestantism: prove it on my pulse, bring me to Thee. I confront Thee directly, or not at all. If you're father, father away. This does not, I repeat, make me superior, but I'm damned if I'm inferior to those who fall back on an accepted, arranged order of things, a complete theology with all the answers. (28 #26)

Aside from his attitude toward organized religion, this statement reflects Roethke's familiar stance before God, a kind of belligerent reverence, defiance and acceptance at the same time. It was this assertion of identity that prevented Roethke from experiencing union in the immediate sense. However, he followed through, in his poetry, on the basis of his firsthand knowledge of the first four stages of the mystic way, extending himself poetically beyond his personal limitations. Roethke knew, not only through his readings in mysticism and philosophy but through his own intuitive powers, what the final stage must be like, and his description of it, particularly in "In a Dark Time," brought him as close to the real experience as he could come. Consequently, we find in Roethke's poetry as accurate an account of union as we are likely to find anywhere.

Throughout this study, I have boldly used the term *mystical* rather than *visionary* or some other substitute, taking Roethke himself as my authority. The notebooks abound with references to mystics and mysticism, far more than I have been able to incorporate into this book. Nevertheless, I do not believe Roethke ever considered himself a mystic. Unquestionably, he felt a strong kinship with the mystics, as he did with the mad poets, because of his manic perceptions, but his extensive readings in mysticism, though they provided him with insights into his own condition, apparently never led him to declare, "I am one of them." Most revealing in this area are Roethke's notes on mysticism, those he apparently used in his classes at the University of Washington. Like most of his teaching notes, these are jotted down in the form of a general outline, with each major point probably leading Roethke into a much longer commentary in which he drew freely from his reading and personal experience. One page is of particular interest here because it reveals Roethke's views of the relationship between poets and mystics:

> *Mystic & poet*
> Both contemplate object
> Both are not passive: doesn't fall bewildered
>   "a selective surrender"
> Both have a total operation of the mind & spirit:
>   a completeness
> Both have that character of "otherness"
>   "Yet it has not come from within me, for
>   it is good, and I know that in me dwelleth no
>   good thing."
>   [The daemon, the unconscious, the oversoul]
> Both have mood of wonder, of surprise (72 #13)

Taken together, these five points of similarity represent the initial movement of the mystic: from contemplation, a time of quiet activity not to be confused with passivity, in which all powers (mind and spirit) focus on the sense of "otherness," to a point of illumination characterized by wonder and surprise. Clearly, this outline also characterizes the movement in Roethke's poetry, the persistent journey "from I to Otherwise."[10]

On another page of notes apparently written at the same time, Roethke identifies some points at which the poet and mystic differ, indicating that he does not think the poetic and mystic processes, however similar, are identical:

> *Differences*
> 1) The *will* plays a larger part in experience
> 2) The frame of reference is vaster [is it] in mystical:
>   "Thou, oh eternal Trinity, art a deep sea, into
>   which the deeper I enter the more I find, and
>   the more I find the more I seek."
>   Catherine of Siena
> 3) Compulsive fever of attention
> 4) A greater tendency toward concentration, toward
>   absorption in the mystic (72 #13)

Items 1 and 3 are problematic because Roethke does not indicate how he is making the distinction. Nevertheless, it seems safe to assume, in the first instance anyway, that he is speaking of the poet. Indeed, as we have seen throughout this study, the will was a significant factor in Roethke's experiences. He never stopped believing that he willed his first manic episode, and in the end it was his will that prevented him from relinquishing himself completely to the experience of union. Certainly, this is a very important point of difference between the poet and the mystic, for the latter accepts the annihilation of the individual will and the consequent loss of individual identity. Without question, Roethke's dominant will, which was largely responsible for making him an exceptional poet, prevented him from taking the final step on the mystic way.

The bracketed question, "is it," in the second item is Roethke's, and it indicates that he was not prepared to grant the mystic a broader scope than the poet. To be sure, his own frame of reference, which extended from birth and before to death and beyond, was enough to make him doubt the validity of this distinction. Though he may have been no Catherine of Siena, he obviously was not willing to abandon the field of perception to her. Significantly, though, within this shared field, he attributes to the mystic "a sharper concentration," a stronger ability of attention, and a greater tendency toward absorption. These qualities characterize the mystic's movement out of self toward some other center, toward an eventual absorption in the vast unity of creation, and return us once again to the individual will, which the mystic relinquishes but the poet clings to. That Roethke understood this fundamental distinction is obvious. More than likely he believed that, through some accident of chemistry or biology, he had been granted a comparable perception, had been admitted through some back or side door into the world of the mystics. Obviously, the significance of his manic-depressiveness cannot be overlooked in this regard. His condition was both a curse and a blessing, at times a danger to his life but also a boon to his poetry, the source both of great pain and of insights far beyond those normally associated with mere artistic sensitivity.

Afterword

"I will be nothing & I will be all."—Roethke Notebooks (39 #126)

In the last year of his life, Roethke made the following self-evaluative comment to the students from San Francisco State College who had come to Seattle to film him:

> We don't grow up, older and older, more and more benign, more and more full of wisdom and so on. I'm still death haunted, I'm afraid, in spite of the fact I say that death is an absurdity. (140)

On the basis of this comment, it would seem that, despite the hard-won sense of reconciliation and joy that concludes *The Far Field*, Roethke was never completely at peace with himself. Death remained for him, until the end, a terrible consequence. For Roethke, as for the protagonist in his poetry, spiritual advancement was always accompanied by some slipping back, and the gains he made in the poems of his final volume were apparently only temporary, though that final struggle did represent, in Roethke's words, some progress. His push toward the Absolute was indeed among those experiences that are "so powerful and so profound . . . that they repeat themselves . . . again and again . . . each time bringing us closer to our own most particular (and thus most universal) reality."[1] In his last poems, it appears that Roethke drew as near to his particular and universal reality as life would allow. To go further meant to go beyond life, to die.

If Roethke was haunted by a fear of death, he was also haunted by an attraction to it. From the very beginning, in *Open House*, those taut little poems of self-loathing such as "Epidermal Macabre" and "Prayer Before Study" reveal something of a death wish. And therein lies the ultimate irony of Roethke's poetry, that his struggle for identity inevitably necessitated the loss of his identity. Roethke discovered that in order to find himself he had to lose himself, and the truth of that paradox produced in him the conflicting drives that are most clearly revealed in "Sequence, Sometimes Metaphysical." His desire was to attain ultimate union, but he could not bear to pay the ultimate cost, the loss of his own individual identity. What he passionately desired was an impossible contradiction, "to be something else, yet still to be!" (*CP*, 244).

I do not wish to claim for Roethke a place among the saints, or even among the great mystics, for that matter. Mysticism is central to Roethke's poetry, and I have tried to account for that mystical element in terms of his own unique psyche. Roethke's manic-depressiveness stands at the center of this study because it was the source of his insights. I do not believe Roethke was a poet because he was a manic-depressive, but that his manic-depressiveness helped to make him the kind of poet he was. In the final sense, Roethke's exploitation of a psychosis, which for most people would be a grave handicap, was a supreme act of courage and revealed an unflagging dedication to the craft of poetry.

As late as January 1963 Roethke proclaimed, "I know, in the final term, something, and perhaps a good deal more than I realize, about mystic experience" (140). To be sure, by the early 1960s Roethke knew quite a lot about mysticism because he had been reading extensively for a number of years in mystical literature and related philosophy. But his contention that he might know even more than he himself realized seems a clear indication that his knowledge of the mystical experience came not only from analytical study; a good portion of it was intuitive. It is apparent that what began for Roethke in 1935, during his first manic episode, as a spontaneous insight into the mystical unity of creation, subsequently became an area of organized study. In an effort to make sense of his unusual experiences, Roethke began to read among the works of such mystics and scholars as Jacob Boehme, John Ruysbroeck, and, most significantly, Evelyn Underhill. Over time, his studies began to influence his work, so the poetry of the last years of his life not surprisingly reveals his sources. However, a complex interchange must be accounted for here lest we mistakenly identify Roethke as a text creeper and random borrower. What he read in those mystical and philosophical treatises was what he had already experienced himself, and his readings, initially undertaken to explain his manic visions, eventually became a way of substantiating, perhaps even of legitimizing them.

The remarkable unity of Roethke's work is attributable to Roethke's persistence, to his "spiritual toughness," for he never once grew lax in the pursuit of his ultimate identity. Like the mystic, Roethke's awareness of another level of reality, one more real and significant than that which is normally perceived, led him to dedicate himself to the attainment of the Absolute. Robert Heilman, Roethke's department chairman at Washington and his good friend for many years, recalls worrying about Roethke during the spring of 1963. He was concerned about the possibility of another manic episode, which appeared to be in the offing, and worried that at any moment he might have to find a substitute to take over Roethke's teaching duties. According to Heilman, Roethke seemed to be on the edge of a mystical vision, walking the periphery of some kind of revelation. Nevertheless, he finished out the term without incident and Heilman was spared the administrative dilemma of finding a replacement teacher in the middle of the semester, though he continued to be concerned for his friend's condition.[2] In a curiously appropriate way, Roethke seems to have spent the last months of his life on the brink of some perception, his final illumination.

Significantly, the last poem Roethke wrote was one that deals with the mystical experience.[3] Titled "Song" (27 #10), the poem is clearly related to "The Lost Son" sequence, with its nonsense rhymes, and to "Sequence, Sometimes Metaphysical," with its approach–avoidance attitude toward death and union. Appropriately, the poem draws together disparate elements of Roethke's work and leaves us with a final enigma, for Roethke, like Mirabell in the poem, has told us all he can in his ambivalent stance on death and union. The rest is silence and a brilliant darkness. Written as a dialogue, the poem begins with an epigram from Underhill:

"This fragrance, as St. Augustine calls it . . . "—Evelyn Underhill

"Witch-me-tiddle-dee Mirabell
Took herself to the wishing well,
She did, she did, my darling dithery."

"What did she do when she got there?
Did she dally and dither,
Your darling dithery?"

"She threw back a lock of her coal-black hair,
Tossed up a penny into the air
And over the edge; and bent to stare."

"What did she see when she looked down there?"

"She stared, and stared, and her face grew small:
'There's nothing down there, there's nothing at all,
Down in the depths of the wishing well,
But a faint, a paradisal smell;
It's sweeter than heaven but straight from hell!' "

"And anything more she would not tell,
Would Witch-me-tiddle-dee Round-the-Well
Hithery-tithery, darling-dithery
Hokey-pokey Mirabell!"

Notes

1. Roethke's Mysticism

1. In addition to the six volumes mentioned here, Roethke published two books of children's verse, *I Am! Says the Lamb* and *Party at the Zoo*.

2. Karl Malkoff, *Theodore Roethke: An Introduction to the Poetry*. Richard Allen Blessing, *Theodore Roethke's Dynamic Vision*.

3. Ralph J. Mills, Jr., "In the Way of Becoming: Roethke's Last Poems," in *Theodore Roethke: Essays on the Poetry*, ed. Arnold Stein, p. 115.

4. Roethke, "Open Letter," in *On the Poet and His Craft: Selected Prose of Theodore Roethke*, ed. Ralph J. Mills, Jr., p. 37.

5. Roethke, *The Collected Poems of Theodore Roethke*, p. 47. Subsequent references to this source will be given in the text using the abbreviation *CP*.

6. "On 'Identity,'" in *On the Poet and His Craft*, p. 20.

7. Blessing, *Roethke's Dynamic Vision*, p. 60.

8. *The Glass House: The Life of Theodore Roethke*, p. 90.

9. Ibid., p. 91.

10. Ibid., p. 101.

11. Evelyn Underhill, *Mysticism: A Study in the Nature and Development of Man's Spiritual Consciousness*, p. 240.

12. Seager, *The Glass House*, p. 101.

13. *Straw for the Fire: From the Notebooks of Theodore Roethke, 1943–63*, ed. David Wagoner, p. 87.

14. Roethke, "On 'Identity,'" p. 26.

15. Seager, *The Glass House*, p. 101.

16. Thomas Freeman, "Observations on Mania," in *Manic–Depressive Illness: History of a Syndrome*, ed. Edward A. Wolpert, p. 257.

17. Underhill, *Mysticism*, p. 168.

18. Freeman, "Observations on Mania," p. 258.

19. Seager, *The Glass House*, p. 224.

20. Raymond Prince and Charles Savage, "Mystical States and the Concept of Regression," in *The Highest State of Consciousness*, ed. John White, p. 123.

21. Karl Abraham, "Notes on the Psycho-Analytical Investigation and Treatment of Manic-Depressive Insanity and Allied Conditions," in *Manic-Depressive Illness*, p. 124.

22. *Theodore Roethke: An American Romantic*, p. 136.

23. Roethke, "On 'Identity,'" p. 26.

24. Ibid.

25. Underhill, *Mysticism*, p. 299.

26. Roethke, *Straw for the Fire*, p. 14.

2. A Definition of Mysticism

1. S. N. Dasgupta, *Hindu Mysticism*, p. 17.

2. Claire Myers Owens, "The Mystical Experience: Facts and Values," in *The Highest State of Consciousness*, ed. John White, p. 145.

3. Evelyn Underhill, *Mysticism: A Study in the Nature and Development of Man's Spiritual Consciousness*, pp. vii, xiv.

4. John Senior, *The Way Down and Out: The Occult in Symbolist Literature*, p. xviii.

5. Ibid., p. 8.

6. This statement, which concludes "The Abyss," is very nearly a direct quotation of a statement made by Underhill in *Mysticism:* "Being, not doing, is the first aim of the mystic," p. 380.

7. Theodore Roethke, "On 'Identity,' " in *On the Poet and His Craft: Selected Prose of Theodore Roethke*, ed. Ralph J. Mills, Jr., p. 24.

8. Bertrand Russell, *Mysticism and Logic*, p. 3.

9. Ibid., pp. 9–11.

10. William James, *The Varieties of Religious Experience: A Study in Human Nature*, pp. 371–72.

11. U. A. Asrani, "The Psychology of Mysticism," in *The Highest State of Consciousness*, ed. John White, p. 226.

12. Owens, "The Mystical Experience," p. 142.

13. Aldous Huxley, "Visionary Experience," in *The Highest State of Consciousness*, p. 47.

14. William Heyen, "The Divine Abyss: Theodore Roethke's Mysticism," in *Profile of Theodore Roethke*, ed. William Heyen, pp. 100–116.

15. Underhill, *Mysticism*, p. 3.

16. Ibid., p. 170.

17. Ibid., pp. 126–27.

3. The Mystical Tradition:
Vaughan, Traherne, Blake, and Yeats

1. David Wagoner, Personal Interview, 23 August 1978, Seattle, Washington.

2. Karl Malkoff, *Theodore Roethke: An Introduction to the Poetry*, p. 65.

3. Jenijoy La Belle, *The Echoing Wood of Theodore Roethke*, p. 20.

4. Roethke, *Selected Letters of Theodore Roethke*, ed. Ralph J. Mills, Jr., p. 10.

5. Ibid., p. 11.

6. Henry Vaughan, "The Retreate," in *Poetry and Selected Prose of Henry Vaughan*, ed. L. C. Martin, p. 250.

7. Roethke, *Selected Letters*, p. 142.

8. Thomas Traherne, "Wonder," in *The Poetical Works of Thomas Traherne, B. D.*, ed. Bertram Dobell, p. 4.

9. Roethke, "Open Letter," in *On the Poet and His Craft: Selected Prose of Theodore Roethke*, ed. Ralph J. Mills, Jr., p. 37.

10. Roethke, "On 'Identity,' " in *On the Poet and His Craft*, p. 19.

11. Ibid.

12. Roethke, *Straw for the Fire: From the Notebooks of Theodore Roethke, 1943–63*, ed. David Wagoner, p. 244.

13. Roethke, "How to Write Like Somebody Else," in *On the Poet and His Craft*, p. 70.

14. Rosemary Sullivan, *Theodore Roethke: The Garden Master*, p. 98.

15. William Butler Yeats, "Among School Children," in *Selected Poems and Two Plays of William Butler Yeats*, ed. M. L. Rosenthal, p. 115.

16. Yeats, "Death," in *Selected Poems and Two Plays of William Butler Yeats*, p. 123.

17. William Meredith, "A Steady Storm of Correspondences: Theodore Roethke's Long Journey Out of the Self," in *Theodore Roethke: Essays on the Poetry*, ed. Arnold Stein, p. 61.

18. Evelyn Underhill, *Mysticism: A Study in the Nature and Development of Man's Spiritual Consciousness*, p. 151. See especially her discussion of mysticism and occultism.

4. The Arrival of Awareness

1. "Theodore Roethke," in *On the Poet and His Craft: Selected Prose of Theodore Roethke*, ed. Ralph J. Mills, Jr., p. 16.

2. Richard Allen Blessing, *Theodore Roethke's Dynamic Vision*, p. 42.

3. Ibid., pp. 31–32.

4. Karl Malkoff, *Theodore Roethke: An Introduction to the Poetry*, p. 45.

5. Roethke, "Open Letter," in *On the Poet and His Craft*, p. 38.

6. Evelyn Underhill, *Mysticism: A Study in the Nature and Development of Man's Spiritual Consciousness*, p. 449.

7. James R. McLeod, *Theodore Roethke: A Manuscript Checklist*, p. 2.

8. Underhill, *Mysticism*, pp. 92–93.

9. Blessing, *Roethke's Dynamic Vision*, p. 56.

10. Malkoff, *Introduction to the Poetry*, pp. 23–26.

11. Ibid.

12. John Donne, "The Relic," in *Renaissance England: Poetry and Prose from the Reformation to the Restoration*, ed. Roy Lamson, p. 800.

13. This comment was found in Box 140 of the Roethke manuscripts on p. 29 of a thirty-page transcript of an interview made in connection with the film *In a Dark Time*. Roethke follows up the comment quoted here with a reference to Proust, who "stumbles going up to the church, and he's suddenly aware that there's another world other than his—a consciousness that is higher."

5. The Start of the Struggle

1. Evelyn Underhill, *Mysticism: A Study in the Nature and Development of Man's Spiritual Consciousness*, p. 200.

2. Ralph J. Mills, Jr., "Theodore Roethke: The Lyric of the Self," in *Poets in Progress: Critical Prefaces to Ten Contemporary Americans*, ed. Edward Hungerford, p. 5.

3. Roethke, "On 'Identity,'" in *On the Poet and His Craft: Selected Prose of Theodore Roethke*, ed. Ralph J. Mills, Jr., p. 21.

4. Claire Myers Owens, "The Mystical Experience: Facts and Values," in *The Highest State of Consciousness*, ed. John White, p. 139.

5. James R. McLeod, *Theodore Roethke: A Manuscript Checklist*, p. 64.

6. Underhill, *Mysticism*, p. 207.

7. Ibid., p. 204.

8. Ibid., p. 129.

9. The concept of poverty is, of course, central to Christian thought, and the abandonment of home and possessions is recommended as a way of life in the New Testament.

10. Roethke, "On 'Identity,' " pp. 22–23.

11. Denis Donoghue, "Roethke's Broken Music," in *Theodore Roethke: Essays on the Poetry*, ed. Arnold Stein, pp. 138–39.

12. Roethke, *Straw for the Fire: From the Notebooks of Theodore Roethke, 1943–63*, ed. David Wagoner, p. 31.

13. Underhill, *Mysticism*, p. 354. This description of the experience of the abyss is taken from the writings of St. John of the Cross.

14. Karl Malkoff, *Escape from the Self: A Study in Contemporary American Poetry and Poetics*, pp. 149–150.

6. *Preparation Through Contemplation*

1. Stephen Baldanza, Review of *Open House* in *Commonweal*, 34 (13 June 1941), p. 188.

2. The poems of Parts II and III, all but three of which were published between 1941 and 1944, closely resemble the poems of *Open House* and reveal few of these stylistic changes.

3. Evelyn Underhill, *Mysticism: A Study in the Nature and Development of Man's Spiritual Consciousness*, pp. 128–29.

4. Theodore Roethke, *Straw for the Fire: From the Notebooks of Theodore Roethke, 1943–63*, ed. David Wagoner, p. 96.

5. Roethke, "Theodore Roethke," in *On the Poet and His Craft: Selected Prose of Theodore Roethke*, ed. Ralph J. Mills, Jr., p. 15.

6. Underhill, *Mysticism*, p. 191.

7. Roethke, "On 'Identity,' " in *On the Poet and His Craft*, p. 25.

8. Underhill, *Mysticism*, p. 300.

9. Arnold Stein, "Introduction," in *Theodore Roethke: Essays on the Poetry*, ed. Arnold Stein, p. xiv.

10. Richard Allen Blessing, *Theodore Roethke's Dynamic Vision*, p. 68.

11. John Ruysbroeck, *De Ornatu Spiritalium Nuptiarum*, as cited in Underhill, p. 48.

12. Roethke, *Straw for the Fire*, p. 96.

13. John Senior, *The Way Down and Out: The Occult in Symbolist Literature*, p. xviii.

14. Karl Malkoff, *Theodore Roethke: An Introduction to the Poetry*, p. 52.

15. Roethke, "Open Letter," in *On the Poet and His Craft*, pp. 37–39.

16. Ibid., p. 38.

17. Ibid.

18. Malkoff, *Introduction to the Poetry*, p. 55.

19. William Meredith, "A Steady Storm of Correspondences: Theodore Roethke's Long Journey Out of the Self," in *Theodore Roethke: Essays on the Poetry*, p. 41.

20. Roethke, "Open Letter," p. 39.

21. Underhill, *Mysticism*, p. 254.

7. *Movement Into the Self*

1. Theodore Roethke, "Open Letter," in *On the Poet and His Craft: Selected Prose of Theodore Roethke*, ed. Ralph J. Mills, Jr., p. 42.

2. Ibid., pp. 37–40.

3. Theodore Roethke, "An American Poet Introduces Himself," in *On the Poet and His Craft*, p. 10.

4. Ibid., p. 12.

5. Evelyn Underhill, *Mysticism: A Study in the Nature and Development of Man's Spiritual Consciousness*, p. 304.

6. Roethke, "Open Letter," p. 39.

7. Theodore Roethke, *Straw for the Fire: From the Notebooks of Theodore Roethke, 1943–63*, ed. David Wagoner, pp. 247–48.

8. Roethke, "Open Letter," pp. 41–42.

9. Theodore Roethke, *Selected Letters of Theodore Roethke*, ed. Ralph J. Mills, Jr., p. 142.

10. Richard Allen Blessing, *Theodore Roethke's Dynamic Vision*, p. 84.

11. Roethke, "Open Letter," pp. 37–42.

12. Roethke, *Selected Letters*, p. 162.

13. Roethke, "Open Letter," p. 37.

14. Roethke, *Straw for the Fire*, p. 229.

15. William Shakespeare, *Romeo and Juliet*, in *Shakespeare: The Complete Works*, ed. G.B. Harrison, p. 492.

16. Allan Seager, *The Glass House: The Life of Theodore Roethke*, p. 142.

17. Ibid., p. 148.

18. Karl Abraham, "Notes on the Psycho-Analytical Investigation and Treatment of Manic-Depressive Insanity and Allied Conditions," in *Manic–Depressive Illness: History of a Syndrome*, ed. Edward A. Wolpert, p. 125.

19. Maurits Katan, "The Role of the Word in Mania," in *Manic–Depressive Illness*, pp. 213–14.

20. Karl Malkoff, *Theodore Roethke: An Introduction to the Poetry*, p. 71.

21. Harry Williams, *"The Edge is What I Have": Theodore Roethke and After*, p. 52.

22. Roethke, "Open Letter," p. 41.

23. Ibid., p. 37.

24. Kenneth Walker, *The Mystic Mind*, p. 146.

25. Underhill, *Mysticism*, p. 158.

26. Roethke, "Open Letter," p. 37.

27. Roethke, *Selected Letters*, p. 141.

28. John Senior, *The Way Down and Out: The Occult in Symbolist Literature*, p. 8.

29. Roethke, "Open Letter," p. 41.

30. Ibid., p. 37.

31. James Joyce, *A Portrait of the Artist as a Young Man*, p. 7.

32. Malkoff, *Introduction to the Poetry*, p. 70.

33. Roethke, "An American Poet Introduces Himself," p. 10.

34. Ibid.

35. Roethke, "Open Letter," p. 41.

36. Ibid., p. 38.

37. Ibid.

38. Roethke, *Selected Letters*, p. 141.

39. Ibid.

40. Ibid., p. 142.

41. Ibid., p. 161.

42. Roethke, "Open Letter," p. 37.

43. Underhill, *Mysticism*, p. 249.

8. *The Lovers*

1. Evelyn Underhill, *Mysticism: A Study in the Nature and Development of Man's Spiritual Consciousness*, pp. 136–37.

2. Theodore Roethke, "On 'Identity,'" in *On the Poet and His Craft: Selected Prose of Theodore Roethke*, ed. Ralph J. Mills, Jr., p. 25.

3. Underhill, *Mysticism*, p. 189.

4. Ibid., pp. 137–38.

5. Ibid., p. 346.

6. Ibid., p. 348.

7. Ibid., pp. 233–34.

8. Ibid., p. 234.

9. *At the Edge of the Abyss*

1. Allan Seager, *The Glass House: The Life of Theodore Roethke*, p. 251.

2. Roethke, "On 'Identity,'" in *On the Poet and His Craft: Selected Prose of Theodore Roethke*, ed. Ralph J. Mills,Jr., p. 23.

3. Ibid., p. 26.

4. Rosemary Sullivan, *Theodore Roethke: The Garden Master*, p. 115.

5. Henry Vaughan, "The Night," in *Poetry and Selected Prose of Henry Vaughan*, ed. L. C. Martin, p. 359.

6. Evelyn Underhill, *Mysticism: A Study in the Nature and Development of Man's Spiritual Consciousness*, p. 73.

7. Roethke, "How to Write Like Somebody Else," in *On the Poet and His Craft*, p. 70.

8. William Butler Yeats, "Sailing to Byzantium," in *Selected Poems and Two Plays of William Butler Yeats*, ed. M. L. Rosenthal, p. 95.

9. Ibid.

10. Karl Malkoff, *Theodore Roethke: An Introduction to the Poetry*, p. 152.

11. In this particular instance, the influence from poem to poem may work in the opposite direction, since "The Dying Man" was originally published a year earlier than "The Sensualists."

12. Roethke, "Open Letter," in *On the Poet and His Craft*, p. 39.

13. Ibid.

14. Underhill, *Mysticism*, p. 204.

15. William Wordsworth, *The Prelude* in *Selected Poems and Prefaces*, ed. Jack Stillinger, p. 345.

16. Malkoff, *Introduction to the Poetry*, p. 159.

17. Ibid., p. 176.

18. Underhill, *Mysticism*, p. 303.

19. Ibid., p. 170.

20. Ibid., p. 401.

10. *Dueling With God*

1. Karl Malkoff, *Theodore Roethke: An Introduction to the Poetry*, p. 195.

2. William Heyen, "The Divine Abyss: Theodore Roethke's Mysticism," in *Profile of Theodore Roethke*, ed. William Heyen, pp. 100–116.

3. Evelyn Underhill, *Mysticism: A Study in the Nature and Development of Man's Spiritual Consciousness*, p. 399.

4. Ibid., p. 350.

5. Ibid., p. 380.

6. Roethke, "On 'Identity,'" in *On the Poet and His Craft: Selected Prose of Theodore Roethke*, ed. Ralph J. Mills, Jr., p. 26.

7. Rosemary Sullivan, *Theodore Roethke: The Garden Master*, p. 178.

8. Roethke, "On 'Identity,'" p. 26.

9. Anthony Ostroff, ed., *The Contemporary Poet as Artist and Critic*.

10. Roethke, "On 'In a Dark Time,'" in *The Contemporary Poet as Artist and Critic*, p. 49.

11. Ibid., p. 50.

12. Jay Parini, *Theodore Roethke: An American Romantic*, p. 180.

13. Underhill, *Mysticism*, p. 170.

14. Ibid., p. 391.

15. In the film *In a Dark Time*, Roethke pronounces the word "târ-ing," emphasizing its violent aspect.

16. Underhill, *Mysticism*, p. 170.

17. Richard Allen Blessing, *Theodore Roethke's Dynamic Vision*, p. 204.

18. Underhill, *Mysticism*, p. 170.

19. Theodore Roethke, *Straw for the Fire: From the Notebooks of Theodore Roethke, 1943–63*, ed. David Wagoner, p. 21.

20. Underhill, *Mysticism*, p. 48.

11. *Poets and Mystics*

1. Jay Parini, *Theodore Roethke: An American Romantic*, p. 180.

2. Rosemary Sullivan, *Theodore Roethke: The Garden Master*, p. 178.

3. Evelyn Underhill, *Mysticism: A Study in the Nature and Development of Man's Spiritual Consciousness*, p. 236.

4. Northrop Frye, *Fearful Symmetry: A Study of William Blake*, p. 431.

5. Ibid., p. 7.

6. W.H. Auden, "Postscript: Christianity & Art," in *The Dyer's Hand and Other Essays*, p. 458.

7. William Butler Yeats, "Vacillation," in *Selected Poems and Two Plays of William Butler Yeats*, ed. M. L. Rosenthal, pp. 135–37.

8. Richard Allen Blessing, *Theodore Roethke's Dynamic Vision*, p. 60.

9. Ibid.

10. Roethke, "On 'Identity,'" in *On the Poet and His Craft: Selected Prose of Theodore Roethke*, ed. Ralph J. Mills, Jr., p. 25.

Afterword

1. Theodore Roethke, "Open Letter," in *On the Poet and His Craft: Selected Prose of Theodore Roethke*, ed. Ralph J. Mills, Jr., p. 39.

2. Robert Heilman, Personal Interview, 21 August 1978, Seattle, Washington.

3. James R. McLeod, *Theodore Roethke: A Manuscript Checklist*, p. 92. McLeod cites Roethke's wife, Beatrice, as the source of his information. Mrs. Roethke indicated that the poem "Song" was completed during the month of July, within a few weeks of Roethke's death.

A Selected Bibliography

Works by Roethke

The Collected Poems of Theodore Roethke. Garden City, N.Y.: Doubleday, 1966.

"On 'In a Dark Time.'" *The Contemporary Poet as Artist and Critic*. Edited by Anthony Ostroff. Boston: Little, Brown and Company, 1964.

On the Poet and His Craft: Selected Prose of Theodore Roethke. Edited by Ralph J. Mills, Jr. Seattle: University of Washington Press, 1965.

Selected Letters of Theodore Roethke. Edited by Ralph J. Mills, Jr. Seattle: University of Washington Press, 1968.

Straw for the Fire: From the Notebooks of Theodore Roethke, 1943–63. Edited by David Wagoner. Garden City, N.Y.: Doubleday and Company, Inc., 1974.

The Theodore Roethke Papers and Notebooks, University of Washington Library, Seattle.

Works about Roethke

Baldanza, Stephen. *Commonweal* 34 (13 June 1941): 188.

Blessing, Richard Allen. *Theodore Roethke's Dynamic Vision*. Bloomington, Ind.: Indiana University Press, 1974.

Burke, Kenneth. "The Vegetal Radicalism of Theodore Roethke." *Sewanee Review* 58 (Winter 1950): 68–108.

Dickey, James. "The Greatest American Poet." *Atlantic* 222 (November 1968): 53–58.

Donoghue, Denis. "Roethke's Broken Music." *Theodore Roethke: Essays on the Poetry*. Edited by Arnold Stein. Seattle: University of Washington Press, 1965.

Eberhart, Richard. "On Theodore Roethke's Poetry." *Southern Review* 1 (1965): 612–20.

Heyen, William, ed. *Profile of Theodore Roethke*. Columbus, Ohio: Charles E. Merrill Publishing Company, 1971.

———. "The Divine Abyss: Theodore Roethke's Mysticism." *A Profile of Theodore Roethke*. Edited by William Heyen. Columbus, Ohio: Charles E. Merrill Publishing Company, 1971.

La Belle, Jenijoy. *The Echoing Wood of Theodore Roethke*. Princeton, N.J.: Princeton University Press, 1976.

Lane, Gary, ed. *A Concordance to the Poems of Theodore Roethke*. Metuchen, N.J.: Scarecrow Press, Inc., 1972.

Malkoff, Karl. *Theodore Roethke: An Introduction to the Poetry*. New York: Columbia University Press, 1966.

Martz, William J. *The Achievement of Theodore Roethke*. Glenview, Ill.: Scott, Foresman and Company, 1966.

McLeod, James R. *Theodore Roethke: A Manuscript Checklist*. Kent, Ohio: Kent State University Press, 1971.

———. *Theodore Roethke: A Bibliography*. Kent, Ohio: Kent State University Press, 1973.

Meredith, William. "A Steady Storm of Correspondences: Theodore Roethke's Long Journey Out of the Self." *Shenandoah* 16:1 (1964): 41–54.

Mills, Ralph J., Jr. "Theodore Roethke: The Lyric of the Self." *Poets in Progress: Critical Prefaces to Ten Contemporary Americans*. Edited by Edward Hungerford. Evanston: Northwestern University Press, 1962.

———. *Theodore Roethke*. Minneapolis: University of Minnesota Press, 1963.

———. "In the Way of Becoming: Roethke's Last Poems." *Theodore Roethke: Essays on the Poetry*. Edited by Arnold Stein. Seattle: University of Washington Press, 1965.

Moul, Keith R. *Theodore Roethke's Career: An Annotated Bibliography*. Boston: G. K. Hall and Company, 1977.

Ostroff, Anthony, ed. *The Contemporary Poet as Artist and Critic*. Boston: Little, Brown and Company, 1964.

Parini, Jay. *Theodore Roethke: An American Romantic*. Amherst, Mass.: University of Massachusetts Press, 1979.

Schwartz, Delmore. "The Cunning and the Craft of the Unconscious and the Preconscious." *Poetry* 904 (1959): 203–5.

Seager, Allan. *The Glass House: The Life of Theodore Roethke*. New York: McGraw–Hill Book Company, 1968.

Snodgrass, W. D. "'That Anguish of Concreteness'—Theodore Roethke's Career." *Theodore Roethke: Essays on the Poetry*. Edited by Arnold Stein. Seattle: University of Washington Press, 1965.

Spender, Stephen. "The Objective Ego." *Theodore Roethke: Essays on the Poetry*. Edited by Arnold Stein. Seattle: University of Washington Press, 1965.

———. "Roethke: The Lost Sun." *New Republic* 155:8 (27 August 1966): 23–5.

Staples, Hugh B. "The Rose in the Sea-Wind: A Reading of Theodore Roethke's 'North American Sequence.'" *American Literature* 36 (1964): 189–203.

Stein, Arnold, ed. *Theodore Roethke: Essays on the Poetry.* Seattle: University of Washington Press, 1965.

Sullivan, Rosemary. *Theodore Roethke: The Garden Master.* Seattle: University of Washington Press, 1975.

Williams, Harry. *"The Edge is What I Have": Theodore Roethke and After.* Cranbury, N.J.: Associated University Presses, Inc., 1977.

General References

Abraham, Karl. "Notes on the Psycho-Analytical Investigation and Treatment of Manic-Depressive Insanity and Allied Conditions." *Manic-Depressive Illness: History of a Syndrome.* Edited by Edward A. Wolpert. New York: International Universities Press, Inc., 1977.

Asrani, U. A. "The Psychology of Mysticism." *The Highest State of Consciousness.* Edited by John White. Garden City, N.Y.: Doubleday/Anchor, 1972.

Auden, W. H. "Postscript: Christianity & Art." *The Dyer's Hand and Other Essays.* New York: Random House, 1948.

Blofeld, John. *The Tantric Mysticism of Tibet: A Practical Guide.* New York: E. P. Dutton and Company, Inc., 1970.

Cheney, Sheldon. *Men Who Have Walked With God.* New York: Alfred A. Knopf, 1945.

Dasgupta, S. N. *Hindu Mysticism.* New York: Frederick Ungar Publishing Company, 1959.

Donne, John. "The Relic." *Renaissance England: Poetry and Prose from the Reformation to the Restoration.* Edited by Roy Lamson and Hallet Smith. New York: W. W. Norton and Company, Inc., 1942.

Durr, R. A. *Poetic Vision and the Psychedelic Experience.* Syracuse: Syracuse University Press, 1970.

Freeman, Thomas. "Observations on Mania." *Manic–Depressive Illness: History of a Syndrome.* Edited by Edward A. Wolpert. New York: International Universities Press, Inc., 1977.

Frye, Northrop. *Fearful Symmetry: A Study of William Blake.* Princeton: Princeton University Press, 1947.

Gaylin, Willard, ed. *The Meaning of Despair: Psychoanalytic Contributions to the Understanding of Depression.* New York: Science House, Inc., 1968.

Harner, Michael J., ed. *Hallucinogens and Shamanism.* London: Oxford University Press, 1973.

Huxley, Aldous. "Visionary Experience." *The Highest State of Consciousness.* Edited by John White. Garden City, N.Y.: Doubleday/Anchor, 1972.

Jacobson, Edith. *Depression: Comparative Studies of Normal, Neurotic, and Psychotic Conditions.* New York: International Universities Press, Inc., 1971.

James, William. *The Varieties of Religious Experience: A Study in Human Nature.* New York: Random House, 1902.

Joyce, James. *A Portrait of the Artist as a Young Man.* New York: Viking Press, 1968.

Katan, Maurits. "The Role of the Word in Mania." *Manic–Depressive Illness: History of a Syndrome.* Edited by Edward A. Wolpert. New York: International Universities Press, Inc., 1977.

Kris, Ernst. *Psychoanalytic Explorations in Art.* New York: International Universities Press, Inc., 1952.

Langer, Susanne K. *Feeling and Form: A Theory of Art.* New York: Charles Scribner's Sons, 1953.

Malkoff, Karl. *Escape from the Self: A Study in Contemporary American Poetry and Poetics.* New York: Columbia University Press, 1977.

Middleton, John, ed. *Gods and Rituals.* Garden City, N.Y.: The Natural History Press, 1967.

Owens, Claire Myers. "The Mystical Experience: Facts and Values." *The Highest State of Consciousness.* Edited by John White. Garden City, N.Y.: Doubleday/Anchor, 1972.

Prescott, Frederick Clarke. *The Poetic Mind.* New York: The Macmillan Company, 1926.

Prince, Raymond and Charles Savage. "Mystical States and the Concept of Regression." *The Highest State of Consciousness.* Edited by John White. Garden City, N.Y.: Doubleday/Anchor, 1972.

Russell, Bertrand. *Mysticism and Logic.* New York: W. W. Norton and Company, Inc., 1929.

Schwartz, Steven, ed. *Language and Cognition in Schizophrenia.* Hillsdale, N.J.: Lawrence Erlbaum Associates, 1978.

Scott, Nathan A., Jr. *Negative Capability: Studies in the New Literature and the Religious Situation.* New Haven: Yale University Press, 1969.

———. *The Wild Prayer of Longing: Poetry and the Sacred.* New Haven: Yale University Press, 1971.

Senior, John. *The Way Down and Out: The Occult in Symbolist Literature.* Ithaca, N.Y.: Cornell University Press, 1959.

Shah, Indries. *The Sufis*. New York: Doubleday and Company, Inc., 1971.

Shakespeare, William. *Romeo and Juliet*, in *Shakespeare: The Complete Works*. Edited by G. B. Harrison. New York: Harcourt, Brace, and World, Inc., 1952.

Snyder, Edward D. *Hypnotic Poetry*. Philadelphia: University of Pennsylvania Press, 1930.

Traherne, Thomas. *The Poetical Works of Thomas Traherne, B. D.* Edited by Bertram Dobell. London: Ballantyne Press, 1903.

Underhill, Evelyn. *The Mystic Way: A Psychological Study in Christian Origins*. London: J. M. Dent and Sons, Ltd., 1913.

———. *Mysticism: A Study in the Nature and Development of Man's Spiritual Consciousness*. New York: Meridian Books, 1955.

Vaughan, Henry. *Poetry and Selected Prose of Henry Vaughan*. Edited by L. C. Martin. London: Oxford University Press, 1963.

Walker, Kenneth. *The Mystic Mind*. New York: Emerson Books, Inc., 1965.

Watkin, E. I. *Poets and Mystics*. London: Sheed and Ward, 1953.

White, Helen C. *The Mysticism of William Blake*. Madison: University of Wisconsin Press, 1927.

White, John, ed. *The Highest State of Consciousness*. Garden City, N.Y.: Doubleday/Anchor, 1972.

Wilson, Colin. *Poetry and Mysticism*. San Francisco: City Lights Books, 1969.

Wolpert, Edward A., ed. *Manic–Depressive Illness: History of a Syndrome*. New York: International Universities Press, Inc., 1977.

Wordsworth, William. *Selected Poems and Prefaces*. Edited by Jack Stillinger. Boston: Houghton Mifflin Company, 1965.

Yeats, William Butler. *Selected Poems and Two Plays of William Butler Yeats*. Edited by M. L. Rosenthal. New York: Collier Books, 1962.

Zaehner, R. C. *Zen, Drugs and Mysticism*. New York: Pantheon Books, 1972.

Index

Theodore Roethke (1908–1963) was a poet of mystical leanings who suffered from chronic manic depression. This is the first study of Roethke's writings to connect the poet's mysticism with his mental disorder. Basing his analysis on extensive study of Roethke's unpublished writings—notebooks, drafts, and finished poems—as well as on his published work, Bowers shows that Roethke found in his manic episodes a way to perceive a higher truth that parallels the experience of mysticism. Bowers begins by defining mysticism and mystic tradition in English poetry. He traces the progressive stages of mysticism—awakening, purgation, illumination, dark night of the soul, and union—and shows how Roethke's writings follow this progression. Unlike other scholars, Bowers pays close attention to the poet's early work, which foreshadows his major writings. Bowers's insights into Roethke's art and his use of hitherto unpublished materials make this a unique and significant analysis of a major twentieth-century poet. Readers interested in the psychology of perception, art, and religion will find this an illuminating case study thoroughly grounded in the author's intimate knowledge of Roethke's life and work.